G.I. JOE

SIREN´S SONG

IDW

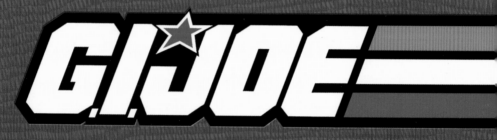

Special thanks to Hasbro's Mike Ballog, Ed Lane, Joe Furfaro, Heather Hopkins, and Michael Kelly for their invaluable assistance.

ISBN: 978-1-63140-012-4

17 16 15 14   2 3 4 5

IDW ® Licensed By: Hasbro

www.IDWPUBLISHING.com
IDW founded by Ted Adams, Alex Garner, Kris Oprisko, and Robbie Robbins

Ted Adams, CEO & Publisher
Greg Goldstein, President & COO
Robbie Robbins, EVP/Sr. Graphic Artist
Chris Ryall, Chief Creative Officer/Editor-in-Chief
Matthew Ruzicka, CPA, Chief Financial Officer
Alan Payne, VP of Sales
Dirk Wood, VP of Marketing
Lorelei Bunjes, VP of Digital Services
Jeff Webber, VP of Digital Publishing & Business Development

Facebook: facebook.com/idwpublishing
Twitter: @idwpublishing
YouTube: youtube.com/idwpublishing
Instagram: instagram.com/idwpublishing
deviantART: idwpublishing.deviantart.com
Pinterest: pinterest.com/idwpublishing/idw-staff-faves

WRITER: PAUL ALLOR

CHAPTERS 1 & 2:
MAIN STORY:
ART: ALEX CAL
COLORS: DAVID GARCIA CRUZ

FLASHBACKS:
"A COWARD'S HEART"
PENCILS: S L GALLANT
INKS: MARC DEERING
COLORS: JOHN-PAUL BOVE

"THE DEBT"
ART: ATILIO ROJO
COLORS: DAVID GARCIA CRUZ

"THE GARDENER"
ART: NICOLE VIRELLA
COLORS: JOHN-PAUL BOVE

"SHADOWS AND LIGHT"
PENCILS: ROBERT ATKINS
INKS: JUAN CASTRO
COLORS: JOANA LAFUENTE

"INFERNO"
ART: CHRIS EVENHUIS
COLORS: JOANA LAFUENTE

CHAPTERS 3 & 4:
ART: STEVE KURTH
INKS: ALLEN MARTINEZ
COLORS: JOANA LAFUENTE

LETTERERS: SHAWN LEE
AND GILBERTO LAZCANO
CONSULTING EDITOR: CARLOS GUZMAN
SERIES EDITOR: JOHN BARBER
SPECIAL THANKS: MAX BROOKS

COVER: STEVE KURTH
COVER COLORS: JOANA LAFUENTE
COLLECTION EDITS: JUSTIN EISINGER
AND ALONZO SIMON
COLLECTION DESIGNER: GILBERTO LAZCANO

CHAPTER ONE

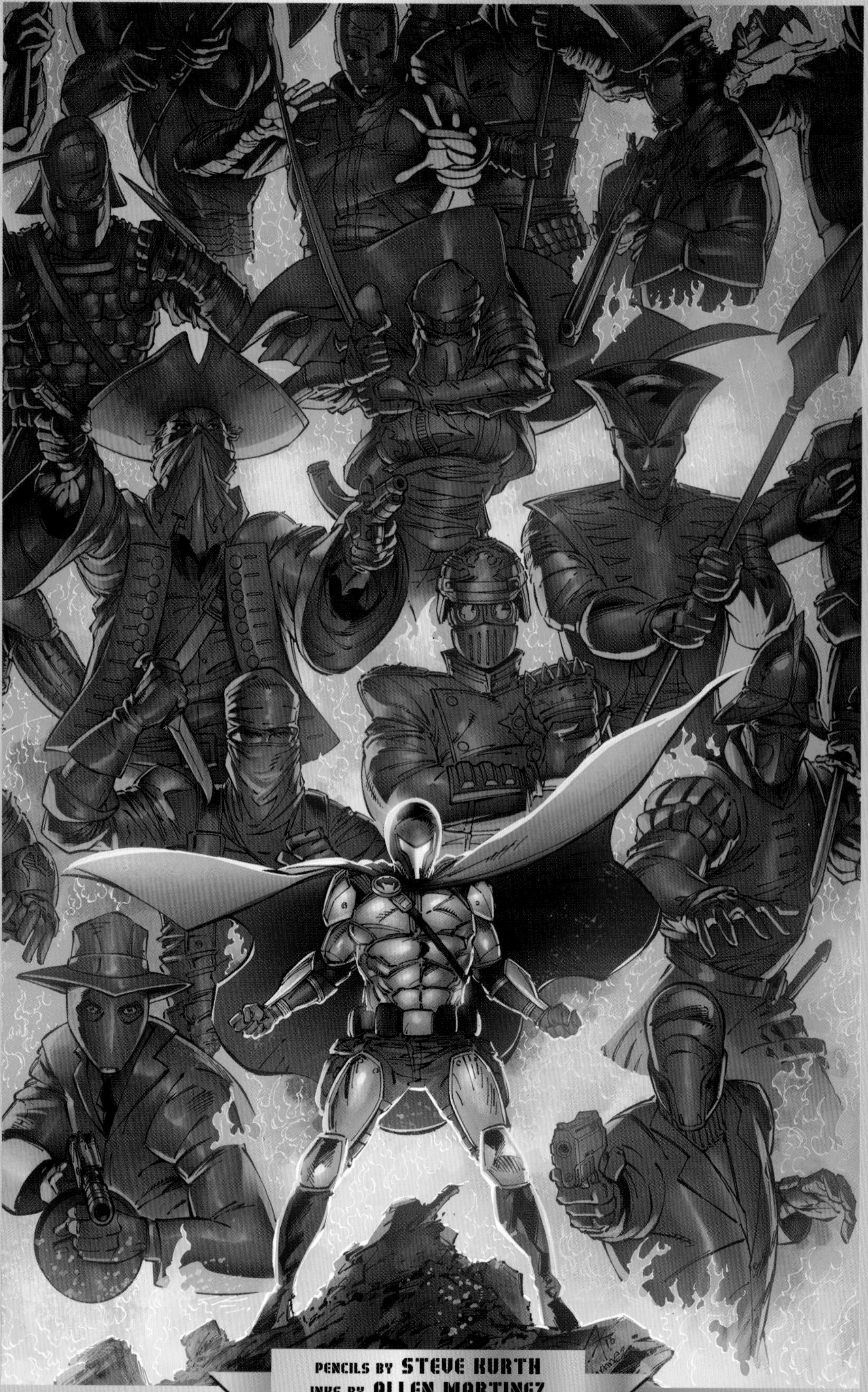

PENCILS BY **STEVE KURTH**
INKS BY **ALLEN MARTINEZ**
COLORS BY **JOANA LAFUENTE**

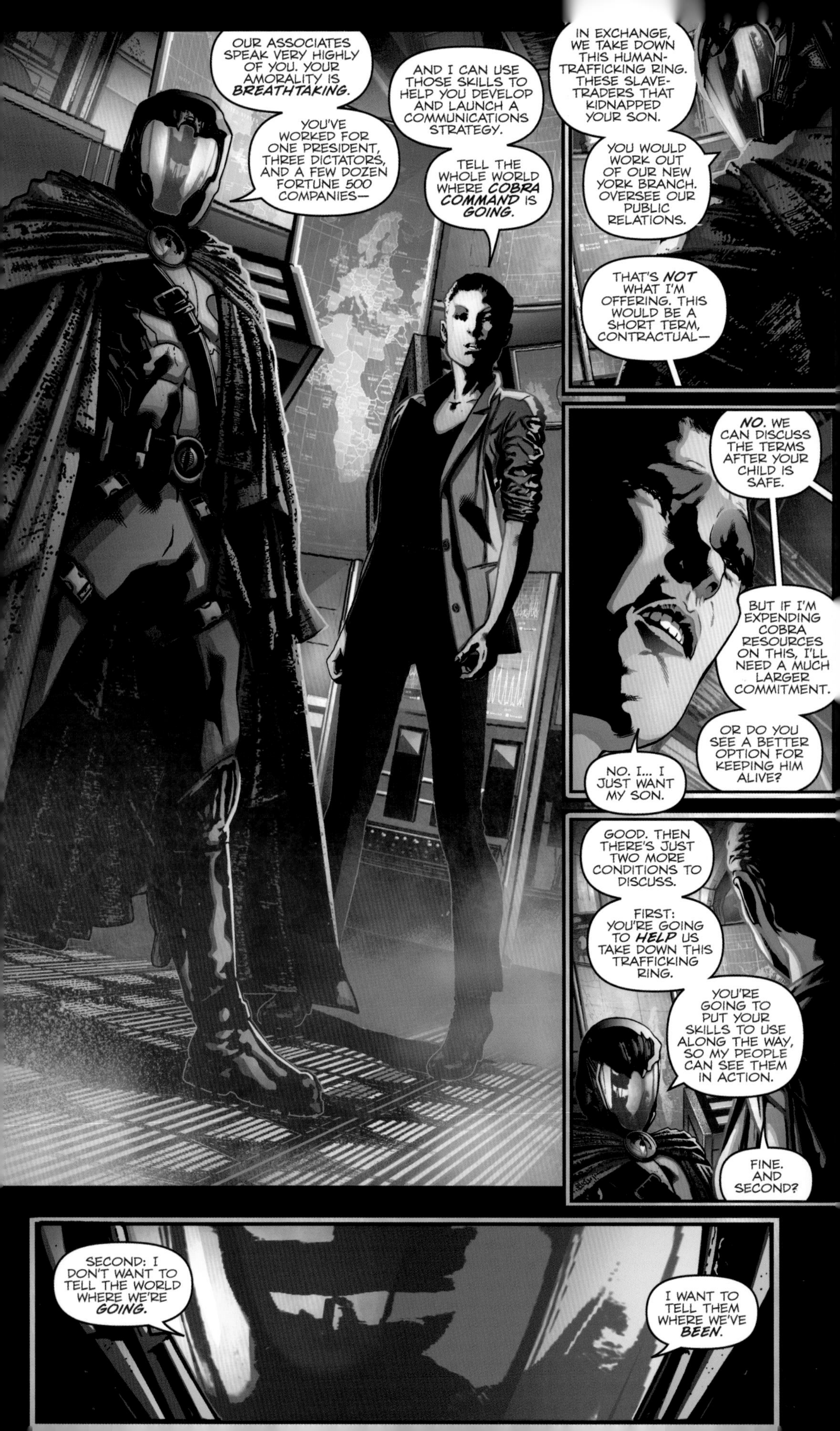
OUR ASSOCIATES SPEAK VERY HIGHLY OF YOU. YOUR AMORALITY IS *BREATHTAKING*.
YOU'VE WORKED FOR ONE PRESIDENT, THREE DICTATORS, AND A FEW DOZEN FORTUNE 500 COMPANIES—
AND I CAN USE THOSE SKILLS TO HELP YOU DEVELOP AND LAUNCH A COMMUNICATIONS STRATEGY.
TELL THE WHOLE WORLD WHERE *COBRA COMMAND* IS *GOING*.
IN EXCHANGE, WE TAKE DOWN THIS HUMAN-TRAFFICKING RING. THESE SLAVE-TRADERS THAT KIDNAPPED YOUR SON.
YOU WOULD WORK OUT OF OUR NEW YORK BRANCH. OVERSEE OUR PUBLIC RELATIONS.
THAT'S *NOT* WHAT I'M OFFERING. THIS WOULD BE A SHORT TERM, CONTRACTUAL—
NO. WE CAN DISCUSS THE TERMS AFTER YOUR CHILD IS SAFE.
BUT IF I'M EXPENDING COBRA RESOURCES ON THIS, I'LL NEED A MUCH LARGER COMMITMENT.
OR DO YOU SEE A BETTER OPTION FOR KEEPING HIM ALIVE?
NO. I... I JUST WANT MY SON.
GOOD. THEN THERE'S JUST TWO MORE CONDITIONS TO DISCUSS.
FIRST: YOU'RE GOING TO *HELP* US TAKE DOWN THIS TRAFFICKING RING.
YOU'RE GOING TO PUT YOUR SKILLS TO USE ALONG THE WAY, SO MY PEOPLE CAN SEE THEM IN ACTION.
FINE. AND SECOND?
SECOND: I DON'T WANT TO TELL THE WORLD WHERE WE'RE *GOING*.
I WANT TO TELL THEM WHERE WE'VE *BEEN*.

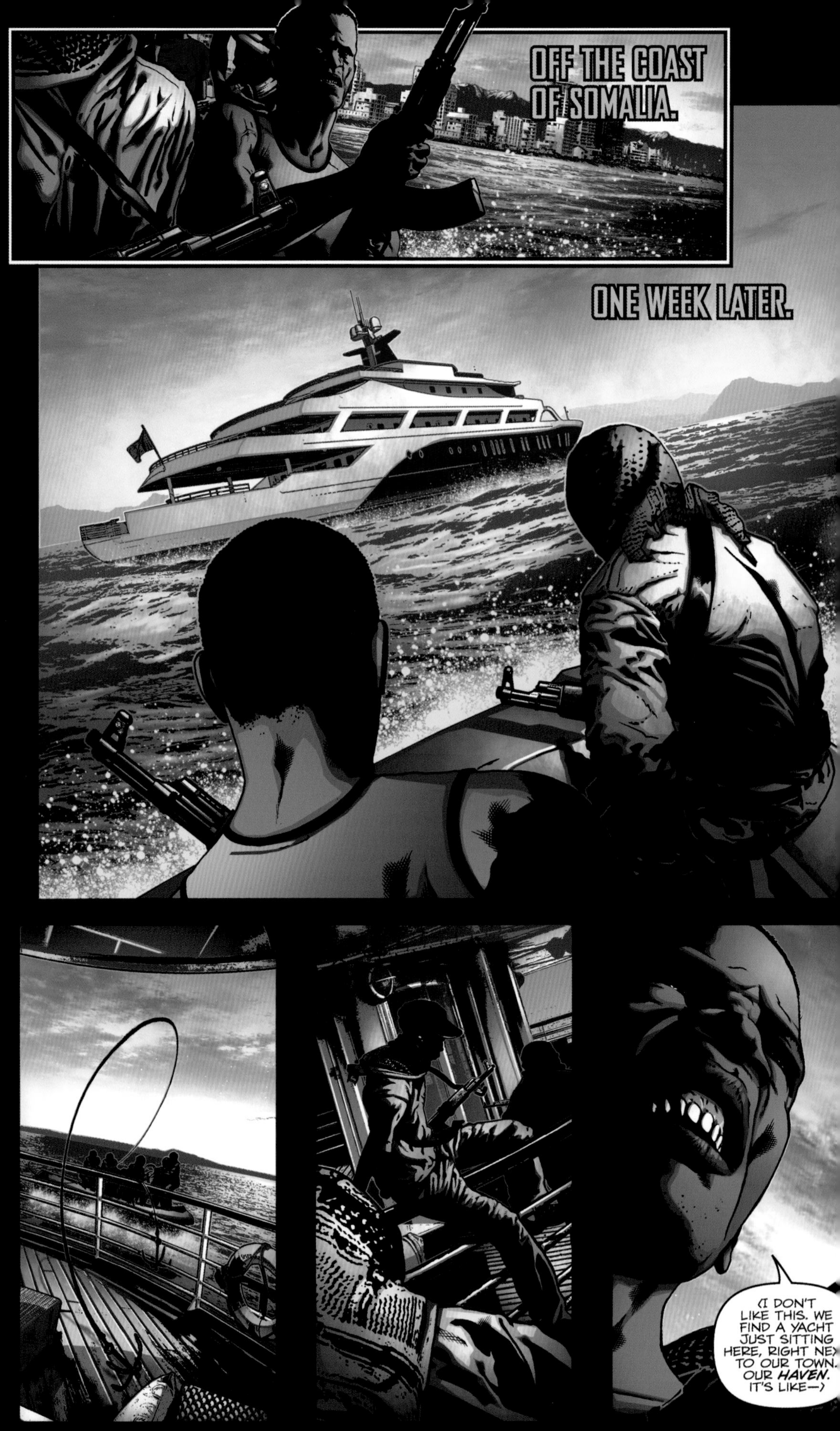
OFF THE COAST OF SOMALIA.
ONE WEEK LATER.
⟨I DON'T LIKE THIS. WE FIND A YACHT JUST SITTING HERE, RIGHT NE TO OUR TOWN. OUR *HAVEN*. IT'S LIKE—⟩

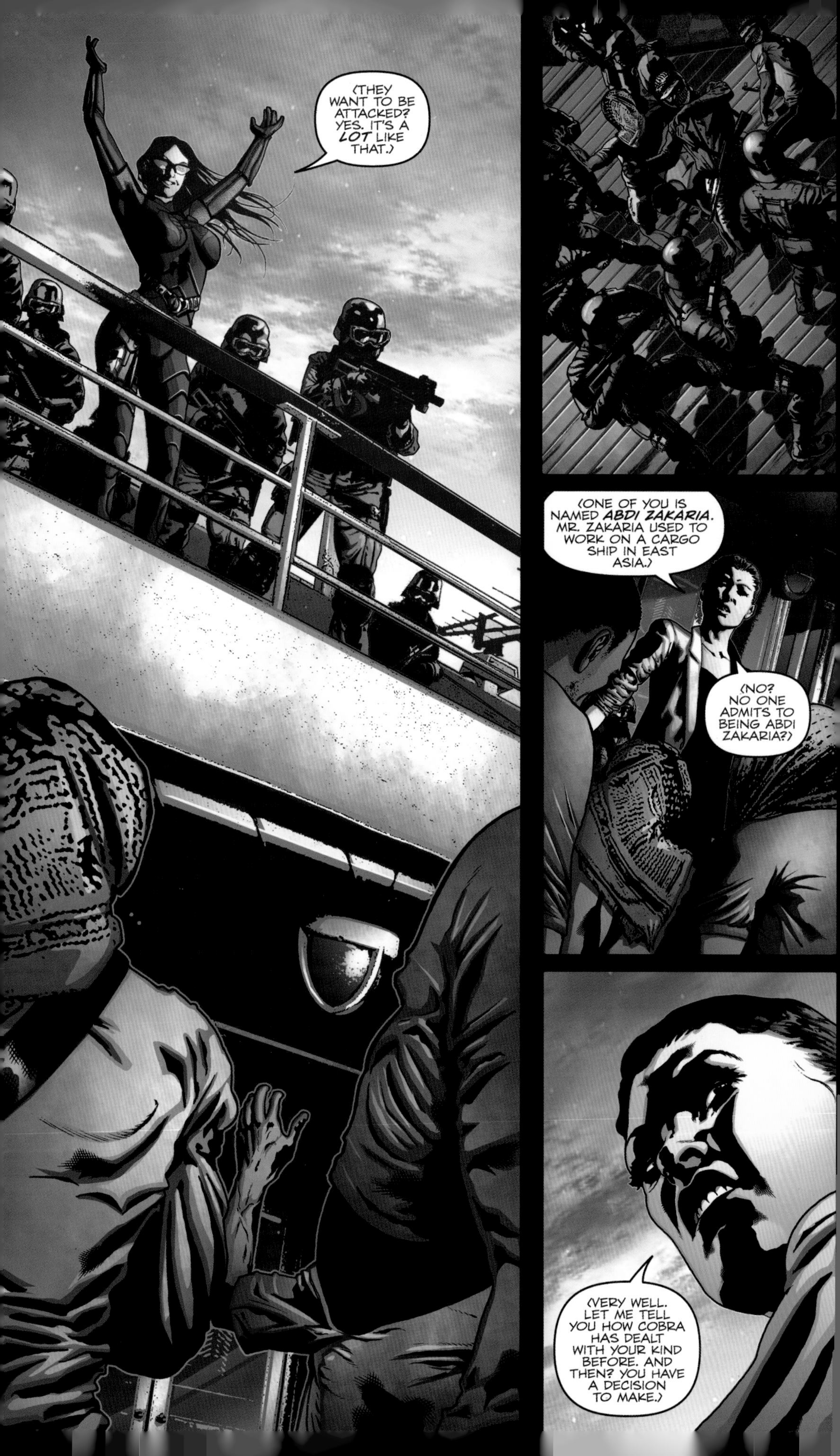
(THEY WANT TO BE ATTACKED? YES. IT'S A LOT LIKE THAT.)
(ONE OF YOU IS NAMED ABDI ZAKARIA. MR. ZAKARIA USED TO WORK ON A CARGO SHIP IN EAST ASIA.)
(NO? NO ONE ADMITS TO BEING ABDI ZAKARIA?)
(VERY WELL. LET ME TELL YOU HOW COBRA HAS DEALT WITH YOUR KIND BEFORE. AND THEN? YOU HAVE A DECISION TO MAKE.)

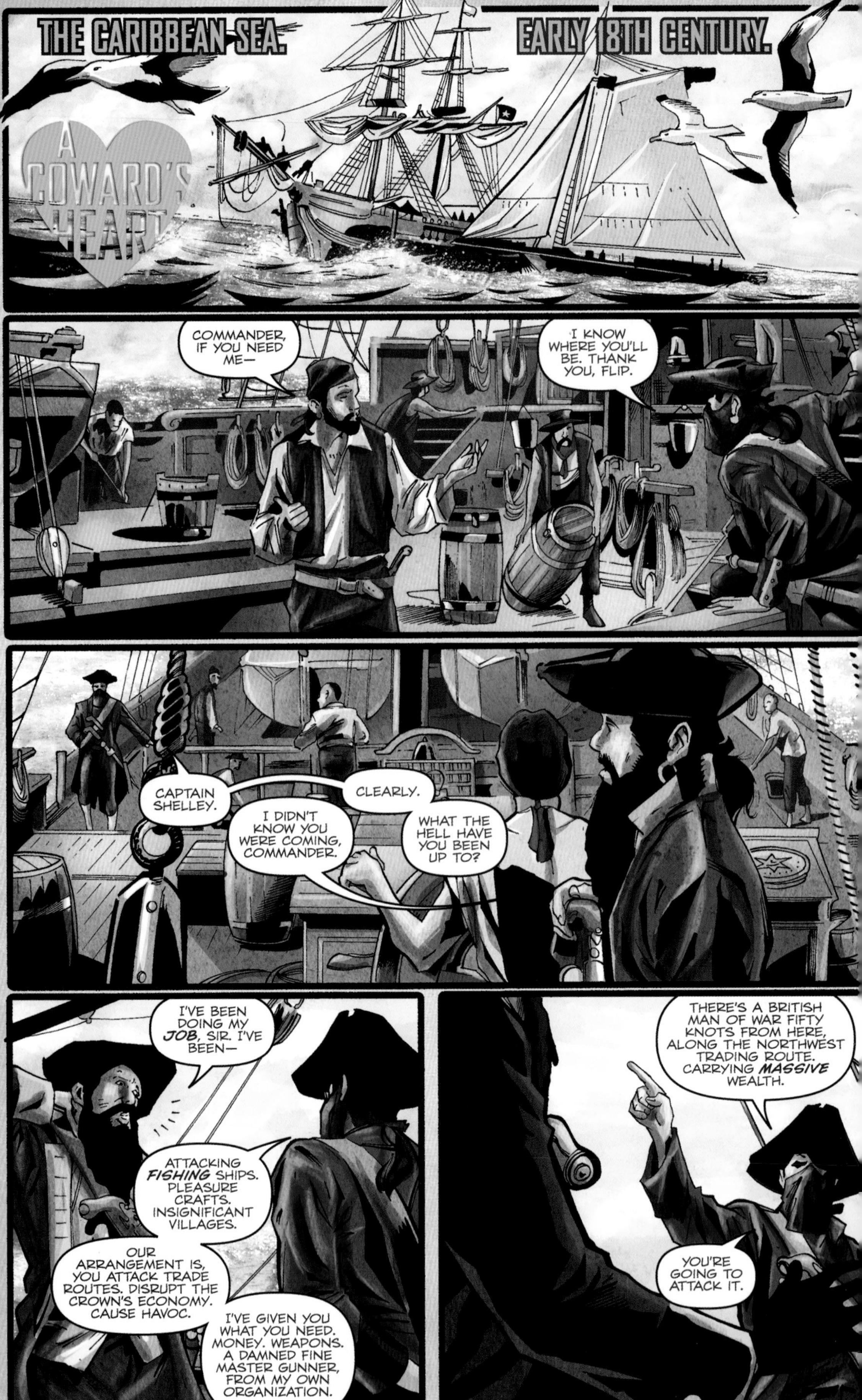

THE CARIBBEAN SEA.
EARLY 18TH CENTURY.
A COWARD'S HEART
COMMANDER, IF YOU NEED ME—
I KNOW WHERE YOU'LL BE. THANK YOU, FLIP.
CAPTAIN SHELLEY.
CLEARLY.
I DIDN'T KNOW YOU WERE COMING, COMMANDER.
WHAT THE HELL HAVE YOU BEEN UP TO?
I'VE BEEN DOING MY JOB, SIR. I'VE BEEN—
ATTACKING FISHING SHIPS. PLEASURE CRAFTS. INSIGNIFICANT VILLAGES.
OUR ARRANGEMENT IS, YOU ATTACK TRADE ROUTES. DISRUPT THE CROWN'S ECONOMY. CAUSE HAVOC.
I'VE GIVEN YOU WHAT YOU NEED. MONEY. WEAPONS. A DAMNED FINE MASTER GUNNER, FROM MY OWN ORGANIZATION.
THERE'S A BRITISH MAN OF WAR FIFTY KNOTS FROM HERE, ALONG THE NORTHWEST TRADING ROUTE. CARRYING MASSIVE WEALTH.
YOU'RE GOING TO ATTACK IT.

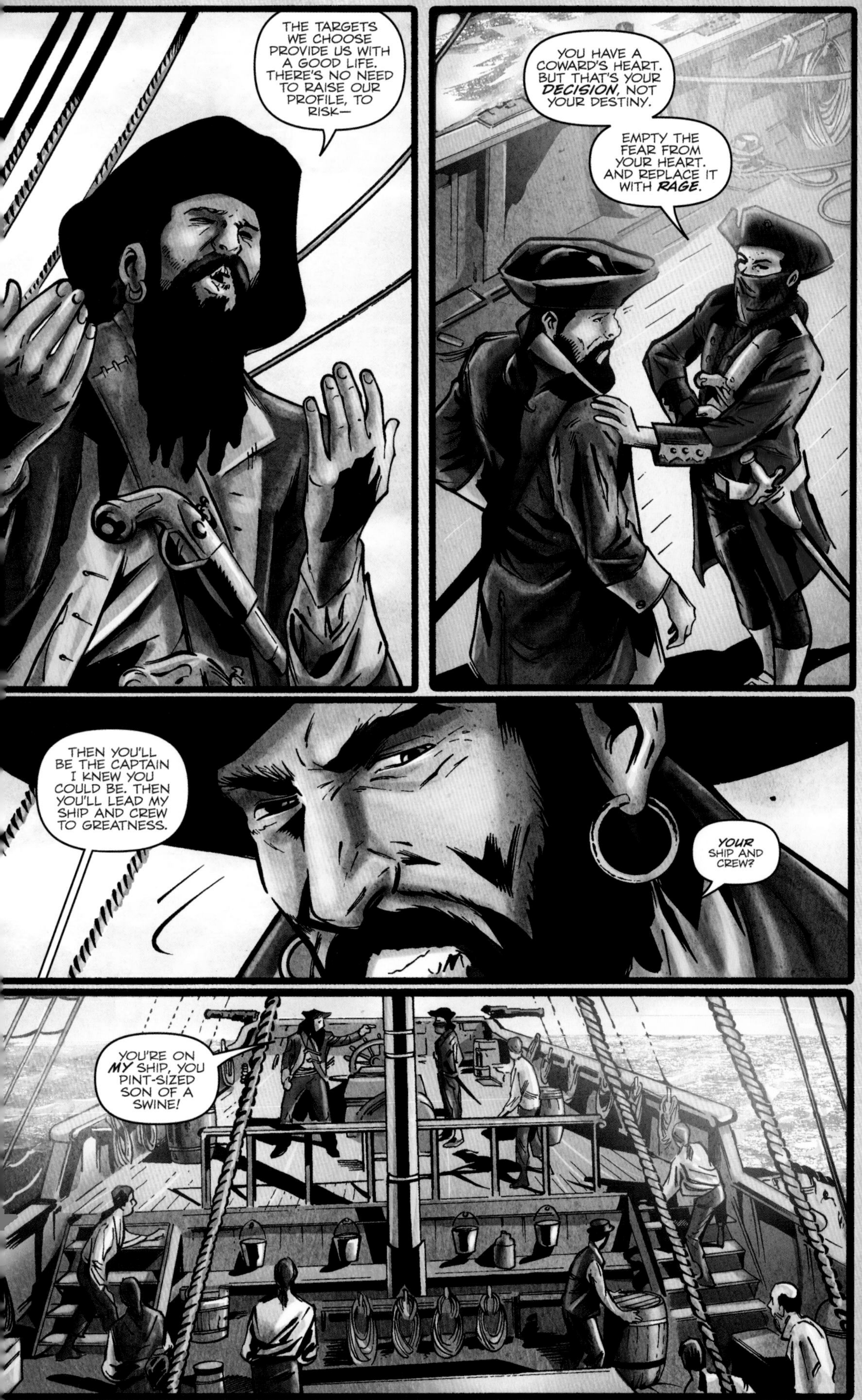
THE TARGETS WE CHOOSE PROVIDE US WITH A GOOD LIFE. THERE'S NO NEED TO RAISE OUR PROFILE, TO RISK—
YOU HAVE A COWARD'S HEART. BUT THAT'S YOUR DECISION, NOT YOUR DESTINY.
EMPTY THE FEAR FROM YOUR HEART. AND REPLACE IT WITH RAGE.
THEN YOU'LL BE THE CAPTAIN I KNEW YOU COULD BE. THEN YOU'LL LEAD MY SHIP AND CREW TO GREATNESS.
YOUR SHIP AND CREW?
YOU'RE ON MY SHIP, YOU PINT-SIZED SON OF A SWINE!

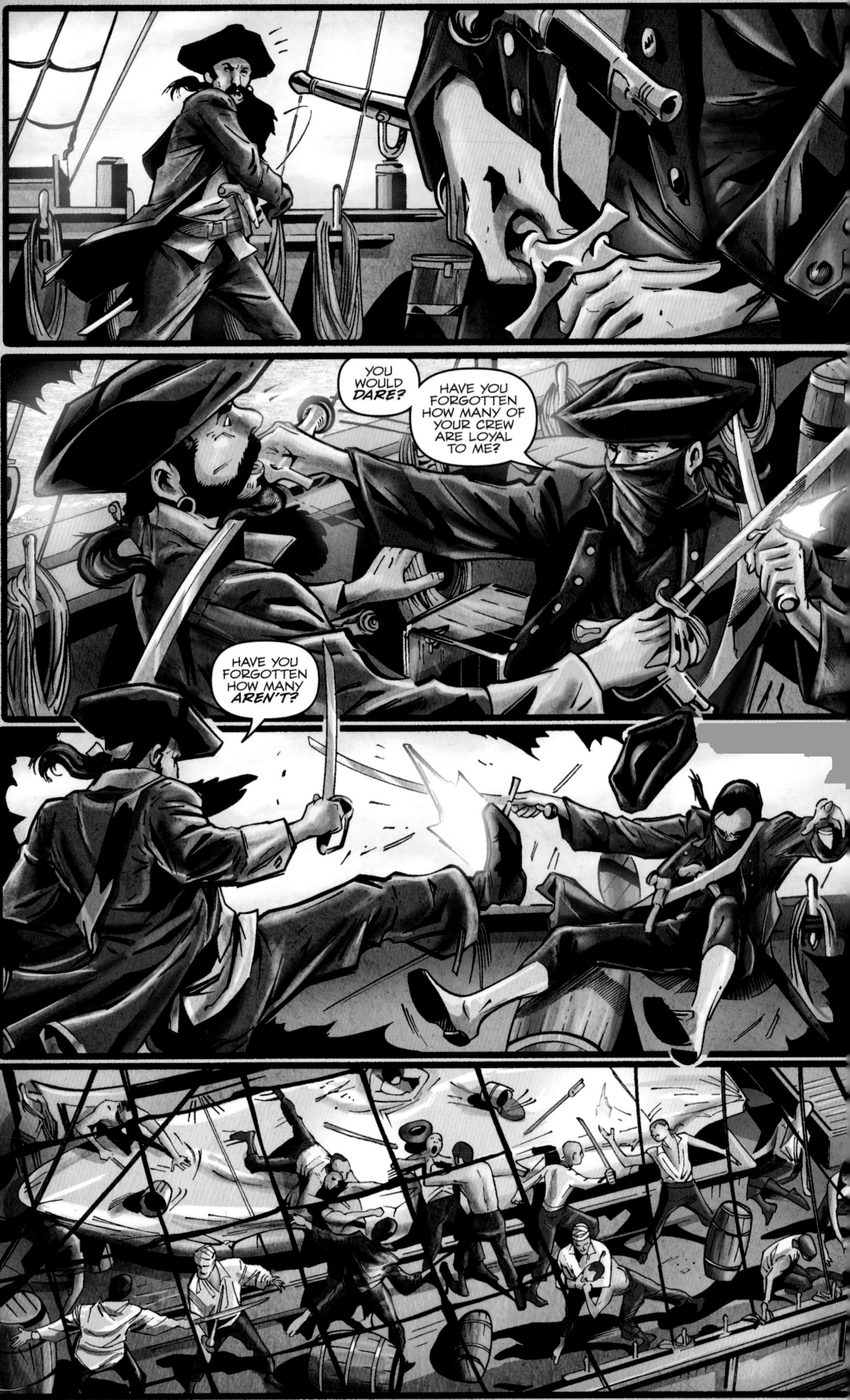
YOU WOULD DARE?
HAVE YOU FORGOTTEN HOW MANY OF YOUR CREW ARE LOYAL TO ME?
HAVE YOU FORGOTTEN HOW MANY AREN'T?

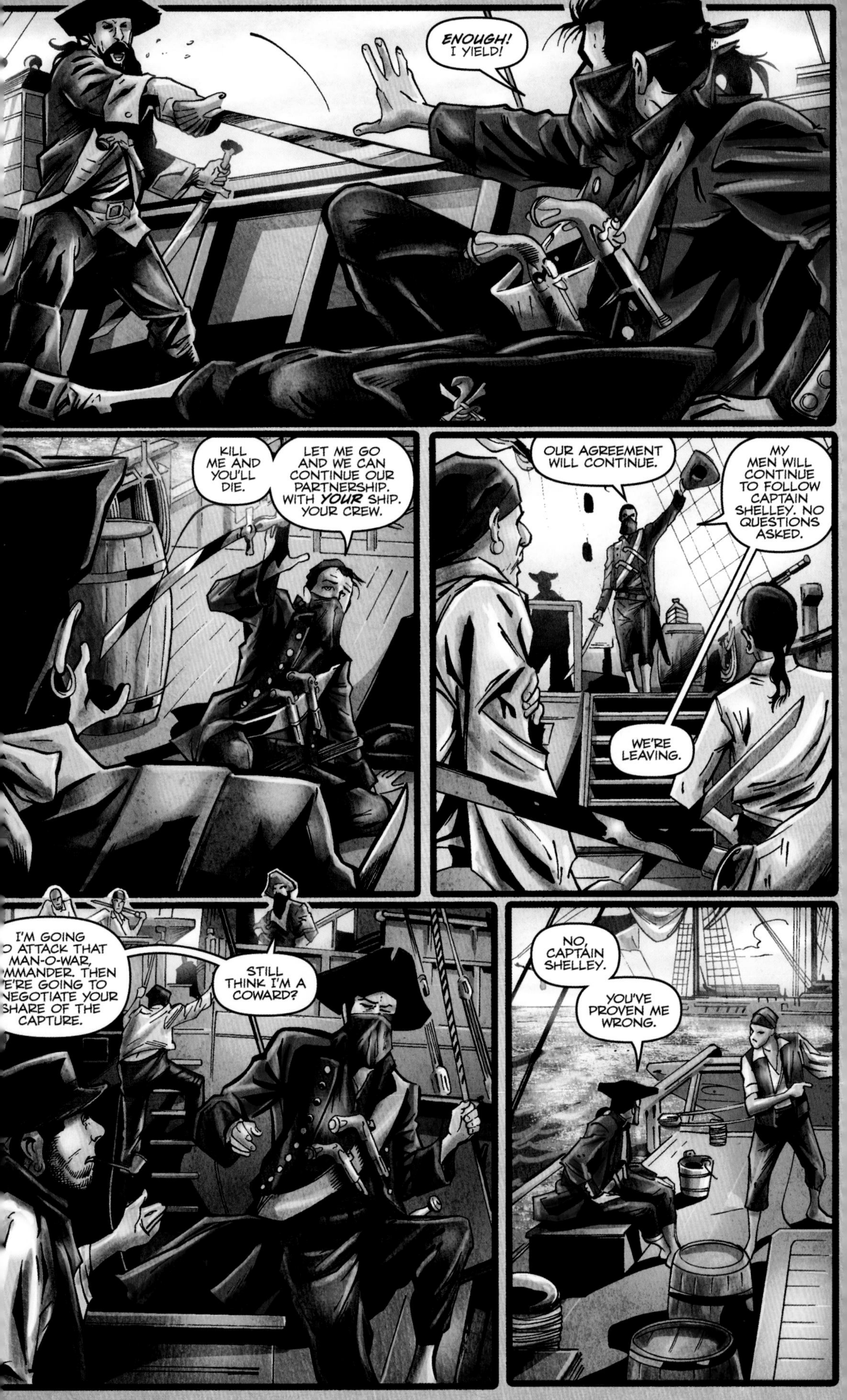
ENOUGH! I YIELD!
KILL ME AND YOU'LL DIE.
LET ME GO AND WE CAN CONTINUE OUR PARTNERSHIP. WITH YOUR SHIP. YOUR CREW.
OUR AGREEMENT WILL CONTINUE.
MY MEN WILL CONTINUE TO FOLLOW CAPTAIN SHELLEY. NO QUESTIONS ASKED.
WE'RE LEAVING.
I'M GOING O ATTACK THAT MAN-O-WAR, OMMANDER. THEN E'RE GOING TO NEGOTIATE YOUR SHARE OF THE CAPTURE.
STILL THINK I'M A COWARD?
NO, CAPTAIN SHELLEY.
YOU'VE PROVEN ME WRONG.

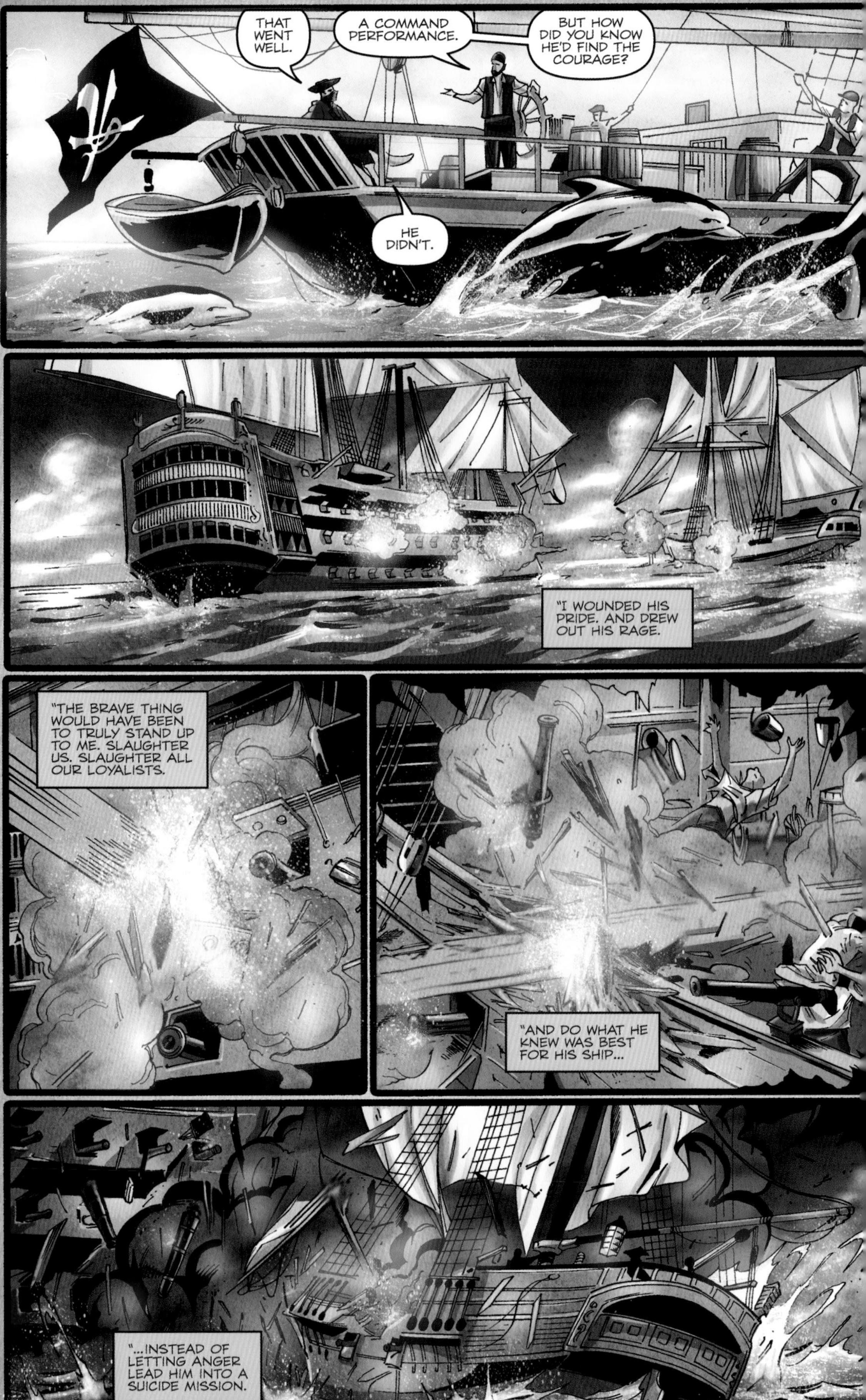

THAT WENT WELL.
A COMMAND PERFORMANCE.
BUT HOW DID YOU KNOW HE'D FIND THE COURAGE?
HE DIDN'T.
"I WOUNDED HIS PRIDE. AND DREW OUT HIS RAGE.
"THE BRAVE THING WOULD HAVE BEEN TO TRULY STAND UP TO ME. SLAUGHTER US. SLAUGHTER ALL OUR LOYALISTS.
"AND DO WHAT HE KNEW WAS BEST FOR HIS SHIP...
"...INSTEAD OF LETTING ANGER LEAD HIM INTO A SUICIDE MISSION.

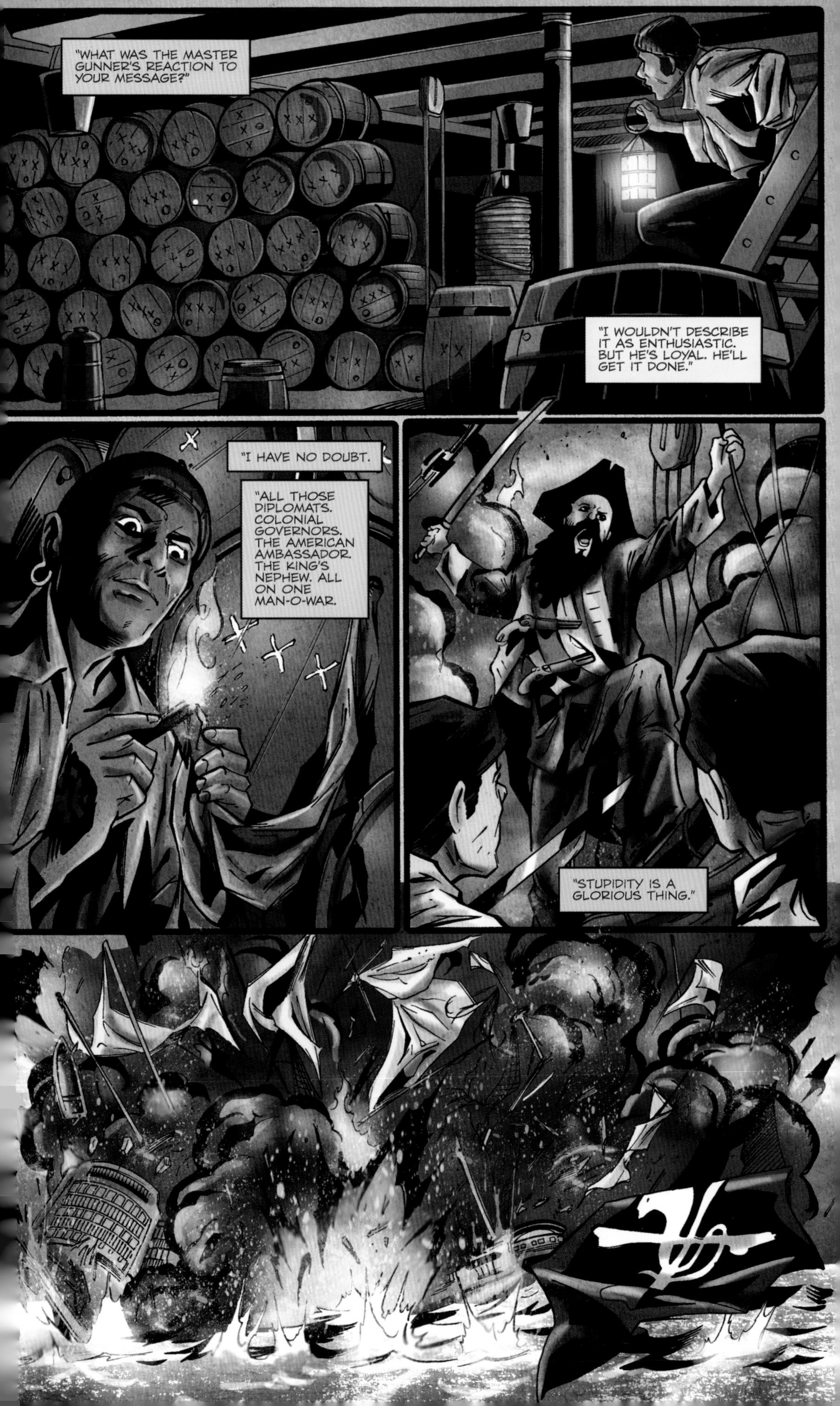
"WHAT WAS THE MASTER GUNNER'S REACTION TO YOUR MESSAGE?"
"I WOULDN'T DESCRIBE IT AS ENTHUSIASTIC. BUT HE'S LOYAL. HE'LL GET IT DONE."
"I HAVE NO DOUBT.
"ALL THOSE DIPLOMATS. COLONIAL GOVERNORS. THE AMERICAN AMBASSADOR. THE KING'S NEPHEW. ALL ON ONE MAN-O-WAR.
"STUPIDITY IS A GLORIOUS THING."

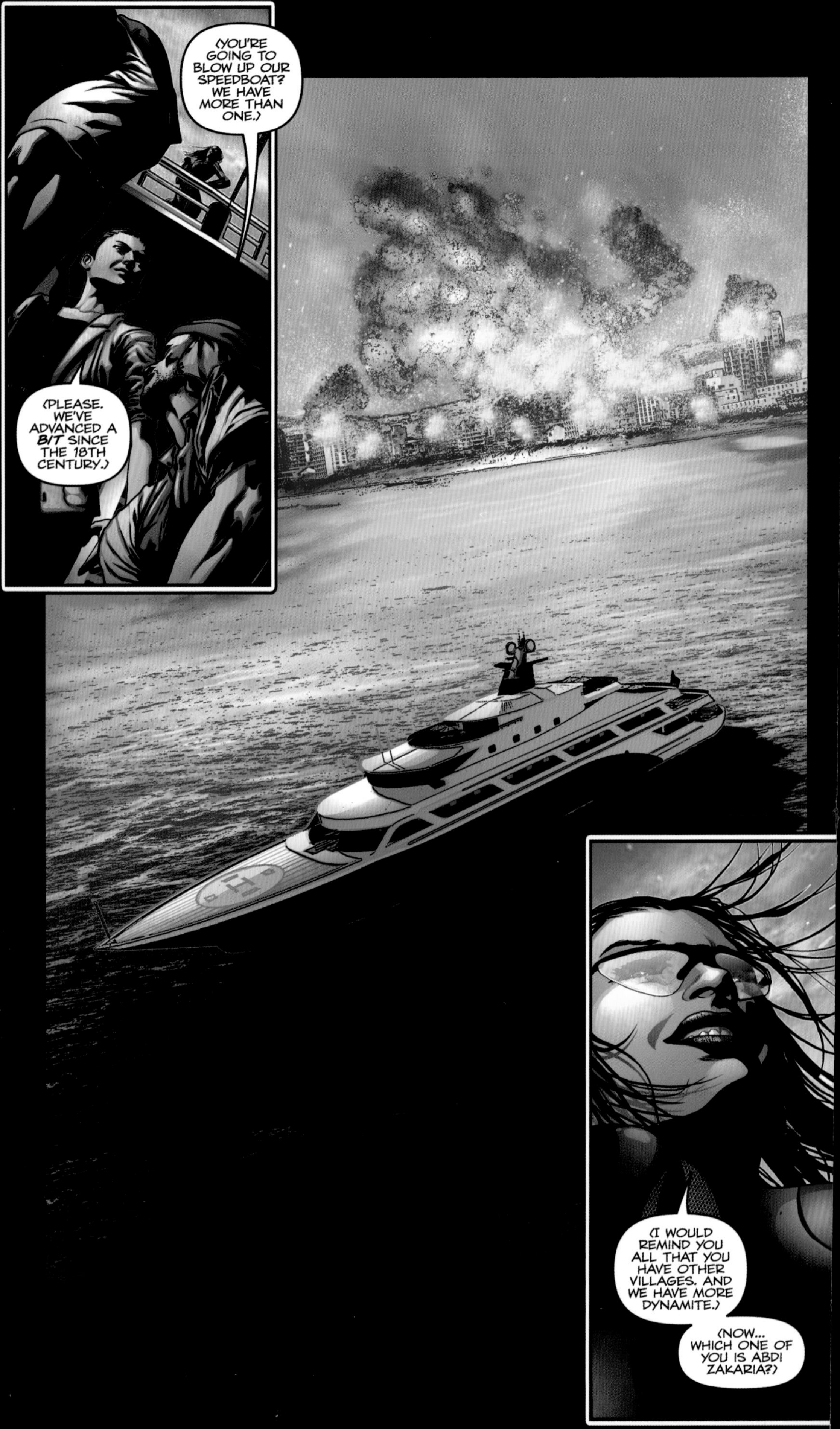
(YOU'RE GOING TO BLOW UP OUR SPEEDBOAT? WE HAVE MORE THAN ONE.)
(PLEASE. WE'VE ADVANCED A *BIT* SINCE THE 18TH CENTURY.)
(I WOULD REMIND YOU ALL THAT YOU HAVE OTHER VILLAGES. AND WE HAVE MORE DYNAMITE.)
(NOW... WHICH ONE OF YOU IS ABDI ZAKARIA?)

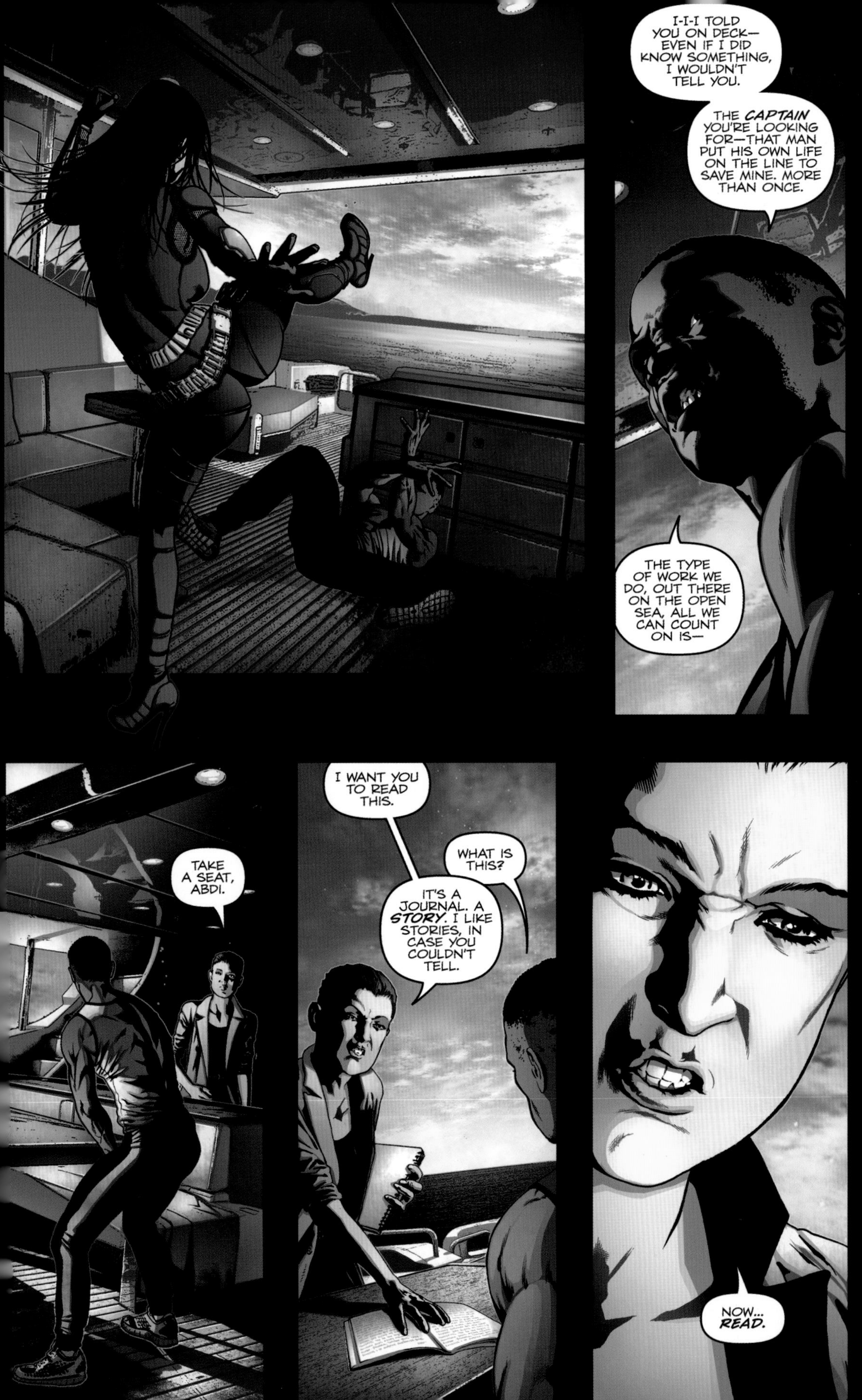
I-I-I TOLD YOU ON DECK—EVEN IF I DID KNOW SOMETHING, I WOULDN'T TELL YOU.
THE CAPTAIN YOU'RE LOOKING FOR—THAT MAN PUT HIS OWN LIFE ON THE LINE TO SAVE MINE. MORE THAN ONCE.
THE TYPE OF WORK WE DO, OUT THERE ON THE OPEN SEA, ALL WE CAN COUNT ON IS—
TAKE A SEAT, ABDI.
I WANT YOU TO READ THIS.
WHAT IS THIS?
IT'S A JOURNAL. A STORY. I LIKE STORIES, IN CASE YOU COULDN'T TELL.
NOW... READ.

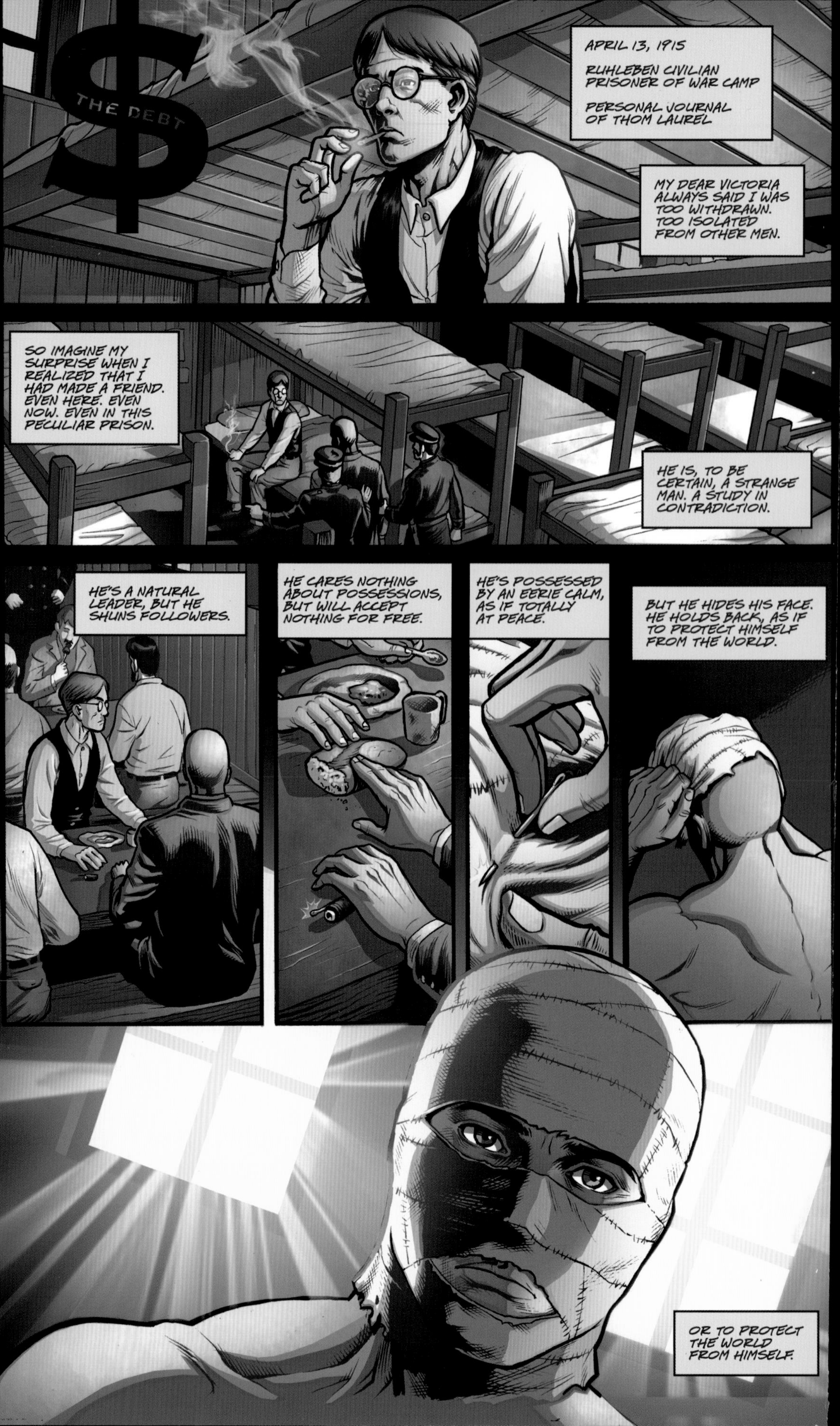
THE DEBT
APRIL 13, 1915
RUHLEBEN CIVILIAN PRISONER OF WAR CAMP
PERSONAL JOURNAL OF THOM LAUREL
MY DEAR VICTORIA ALWAYS SAID I WAS TOO WITHDRAWN. TOO ISOLATED FROM OTHER MEN.
SO IMAGINE MY SURPRISE WHEN I REALIZED THAT I HAD MADE A FRIEND. EVEN HERE. EVEN NOW. EVEN IN THIS PECULIAR PRISON.
HE IS, TO BE CERTAIN, A STRANGE MAN. A STUDY IN CONTRADICTION.
HE'S A NATURAL LEADER, BUT HE SHUNS FOLLOWERS.
HE CARES NOTHING ABOUT POSSESSIONS, BUT WILL ACCEPT NOTHING FOR FREE.
HE'S POSSESSED BY AN EERIE CALM, AS IF TOTALLY AT PEACE.
BUT HE HIDES HIS FACE. HE HOLDS BACK, AS IF TO PROTECT HIMSELF FROM THE WORLD.
OR TO PROTECT THE WORLD FROM HIMSELF.

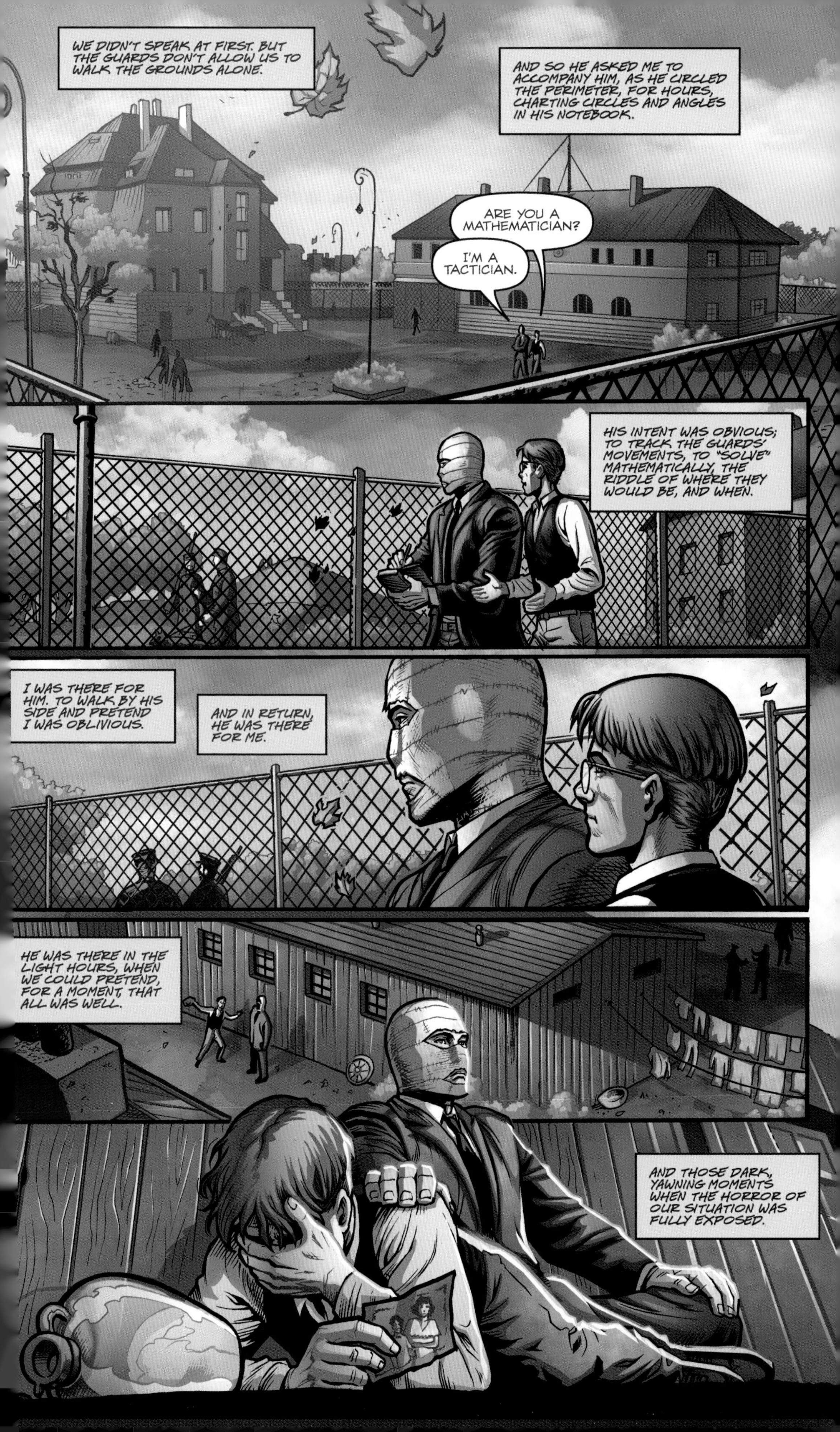
WE DIDN'T SPEAK AT FIRST. BUT THE GUARDS DON'T ALLOW US TO WALK THE GROUNDS ALONE.
AND SO HE ASKED ME TO ACCOMPANY HIM, AS HE CIRCLED THE PERIMETER, FOR HOURS, CHARTING CIRCLES AND ANGLES IN HIS NOTEBOOK.
ARE YOU A MATHEMATICIAN?
I'M A TACTICIAN.
HIS INTENT WAS OBVIOUS; TO TRACK THE GUARDS' MOVEMENTS, TO "SOLVE" MATHEMATICALLY, THE RIDDLE OF WHERE THEY WOULD BE, AND WHEN.
I WAS THERE FOR HIM. TO WALK BY HIS SIDE AND PRETEND I WAS OBLIVIOUS.
AND IN RETURN, HE WAS THERE FOR ME.
HE WAS THERE IN THE LIGHT HOURS, WHEN WE COULD PRETEND, FOR A MOMENT, THAT ALL WAS WELL.
AND THOSE DARK, YAWNING MOMENTS WHEN THE HORROR OF OUR SITUATION WAS FULLY EXPOSED.

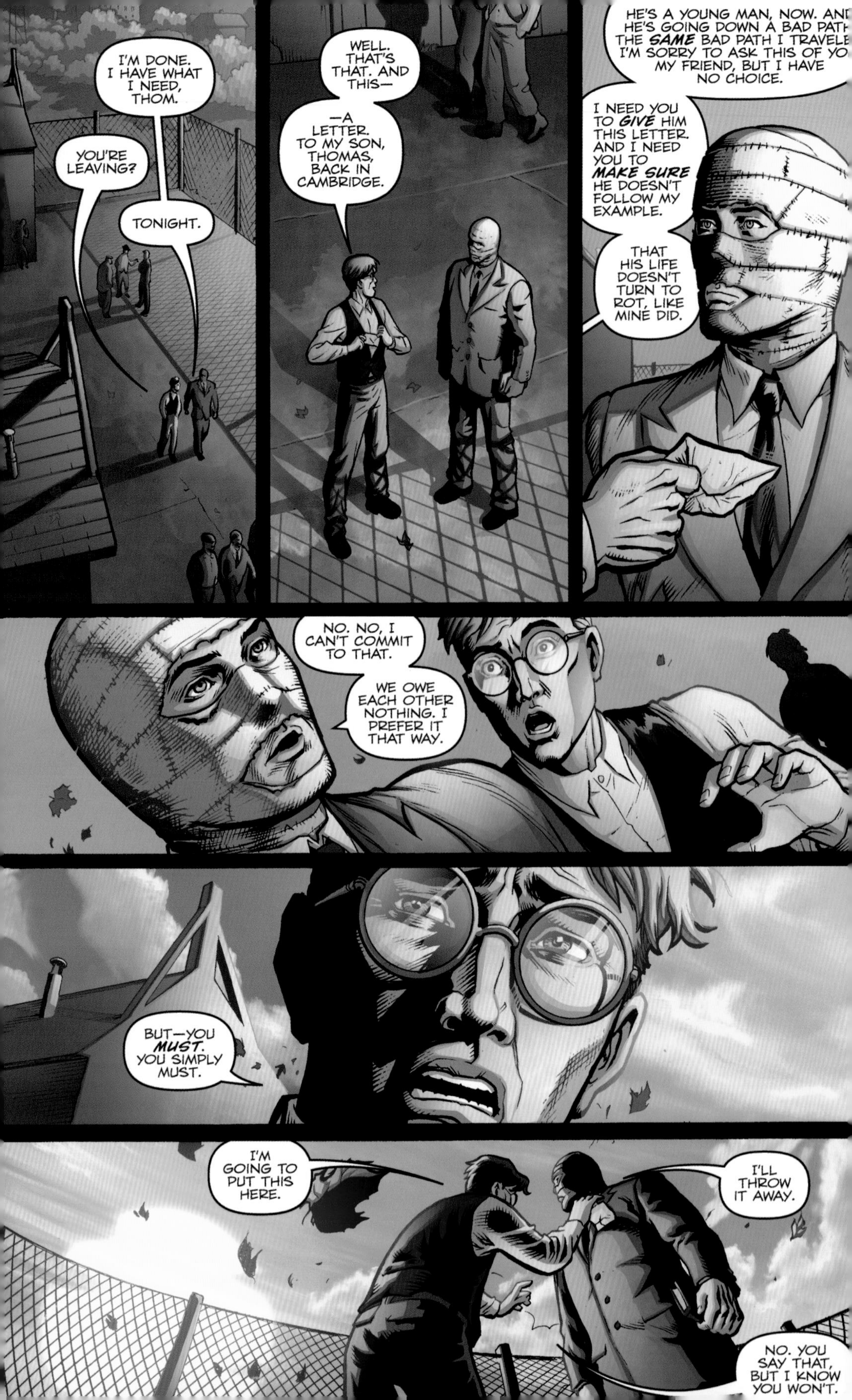
I'M DONE. I HAVE WHAT I NEED, THOM.
YOU'RE LEAVING?
TONIGHT.
WELL. THAT'S THAT. AND THIS—
—A LETTER. TO MY SON, THOMAS, BACK IN CAMBRIDGE.
HE'S A YOUNG MAN, NOW. AND HE'S GOING DOWN A BAD PATH THE SAME BAD PATH I TRAVELE I'M SORRY TO ASK THIS OF YO MY FRIEND, BUT I HAVE NO CHOICE.
I NEED YOU TO GIVE HIM THIS LETTER. AND I NEED YOU TO MAKE SURE HE DOESN'T FOLLOW MY EXAMPLE.
THAT HIS LIFE DOESN'T TURN TO ROT, LIKE MINE DID.
NO. NO, I CAN'T COMMIT TO THAT.
WE OWE EACH OTHER NOTHING. I PREFER IT THAT WAY.
BUT—YOU MUST. YOU SIMPLY MUST.
I'M GOING TO PUT THIS HERE.
I'LL THROW IT AWAY.
NO. YOU SAY THAT, BUT I KNOW YOU WON'T.

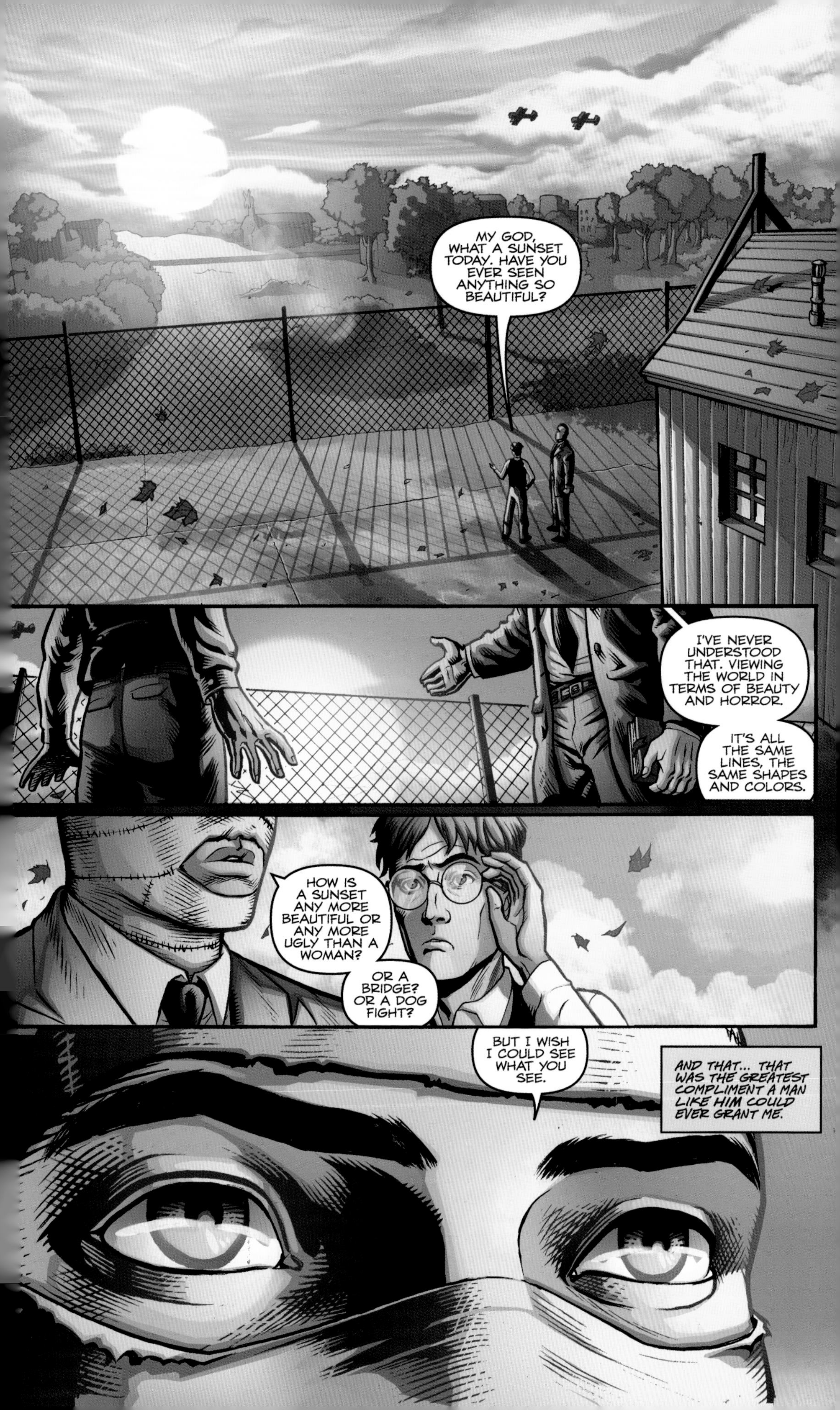
MY GOD, WHAT A SUNSET TODAY. HAVE YOU EVER SEEN ANYTHING SO BEAUTIFUL?
I'VE NEVER UNDERSTOOD THAT. VIEWING THE WORLD IN TERMS OF BEAUTY AND HORROR.
IT'S ALL THE SAME LINES, THE SAME SHAPES AND COLORS.
HOW IS A SUNSET ANY MORE BEAUTIFUL OR ANY MORE UGLY THAN A WOMAN?
OR A BRIDGE? OR A DOG FIGHT?
BUT I WISH I COULD SEE WHAT YOU SEE.
AND THAT... THAT WAS THE GREATEST COMPLIMENT A MAN LIKE HIM COULD EVER GRANT ME.

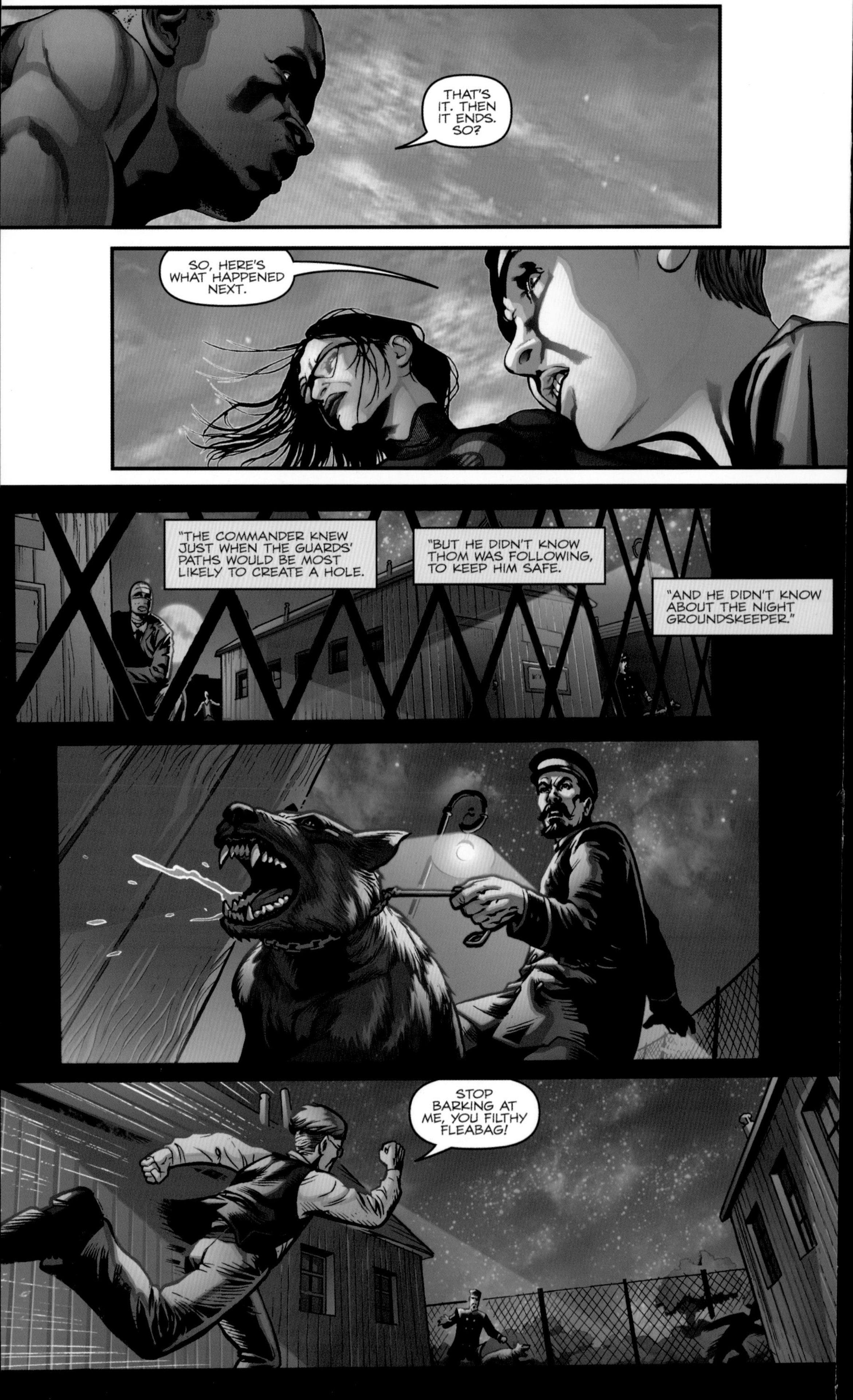
THAT'S IT. THEN IT ENDS. SO?
SO, HERE'S WHAT HAPPENED NEXT.
"THE COMMANDER KNEW JUST WHEN THE GUARDS' PATHS WOULD BE MOST LIKELY TO CREATE A HOLE.
"BUT HE DIDN'T KNOW THOM WAS FOLLOWING, TO KEEP HIM SAFE.
"AND HE DIDN'T KNOW ABOUT THE NIGHT GROUNDSKEEPER."
STOP BARKING AT ME, YOU FILTHY FLEABAG!

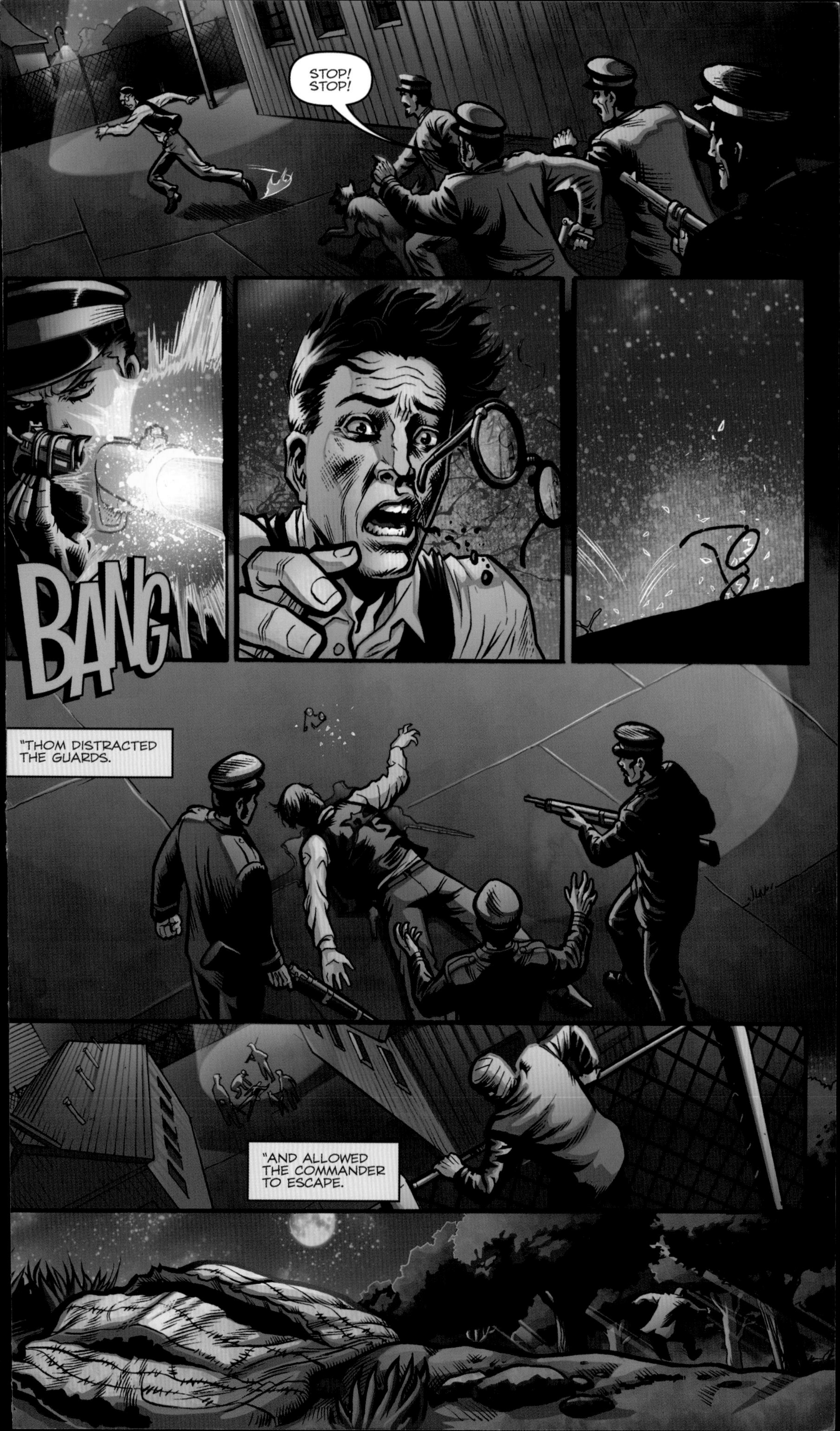
STOP! STOP!
BANG
"THOM DISTRACTED THE GUARDS.
"AND ALLOWED THE COMMANDER TO ESCAPE.

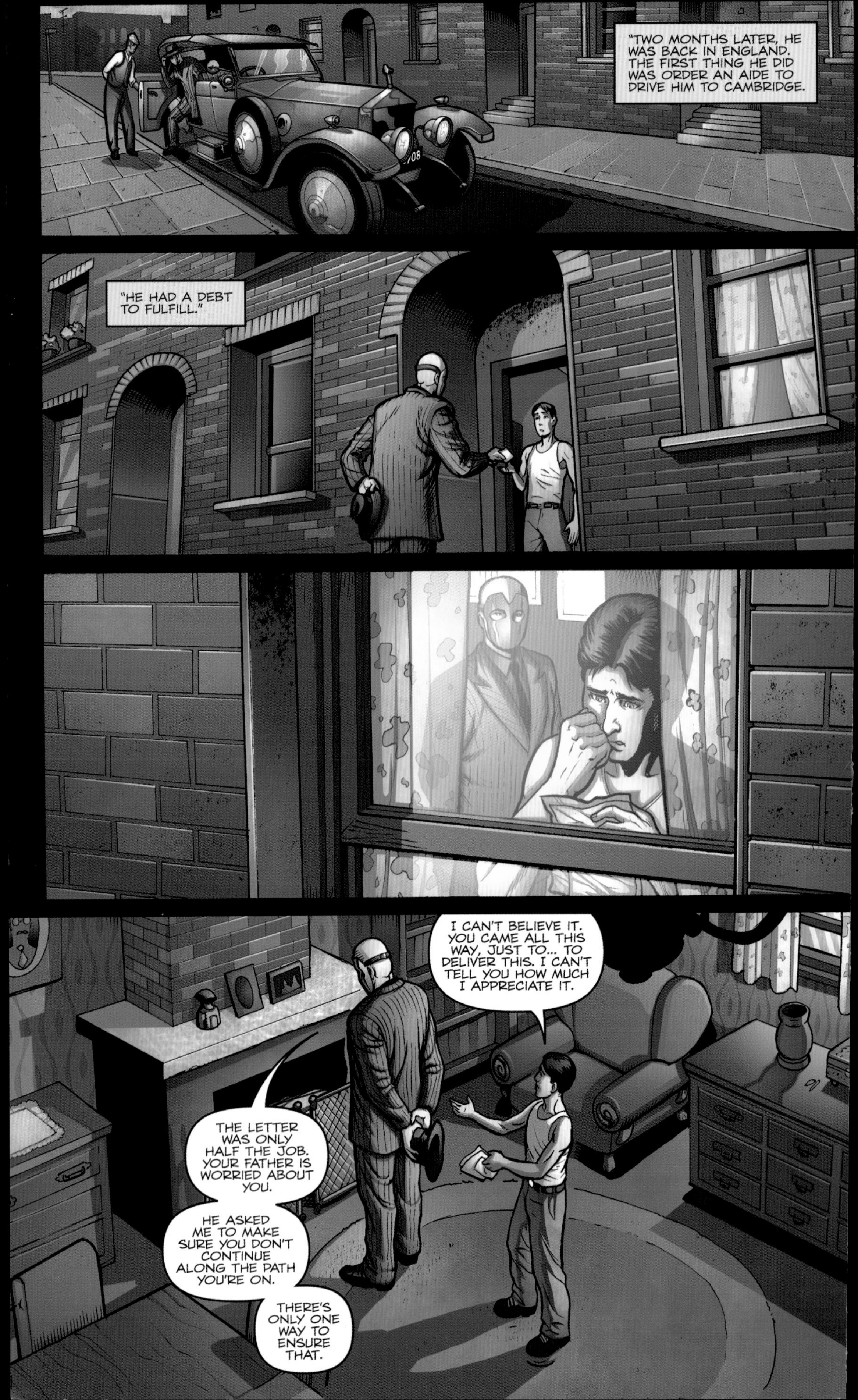
"TWO MONTHS LATER, HE WAS BACK IN ENGLAND. THE FIRST THING HE DID WAS ORDER AN AIDE TO DRIVE HIM TO CAMBRIDGE.
"HE HAD A DEBT TO FULFILL."
I CAN'T BELIEVE IT. YOU CAME ALL THIS WAY, JUST TO... TO DELIVER THIS. I CAN'T TELL YOU HOW MUCH I APPRECIATE IT.
THE LETTER WAS ONLY HALF THE JOB. YOUR FATHER IS WORRIED ABOUT YOU.
HE ASKED ME TO MAKE SURE YOU DON'T CONTINUE ALONG THE PATH YOU'RE ON.
THERE'S ONLY ONE WAY TO ENSURE THAT.

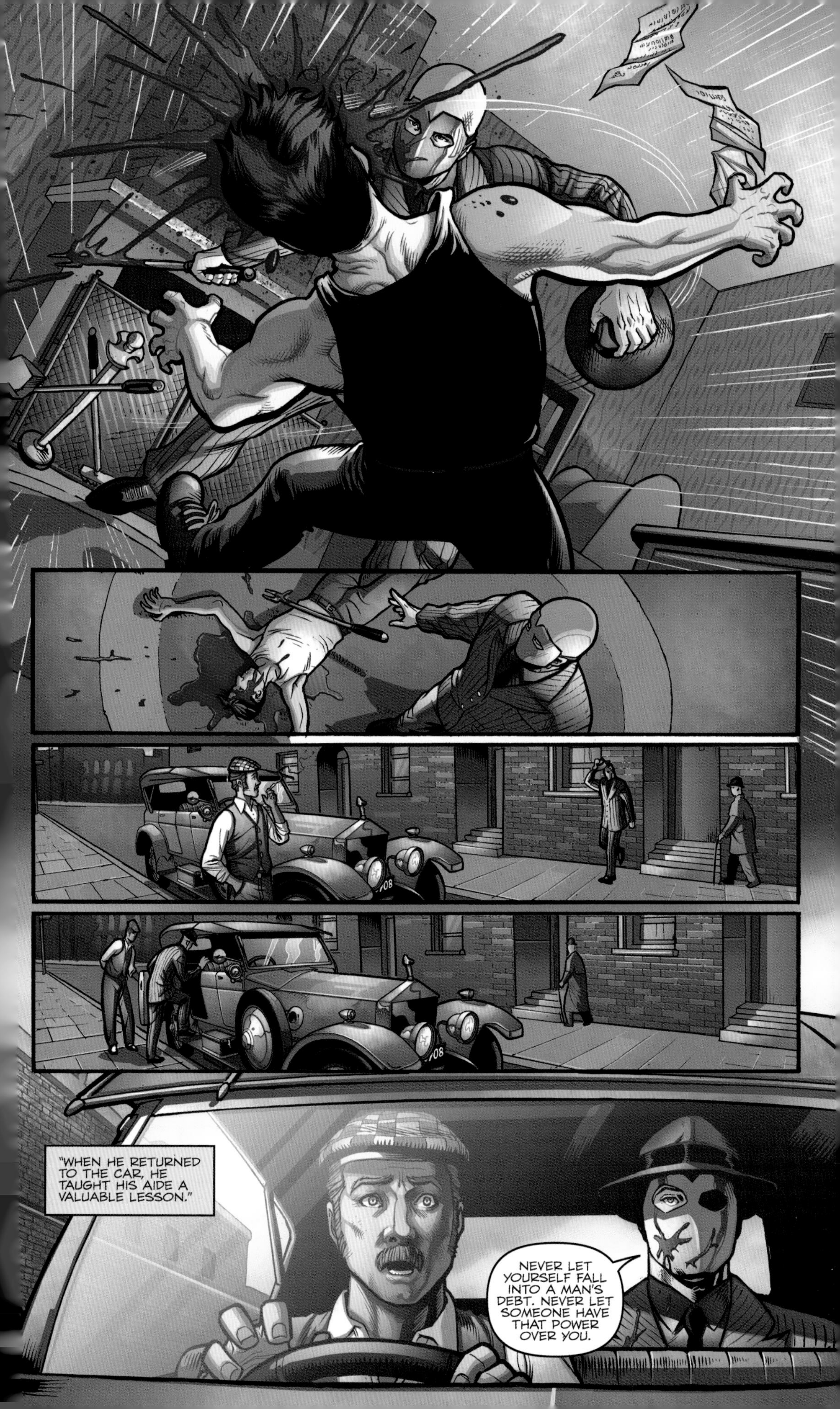
"WHEN HE RETURNED TO THE CAR, HE TAUGHT HIS AIDE A VALUABLE LESSON."
NEVER LET YOURSELF FALL INTO A MAN'S DEBT. NEVER LET SOMEONE HAVE THAT POWER OVER YOU.

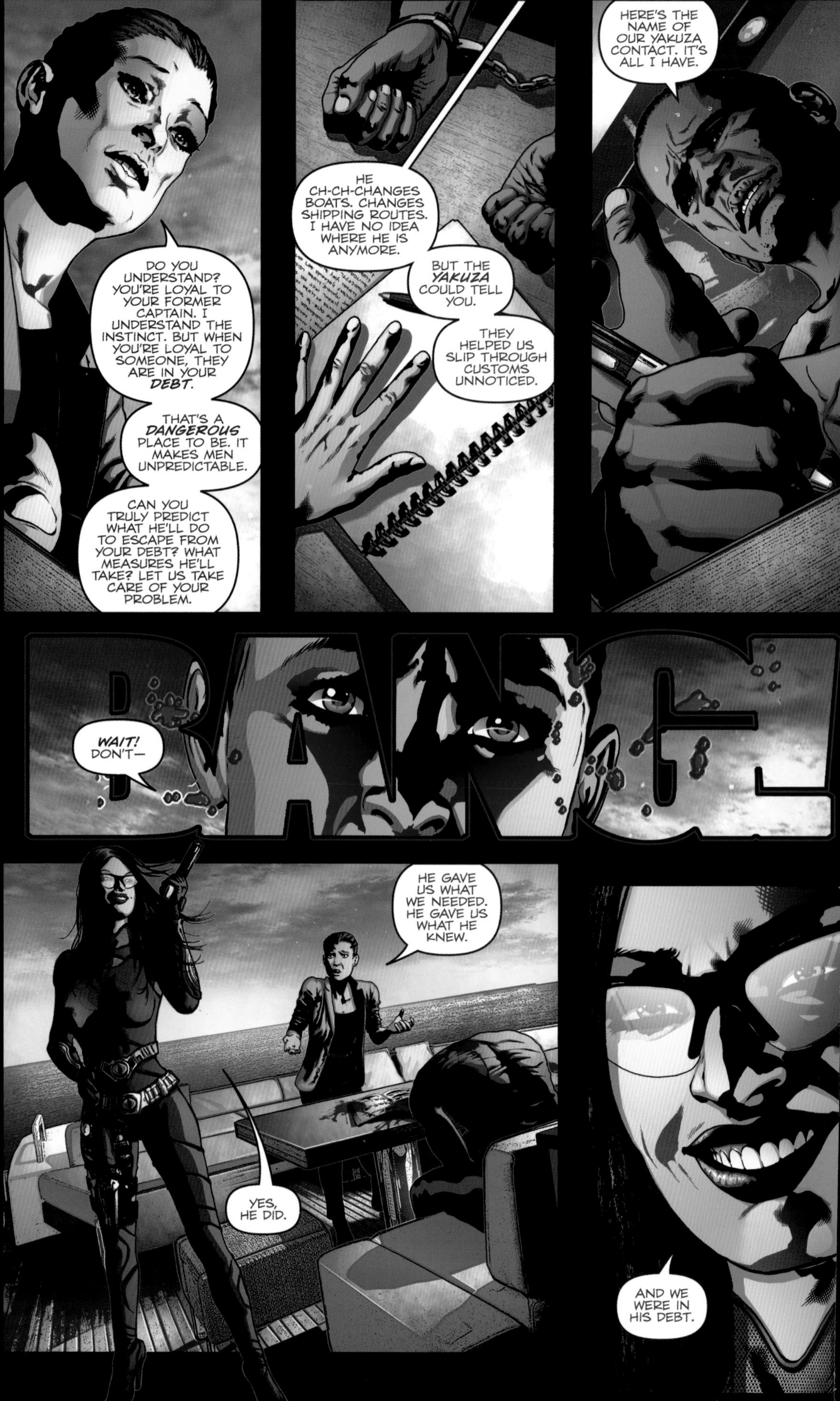
DO YOU UNDERSTAND? YOU'RE LOYAL TO YOUR FORMER CAPTAIN. I UNDERSTAND THE INSTINCT. BUT WHEN YOU'RE LOYAL TO SOMEONE, THEY ARE IN YOUR *DEBT*.
THAT'S A ***DANGEROUS*** PLACE TO BE. IT MAKES MEN UNPREDICTABLE.
CAN YOU TRULY PREDICT WHAT HE'LL DO TO ESCAPE FROM YOUR DEBT? WHAT MEASURES HE'LL TAKE? LET US TAKE CARE OF YOUR PROBLEM.
HE CH-CH-CHANGES BOATS. CHANGES SHIPPING ROUTES. I HAVE NO IDEA WHERE HE IS ANYMORE.
BUT THE *YAKUZA* COULD TELL YOU.
THEY HELPED US SLIP THROUGH CUSTOMS UNNOTICED.
HERE'S THE NAME OF OUR YAKUZA CONTACT. IT'S ALL I HAVE.
WAIT! DON'T—
HE GAVE US WHAT WE NEEDED. HE GAVE US WHAT HE KNEW.
YES, HE DID.
AND WE WERE IN HIS DEBT.

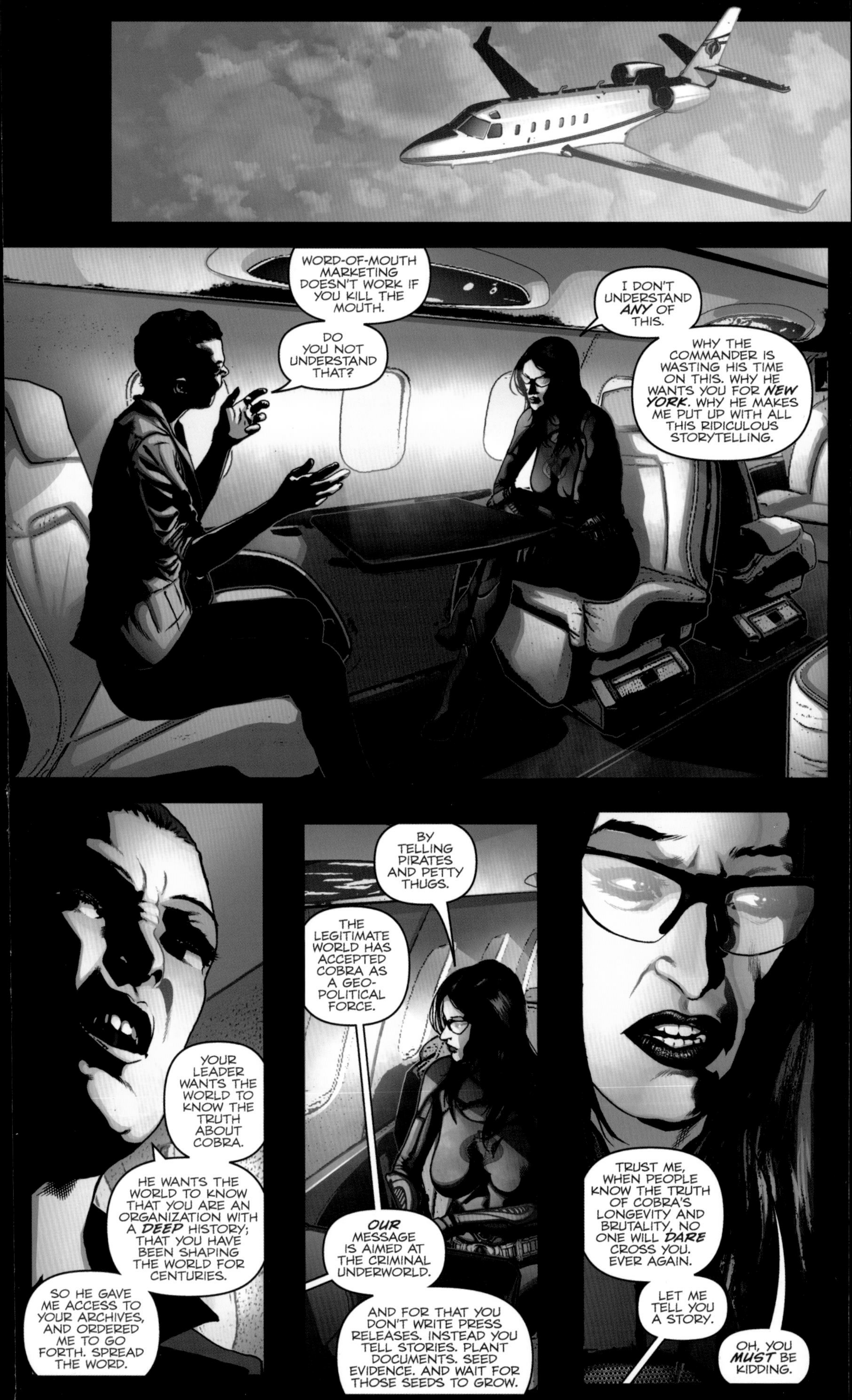
WORD-OF-MOUTH MARKETING DOESN'T WORK IF YOU KILL THE MOUTH.
DO YOU NOT UNDERSTAND THAT?
I DON'T UNDERSTAND ANY OF THIS.
WHY THE COMMANDER IS WASTING HIS TIME ON THIS. WHY HE WANTS YOU FOR NEW YORK. WHY HE MAKES ME PUT UP WITH ALL THIS RIDICULOUS STORYTELLING.
YOUR LEADER WANTS THE WORLD TO KNOW THE TRUTH ABOUT COBRA.
HE WANTS THE WORLD TO KNOW THAT YOU ARE AN ORGANIZATION WITH A DEEP HISTORY; THAT YOU HAVE BEEN SHAPING THE WORLD FOR CENTURIES.
SO HE GAVE ME ACCESS TO YOUR ARCHIVES, AND ORDERED ME TO GO FORTH. SPREAD THE WORD.
BY TELLING PIRATES AND PETTY THUGS.
THE LEGITIMATE WORLD HAS ACCEPTED COBRA AS A GEO-POLITICAL FORCE.
OUR MESSAGE IS AIMED AT THE CRIMINAL UNDERWORLD.
AND FOR THAT YOU DON'T WRITE PRESS RELEASES. INSTEAD YOU TELL STORIES. PLANT DOCUMENTS. SEED EVIDENCE. AND WAIT FOR THOSE SEEDS TO GROW.
TRUST ME, WHEN PEOPLE KNOW THE TRUTH OF COBRA'S LONGEVITY AND BRUTALITY, NO ONE WILL DARE CROSS YOU. EVER AGAIN.
LET ME TELL YOU A STORY.
OH, YOU MUST BE KIDDING.

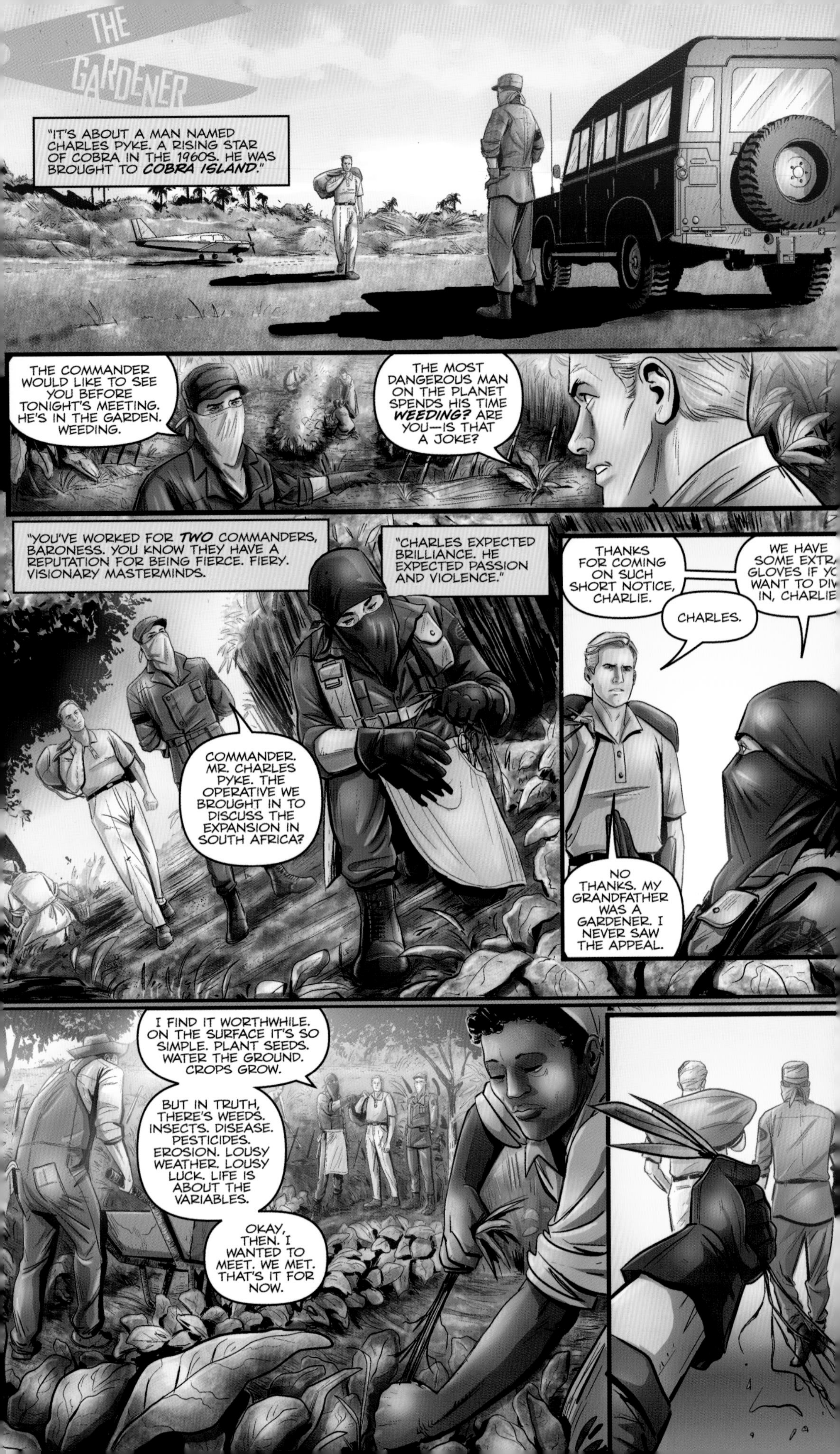
THE GARDENER
"IT'S ABOUT A MAN NAMED CHARLES PYKE. A RISING STAR OF COBRA IN THE 1960S. HE WAS BROUGHT TO COBRA ISLAND."
THE COMMANDER WOULD LIKE TO SEE YOU BEFORE TONIGHT'S MEETING. HE'S IN THE GARDEN. WEEDING.
THE MOST DANGEROUS MAN ON THE PLANET SPENDS HIS TIME WEEDING? ARE YOU—IS THAT A JOKE?
"YOU'VE WORKED FOR TWO COMMANDERS, BARONESS. YOU KNOW THEY HAVE A REPUTATION FOR BEING FIERCE. FIERY. VISIONARY MASTERMINDS.
"CHARLES EXPECTED BRILLIANCE. HE EXPECTED PASSION AND VIOLENCE."
COMMANDER. MR. CHARLES PYKE. THE OPERATIVE WE BROUGHT IN TO DISCUSS THE EXPANSION IN SOUTH AFRICA?
THANKS FOR COMING ON SUCH SHORT NOTICE, CHARLIE.
CHARLES.
WE HAVE SOME EXTR GLOVES IF YO WANT TO DIV IN, CHARLIE
NO THANKS. MY GRANDFATHER WAS A GARDENER. I NEVER SAW THE APPEAL.
I FIND IT WORTHWHILE. ON THE SURFACE IT'S SO SIMPLE. PLANT SEEDS. WATER THE GROUND. CROPS GROW.
BUT IN TRUTH, THERE'S WEEDS. INSECTS. DISEASE. PESTICIDES. EROSION. LOUSY WEATHER. LOUSY LUCK. LIFE IS ABOUT THE VARIABLES.
OKAY, THEN. I WANTED TO MEET. WE MET. THAT'S IT FOR NOW.

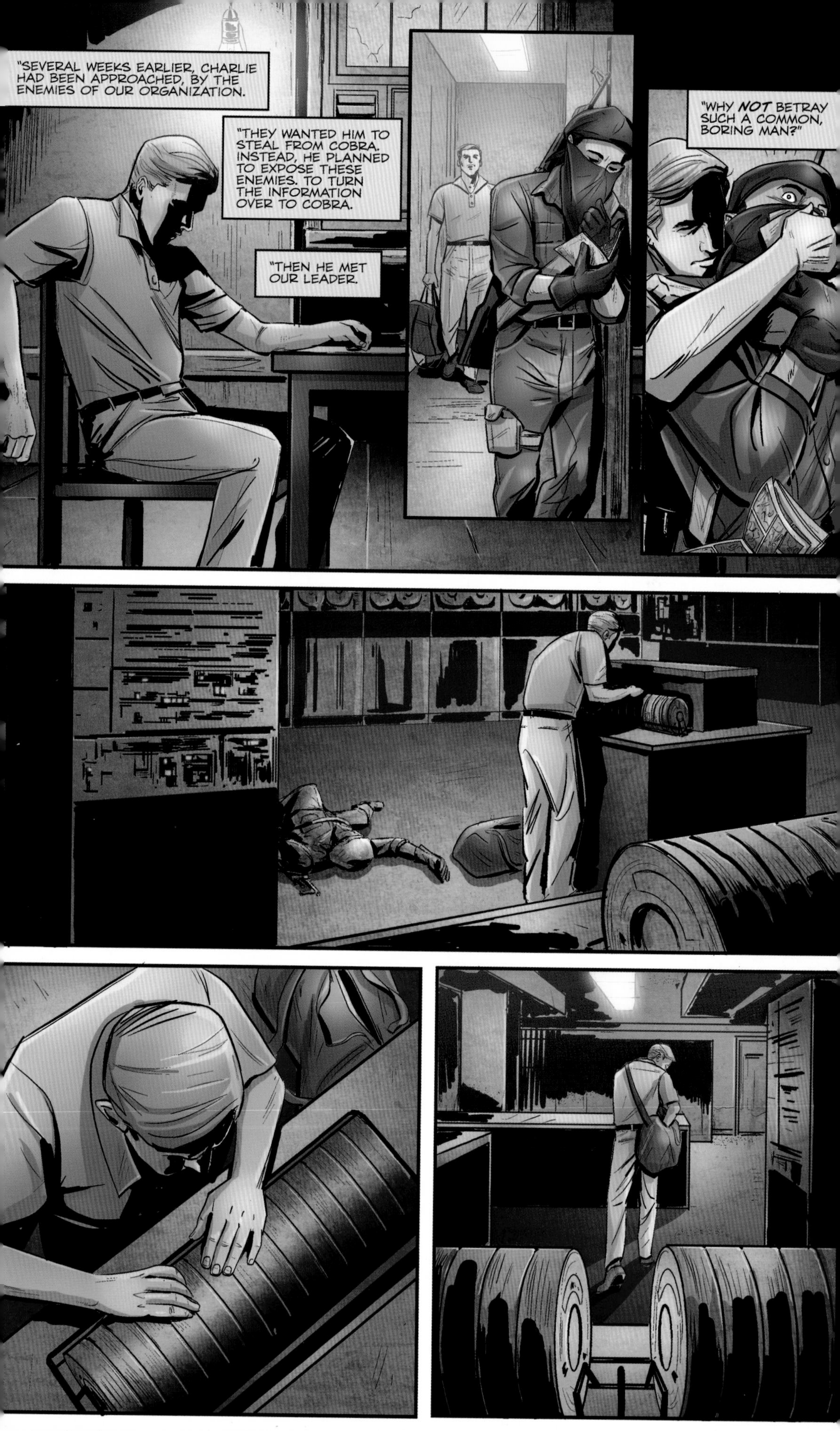
"SEVERAL WEEKS EARLIER, CHARLIE HAD BEEN APPROACHED, BY THE ENEMIES OF OUR ORGANIZATION.
"THEY WANTED HIM TO STEAL FROM COBRA. INSTEAD, HE PLANNED TO EXPOSE THESE ENEMIES. TO TURN THE INFORMATION OVER TO COBRA.
"THEN HE MET OUR LEADER.
"WHY NOT BETRAY SUCH A COMMON, BORING MAN?"

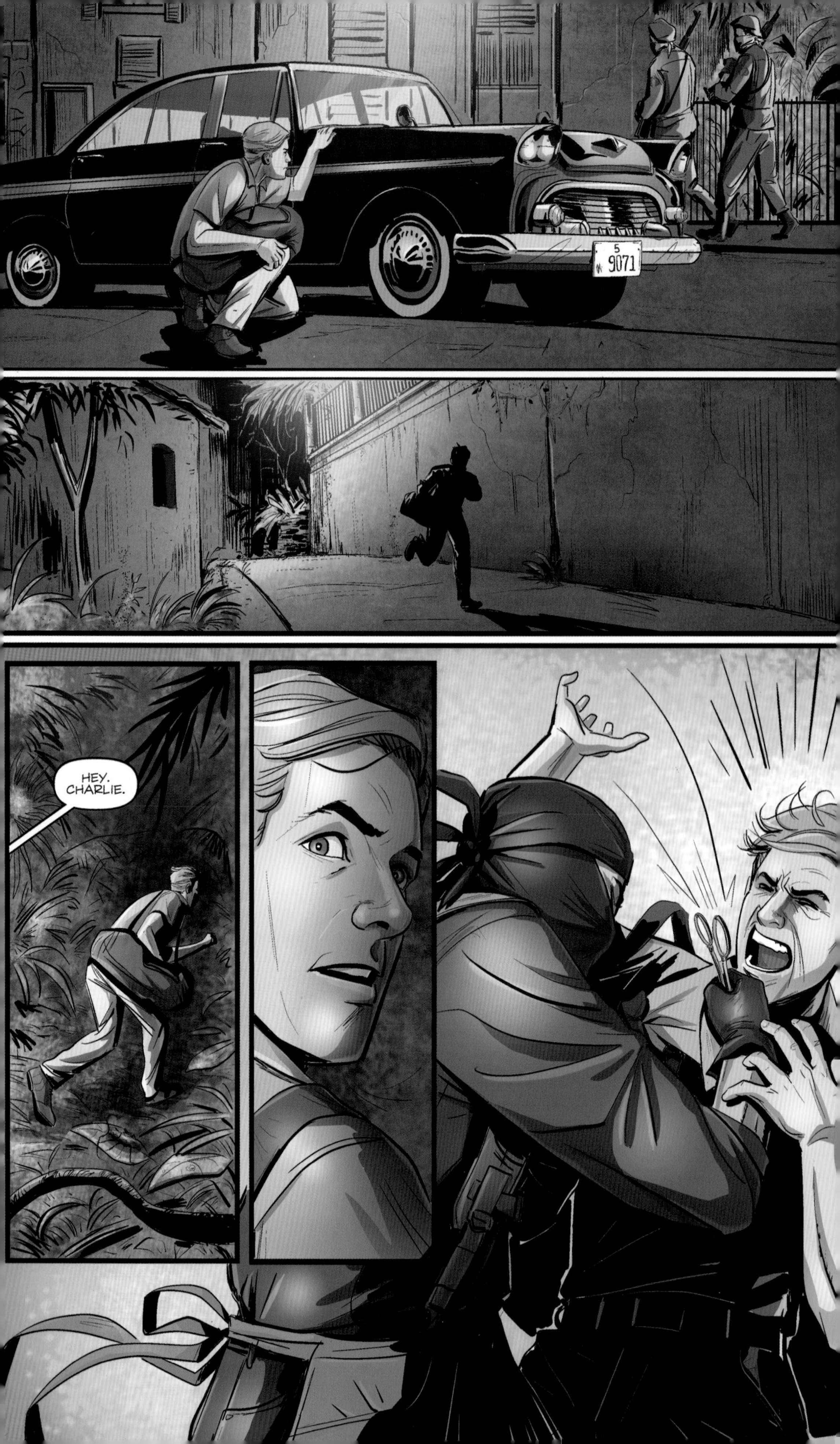
5
9071
HEY. CHARLIE.

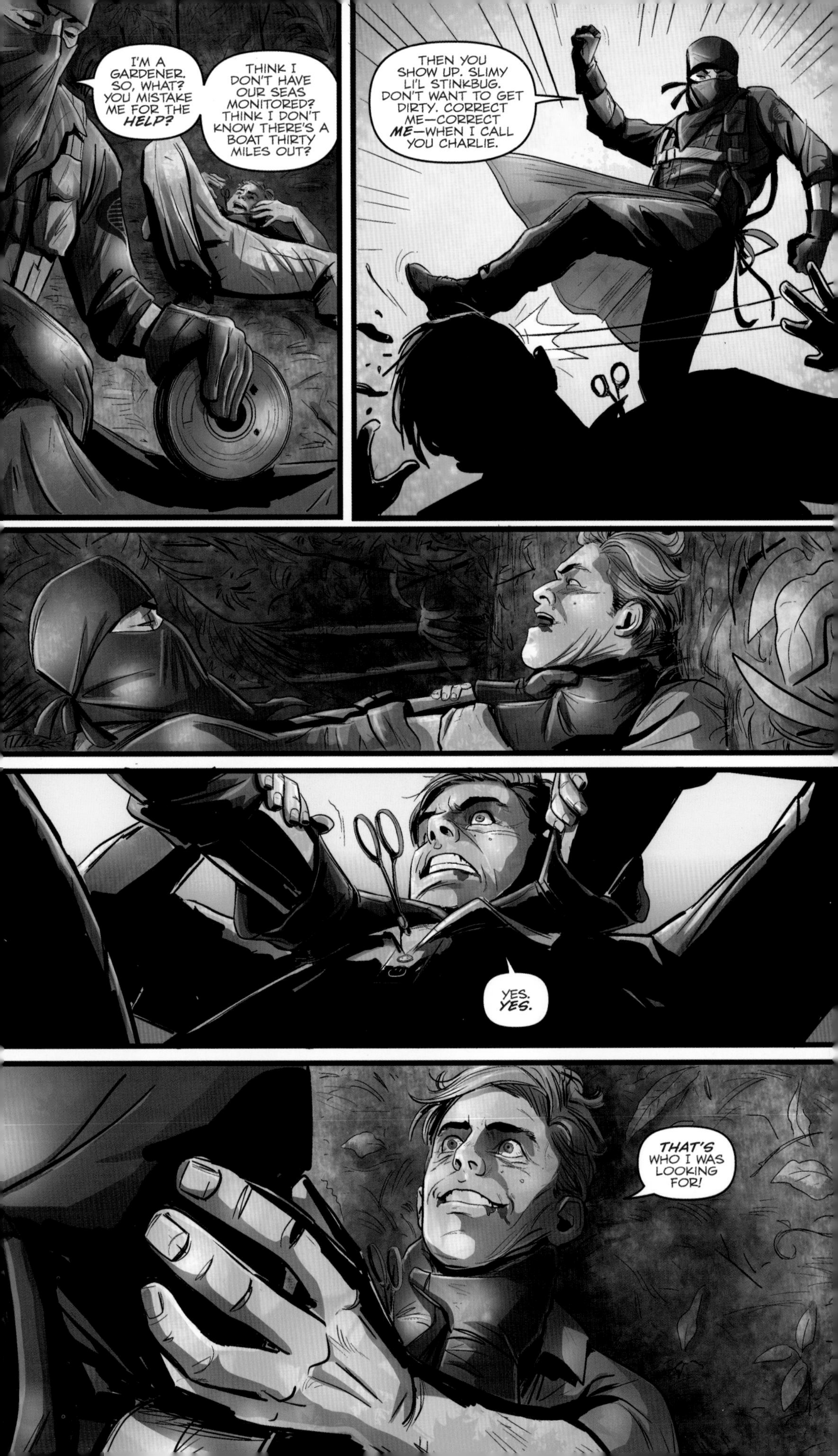
I'M A GARDENER. SO, WHAT? YOU MISTAKE ME FOR THE **HELP?**
THINK I DON'T HAVE OUR SEAS MONITORED? THINK I DON'T KNOW THERE'S A BOAT THIRTY MILES OUT?
THEN YOU SHOW UP. SLIMY LI'L STINKBUG. DON'T WANT TO GET DIRTY. CORRECT ME—CORRECT **ME**—WHEN I CALL YOU CHARLIE.
YES. **YES.**
THAT'S WHO I WAS LOOKING FOR!

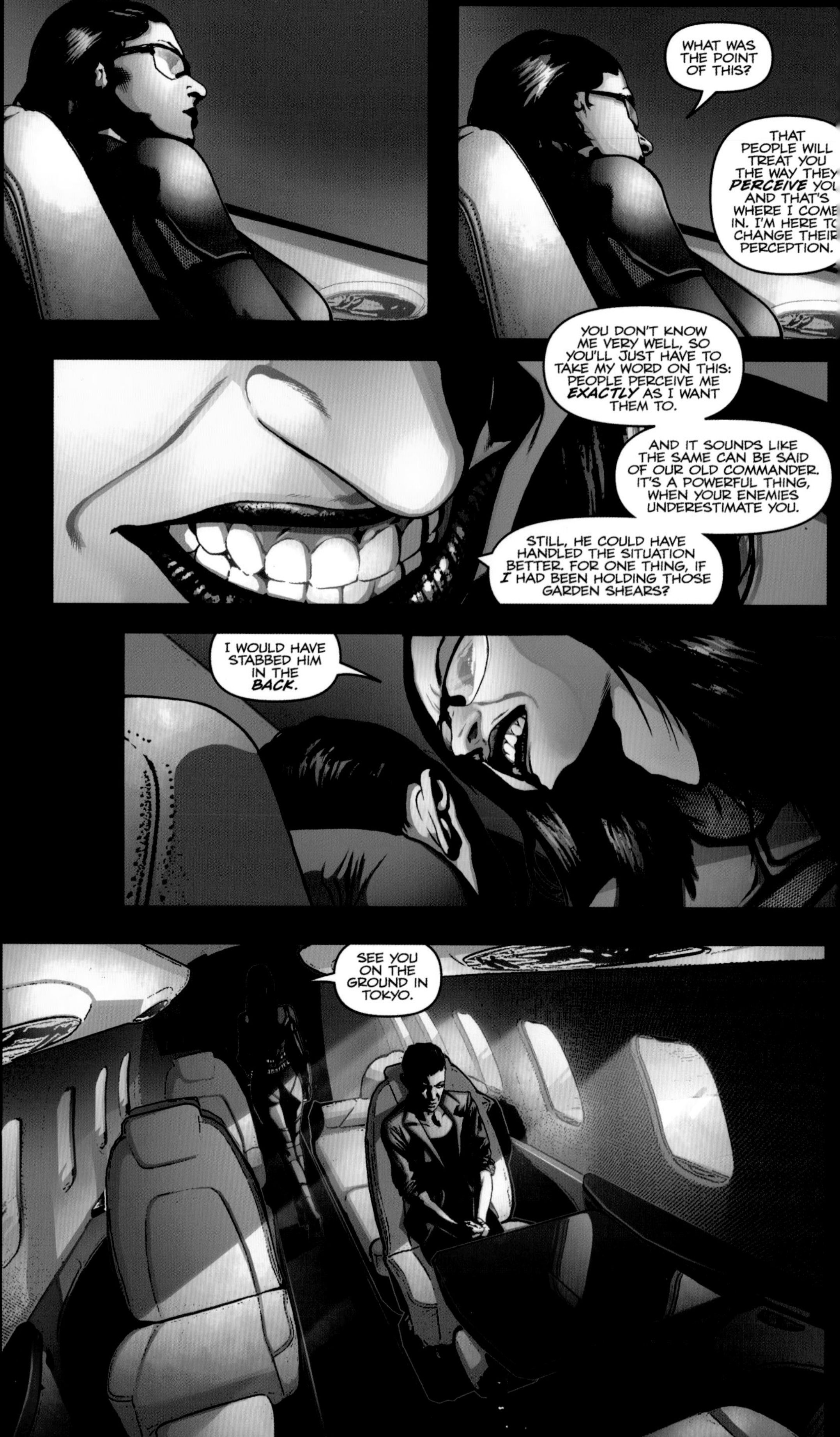
WHAT WAS THE POINT OF THIS?
THAT PEOPLE WILL TREAT YOU THE WAY THEY PERCEIVE YOU AND THAT'S WHERE I COME IN. I'M HERE TO CHANGE THEIR PERCEPTION.
YOU DON'T KNOW ME VERY WELL, SO YOU'LL JUST HAVE TO TAKE MY WORD ON THIS: PEOPLE PERCEIVE ME EXACTLY AS I WANT THEM TO.
AND IT SOUNDS LIKE THE SAME CAN BE SAID OF OUR OLD COMMANDER. IT'S A POWERFUL THING, WHEN YOUR ENEMIES UNDERESTIMATE YOU.
STILL, HE COULD HAVE HANDLED THE SITUATION BETTER. FOR ONE THING, IF I HAD BEEN HOLDING THOSE GARDEN SHEARS?
I WOULD HAVE STABBED HIM IN THE BACK.
SEE YOU ON THE GROUND IN TOKYO.

CHAPTER TWO

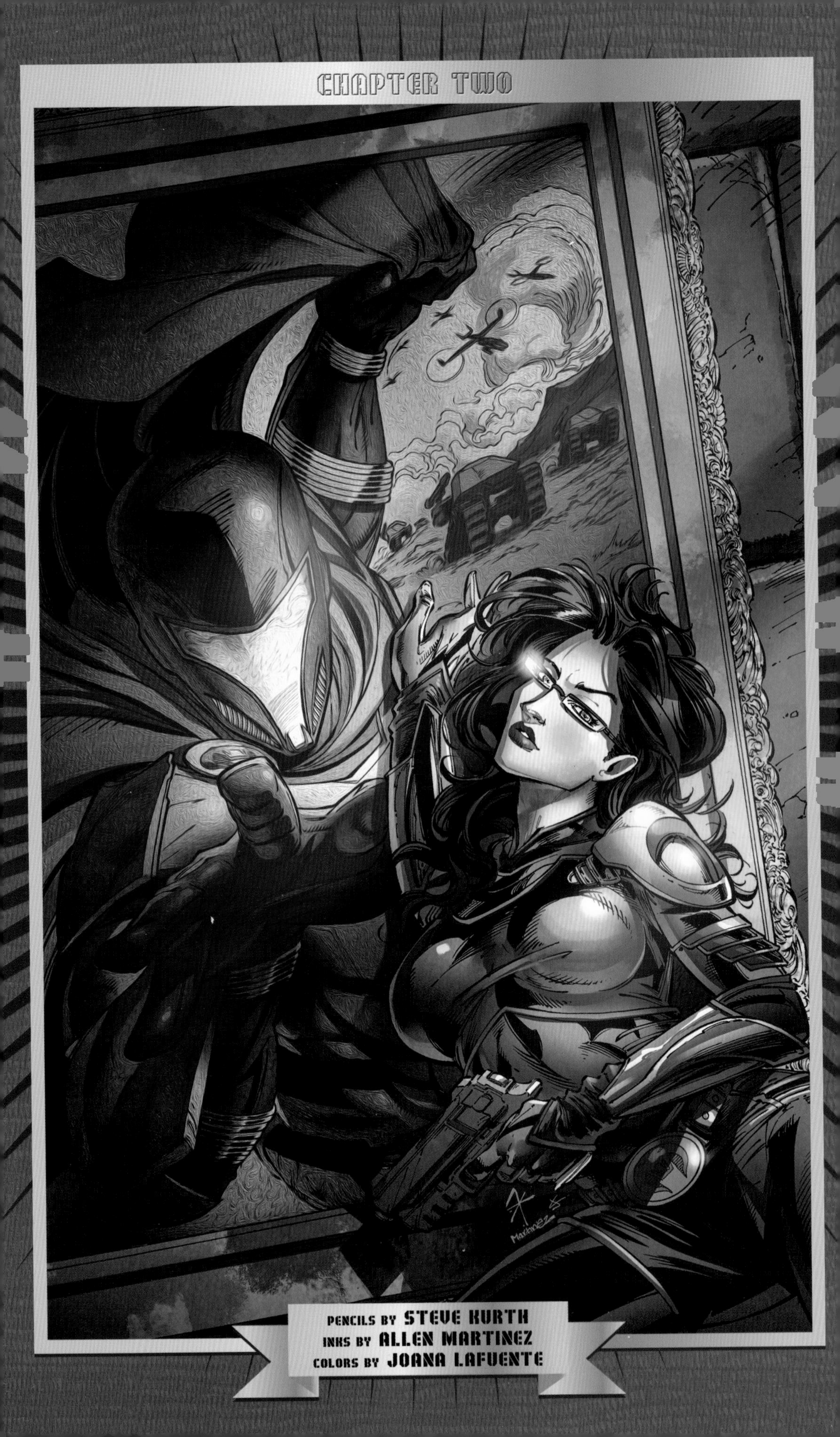
Martinez

PENCILS BY **STEVE KURTH**
INKS BY **ALLEN MARTINEZ**
COLORS BY **JOANA LAFUENTE**

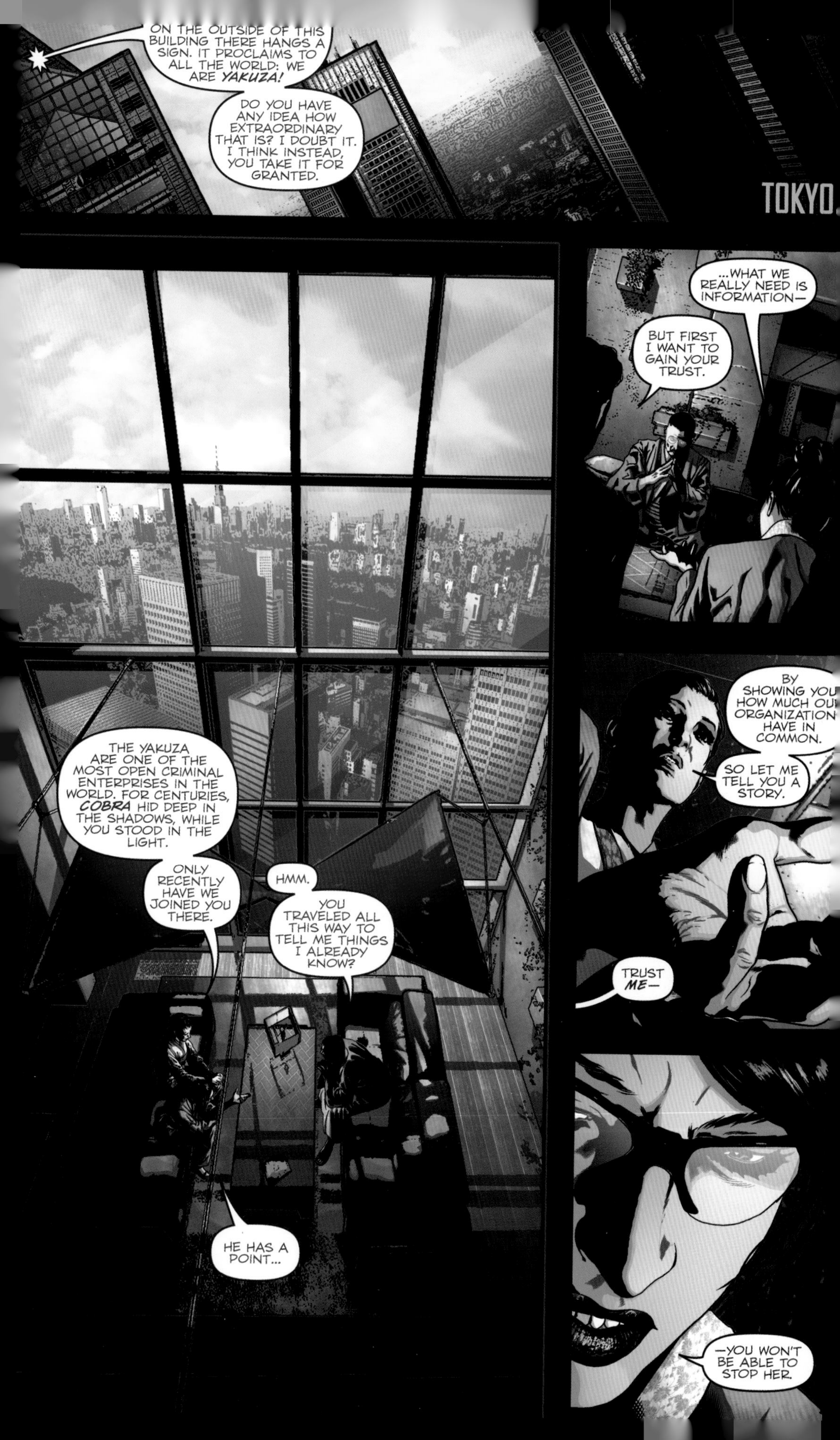
ON THE OUTSIDE OF THIS BUILDING THERE HANGS A SIGN. IT PROCLAIMS TO ALL THE WORLD: WE ARE YAKUZA!
DO YOU HAVE ANY IDEA HOW EXTRAORDINARY THAT IS? I DOUBT IT. I THINK INSTEAD, YOU TAKE IT FOR GRANTED.
TOKYO.
THE YAKUZA ARE ONE OF THE MOST OPEN CRIMINAL ENTERPRISES IN THE WORLD. FOR CENTURIES, COBRA HID DEEP IN THE SHADOWS, WHILE YOU STOOD IN THE LIGHT.
ONLY RECENTLY HAVE WE JOINED YOU THERE.
HMM.
YOU TRAVELED ALL THIS WAY TO TELL ME THINGS I ALREADY KNOW?
HE HAS A POINT...
...WHAT WE REALLY NEED IS INFORMATION—
BUT FIRST I WANT TO GAIN YOUR TRUST.
SO LET ME TELL YOU A STORY.
TRUST ME—
—YOU WON'T BE ABLE TO STOP HER.

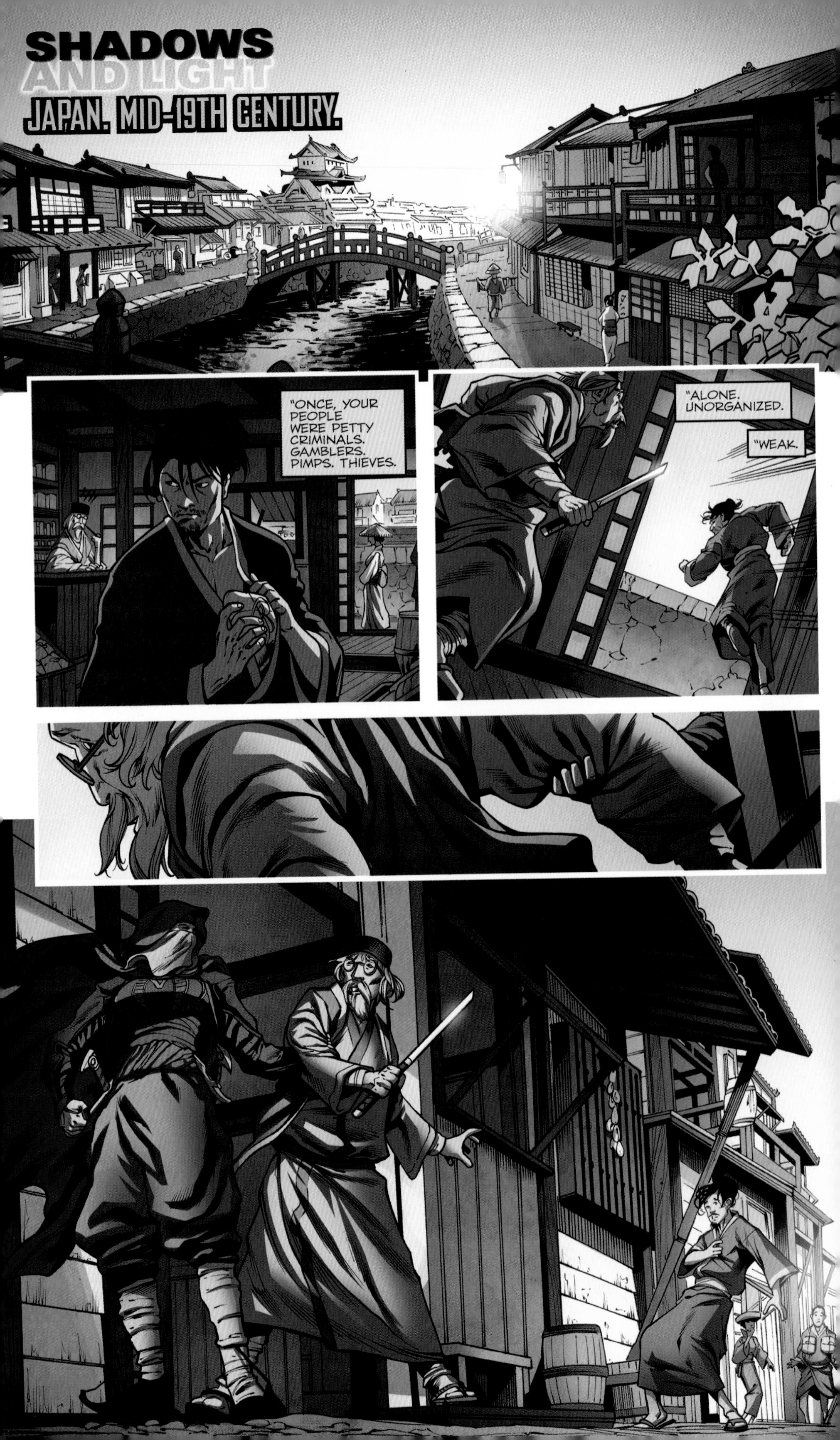
SHADOWS AND LIGHT
JAPAN. MID-19TH CENTURY.
"ONCE, YOUR PEOPLE WERE PETTY CRIMINALS. GAMBLERS. PIMPS. THIEVES.
"ALONE. UNORGANIZED.
"WEAK.

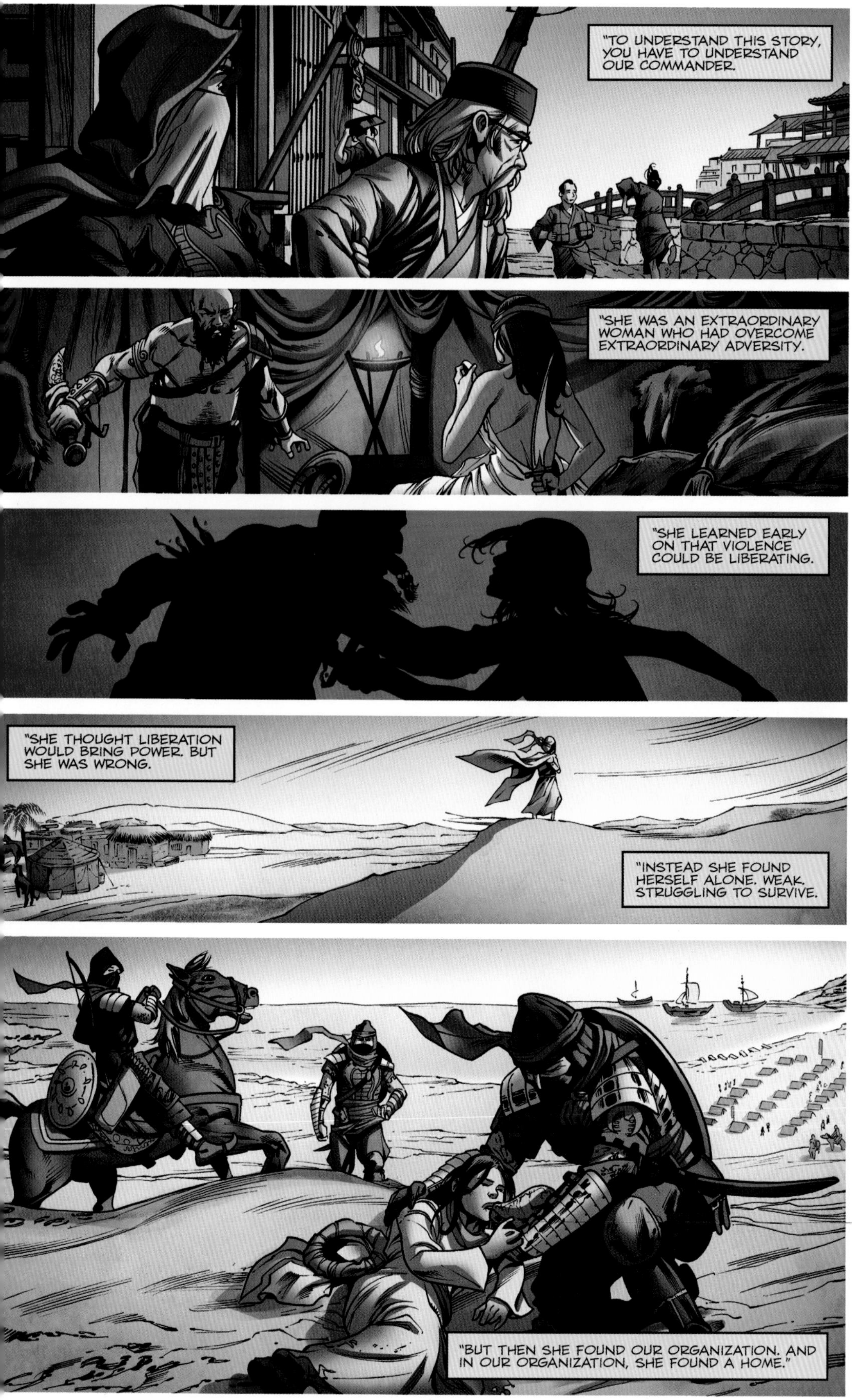
"TO UNDERSTAND THIS STORY, YOU HAVE TO UNDERSTAND OUR COMMANDER.
"SHE WAS AN EXTRAORDINARY WOMAN WHO HAD OVERCOME EXTRAORDINARY ADVERSITY.
"SHE LEARNED EARLY ON THAT VIOLENCE COULD BE LIBERATING.
"SHE THOUGHT LIBERATION WOULD BRING POWER. BUT SHE WAS WRONG.
"INSTEAD SHE FOUND HERSELF ALONE. WEAK. STRUGGLING TO SURVIVE.
"BUT THEN SHE FOUND OUR ORGANIZATION. AND IN OUR ORGANIZATION, SHE FOUND A HOME."

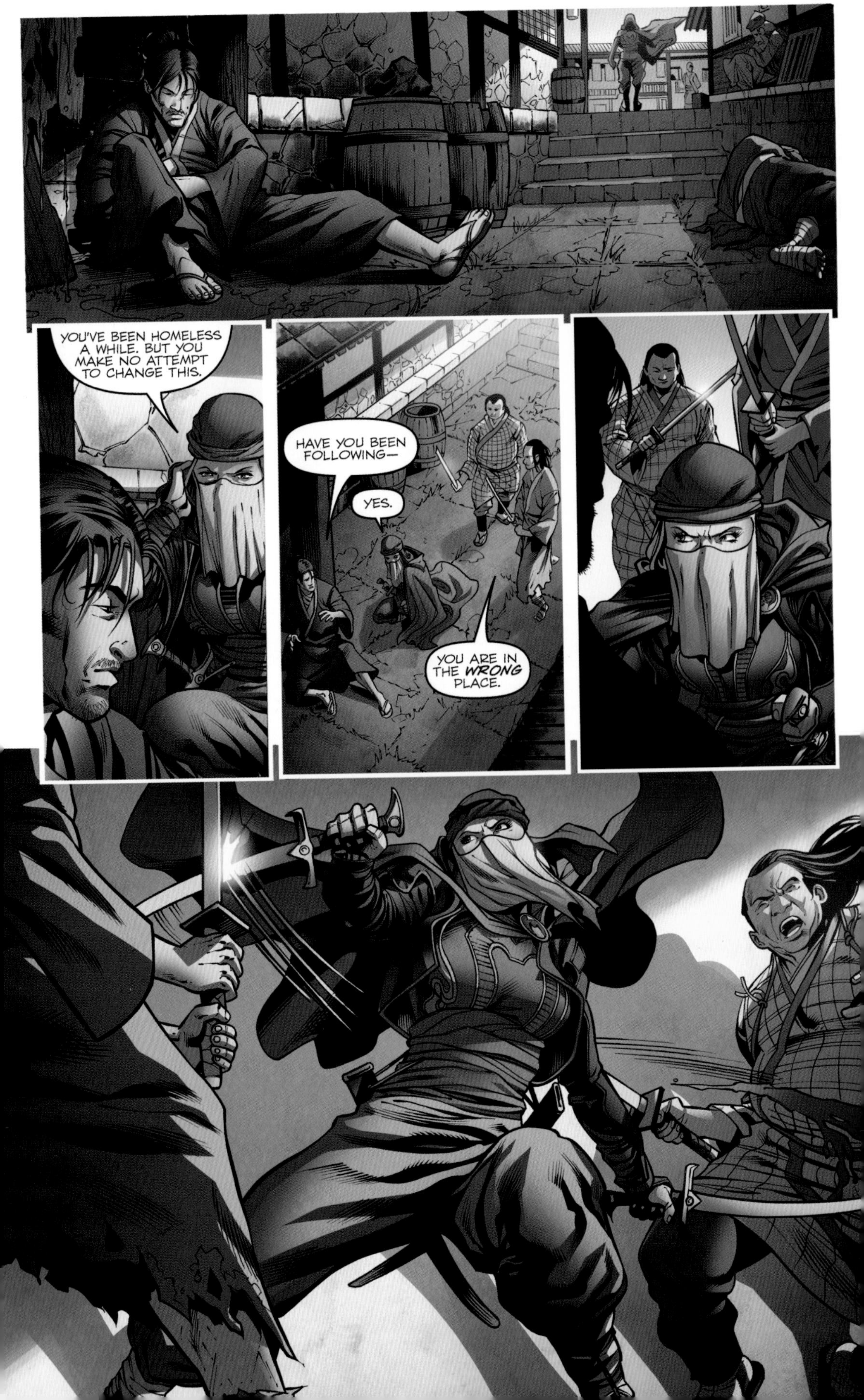

YOU'VE BEEN HOMELESS A WHILE. BUT YOU MAKE NO ATTEMPT TO CHANGE THIS.
HAVE YOU BEEN FOLLOWING—
YES.
YOU ARE IN THE *WRONG* PLACE.

I KNOW YOU. I *WAS* YOU. THERE'S A BETTER WAY TO LIVE.

POWER COMES NOT FROM A SINGLE, LOUD STRUGGLING VOICE, BUT FROM A SILENT, UNIFIED FORCE.

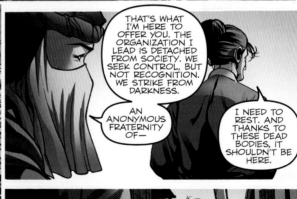

THAT'S WHAT I'M HERE TO OFFER YOU. THE ORGANIZATION I LEAD IS DETACHED FROM SOCIETY. WE SEEK CONTROL, BUT NOT RECOGNITION. WE STRIKE FROM DARKNESS.

AN ANONYMOUS FRATERNITY OF—

I NEED TO REST. AND THANKS TO THESE DEAD BODIES, IT SHOULDN'T BE HERE.

"THIS HAD NEVER HAPPENED BEFORE. THE COMMANDER HAD DELIVERED HER MESSAGE AROUND THE WORLD. IN THAT TIME SHE HAD FACED VIOLENCE. CURIOSITY. FASCINATION. HOSTILITY. BEGRUDGING RESPECT.

"BUT NEVER INDIFFERENCE."

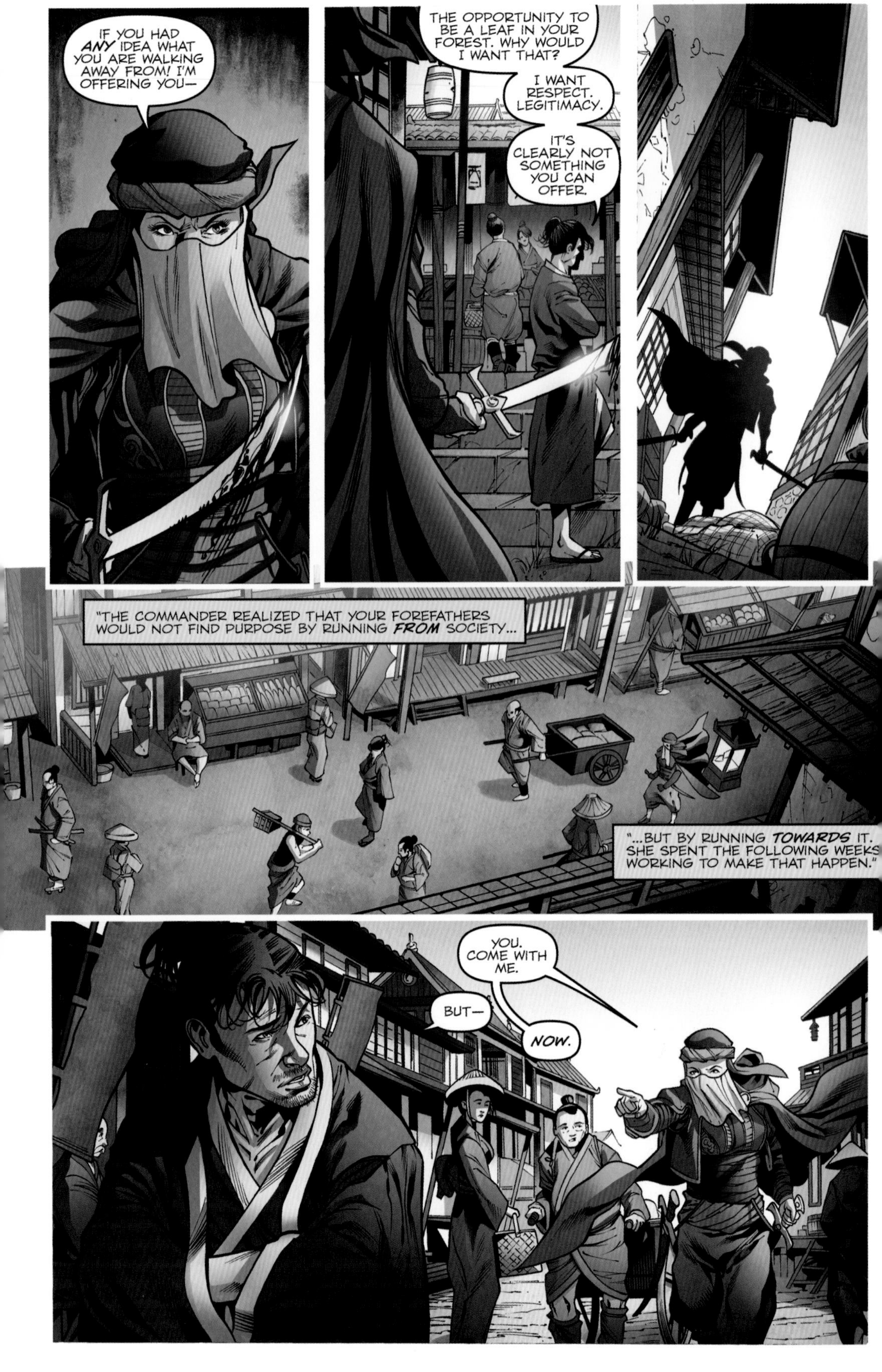
IF YOU HAD *ANY* IDEA WHAT YOU ARE WALKING AWAY FROM! I'M OFFERING YOU—
THE OPPORTUNITY TO BE A LEAF IN YOUR FOREST. WHY WOULD I WANT THAT?
I WANT RESPECT. LEGITIMACY.
IT'S CLEARLY NOT SOMETHING YOU CAN OFFER.
"THE COMMANDER REALIZED THAT YOUR FOREFATHERS WOULD NOT FIND PURPOSE BY RUNNING *FROM* SOCIETY...
"...BUT BY RUNNING *TOWARDS* IT. SHE SPENT THE FOLLOWING WEEKS WORKING TO MAKE THAT HAPPEN."
YOU. COME WITH ME.
BUT—
NOW.

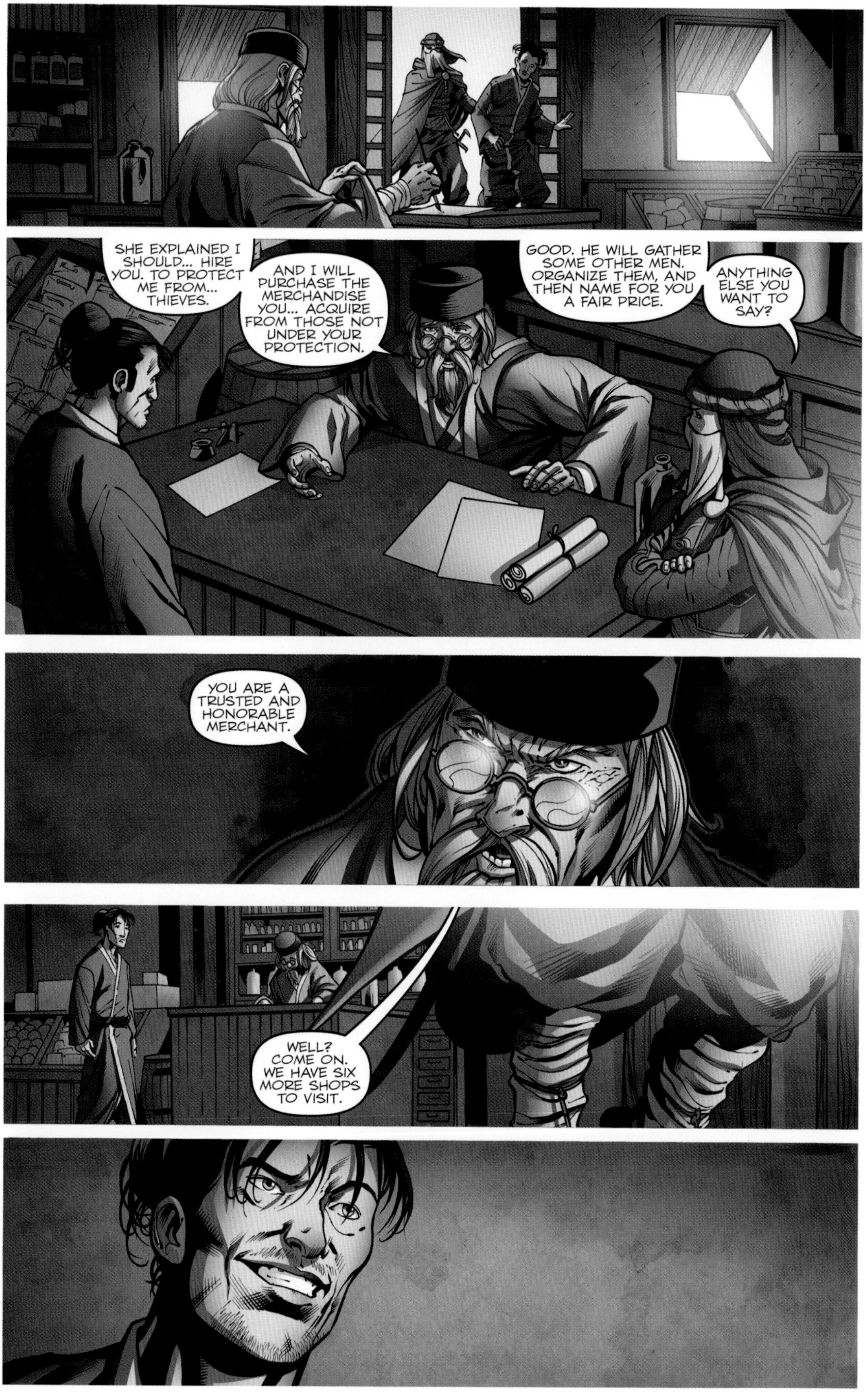

SHE EXPLAINED I SHOULD... HIRE YOU. TO PROTECT ME FROM... THIEVES.
AND I WILL PURCHASE THE MERCHANDISE YOU... ACQUIRE FROM THOSE NOT UNDER YOUR PROTECTION.
GOOD. HE WILL GATHER SOME OTHER MEN. ORGANIZE THEM, AND THEN NAME FOR YOU A FAIR PRICE.
ANYTHING ELSE YOU WANT TO SAY?
YOU ARE A TRUSTED AND HONORABLE MERCHANT.
WELL? COME ON. WE HAVE SIX MORE SHOPS TO VISIT.

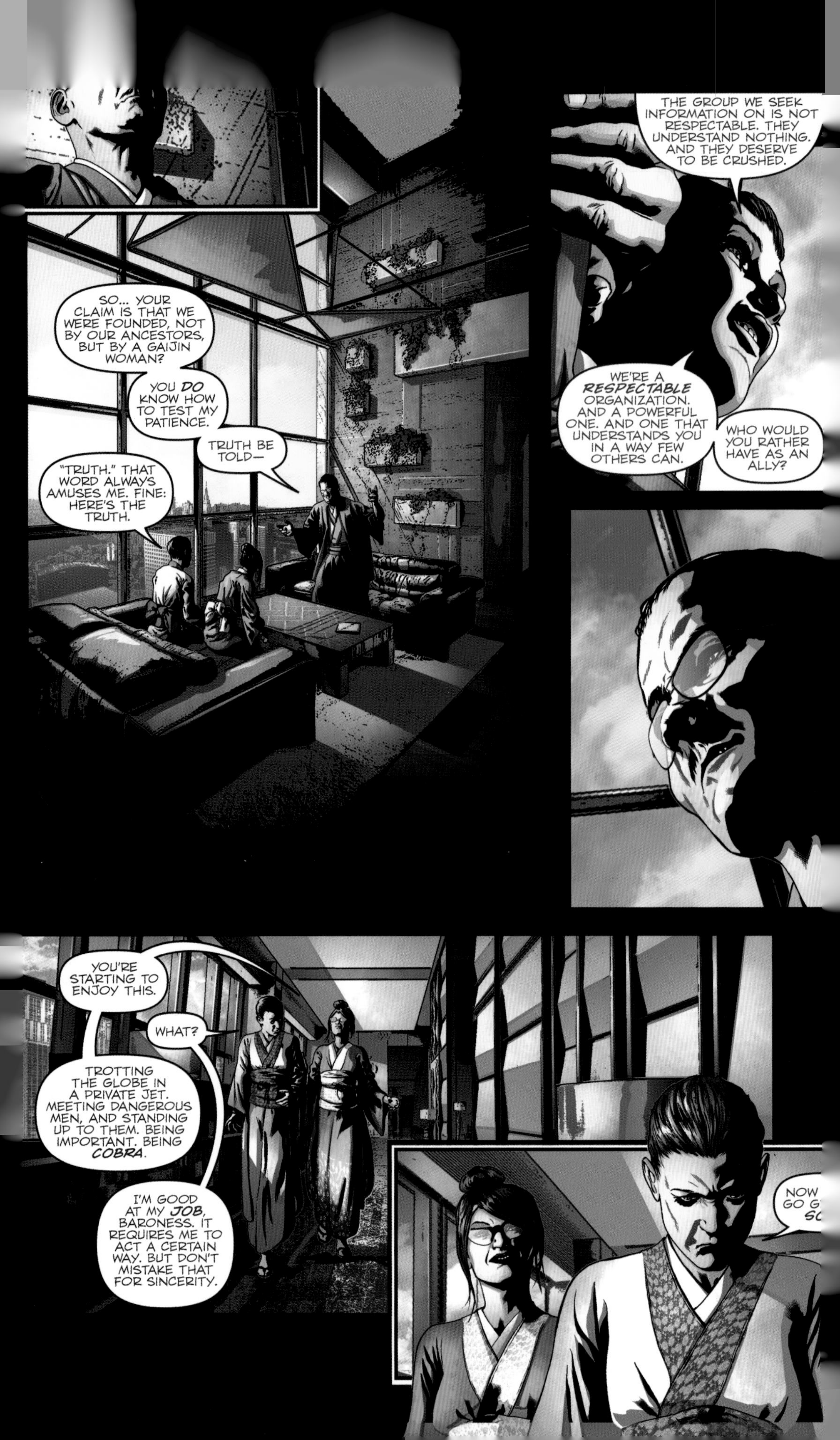
SO... YOUR CLAIM IS THAT WE WERE FOUNDED, NOT BY OUR ANCESTORS, BUT BY A GAIJIN WOMAN?
YOU DO KNOW HOW TO TEST MY PATIENCE.
TRUTH BE TOLD—
"TRUTH." THAT WORD ALWAYS AMUSES ME. FINE: HERE'S THE TRUTH.
THE GROUP WE SEEK INFORMATION ON IS NOT RESPECTABLE. THEY UNDERSTAND NOTHING. AND THEY DESERVE TO BE CRUSHED.
WE'RE A RESPECTABLE ORGANIZATION. AND A POWERFUL ONE. AND ONE THAT UNDERSTANDS YOU IN A WAY FEW OTHERS CAN.
WHO WOULD YOU RATHER HAVE AS AN ALLY?
YOU'RE STARTING TO ENJOY THIS.
WHAT?
TROTTING THE GLOBE IN A PRIVATE JET. MEETING DANGEROUS MEN, AND STANDING UP TO THEM. BEING IMPORTANT. BEING COBRA.
I'M GOOD AT MY JOB, BARONESS. IT REQUIRES ME TO ACT A CERTAIN WAY. BUT DON'T MISTAKE THAT FOR SINCERITY.

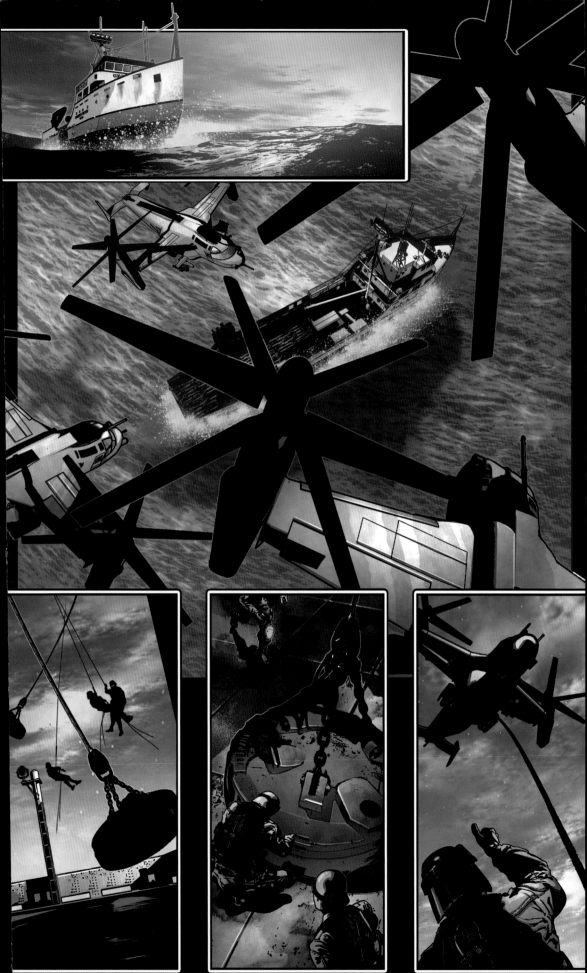

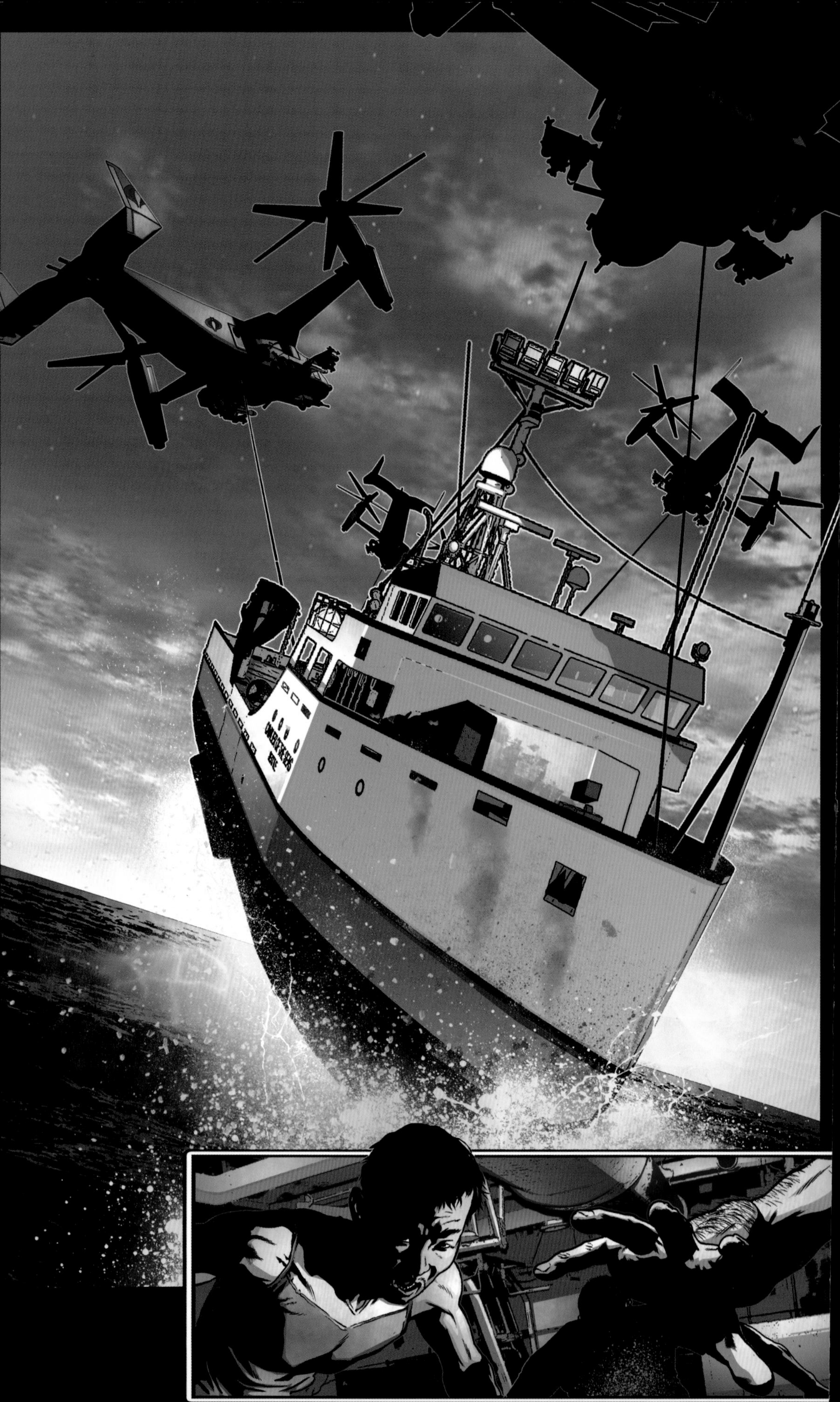

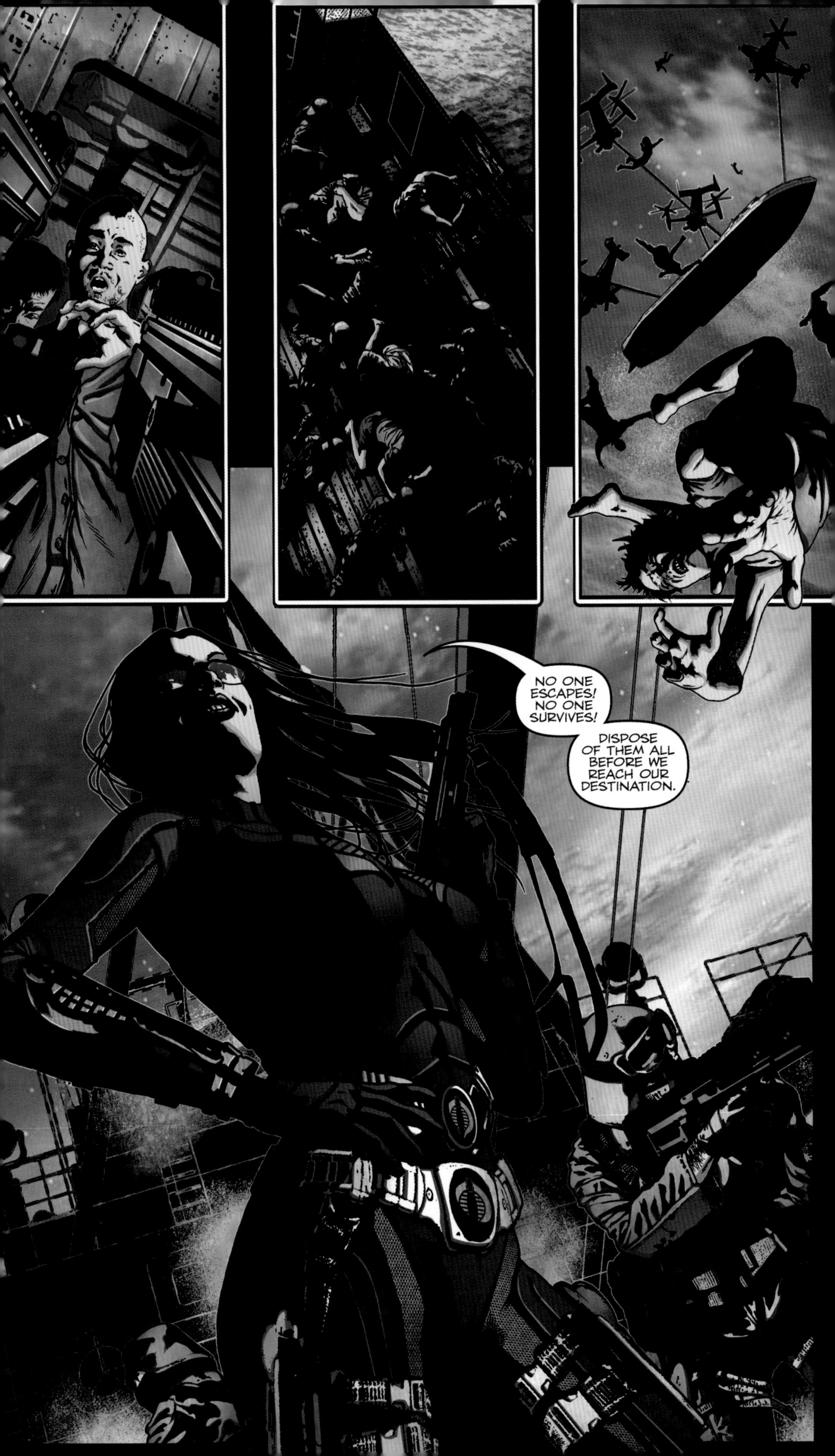
NO ONE ESCAPES! NO ONE SURVIVES!
DISPOSE OF THEM ALL BEFORE WE REACH OUR DESTINATION.

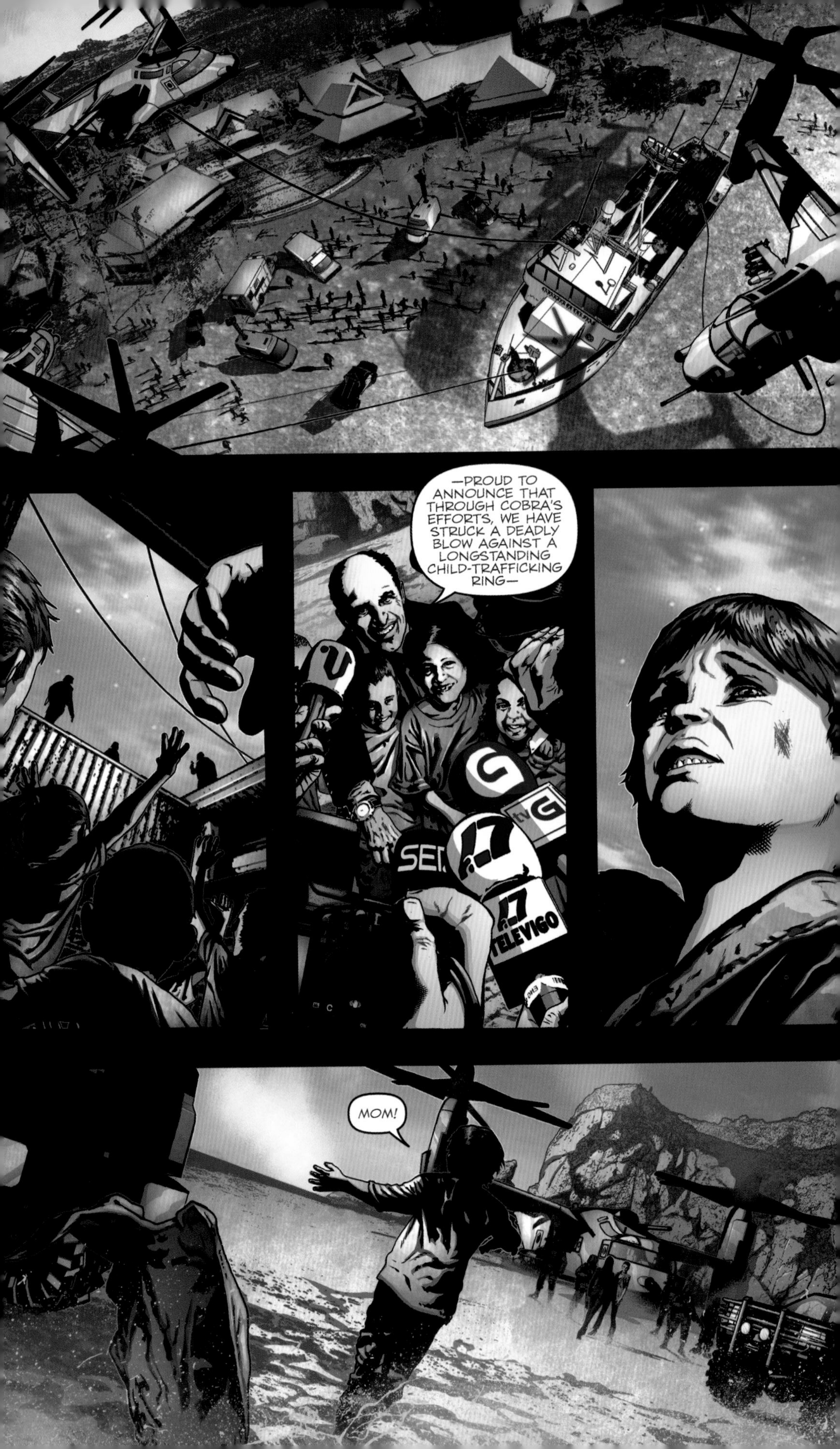
—PROUD TO ANNOUNCE THAT THROUGH COBRA'S EFFORTS, WE HAVE STRUCK A DEADLY BLOW AGAINST A LONGSTANDING CHILD-TRAFFICKING RING—
MOM!

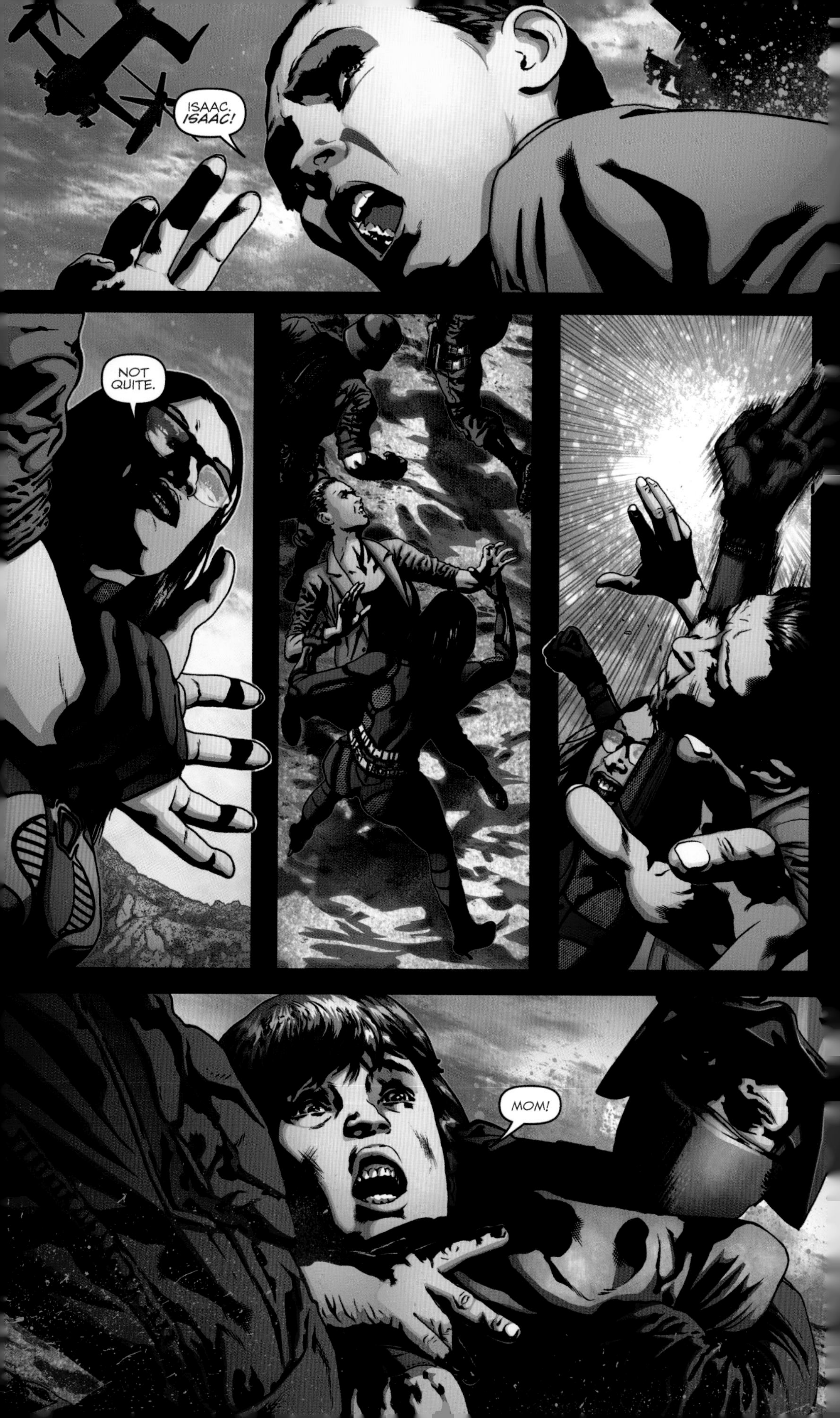
ISAAC. *ISAAC!*
NOT QUITE.
MOM!

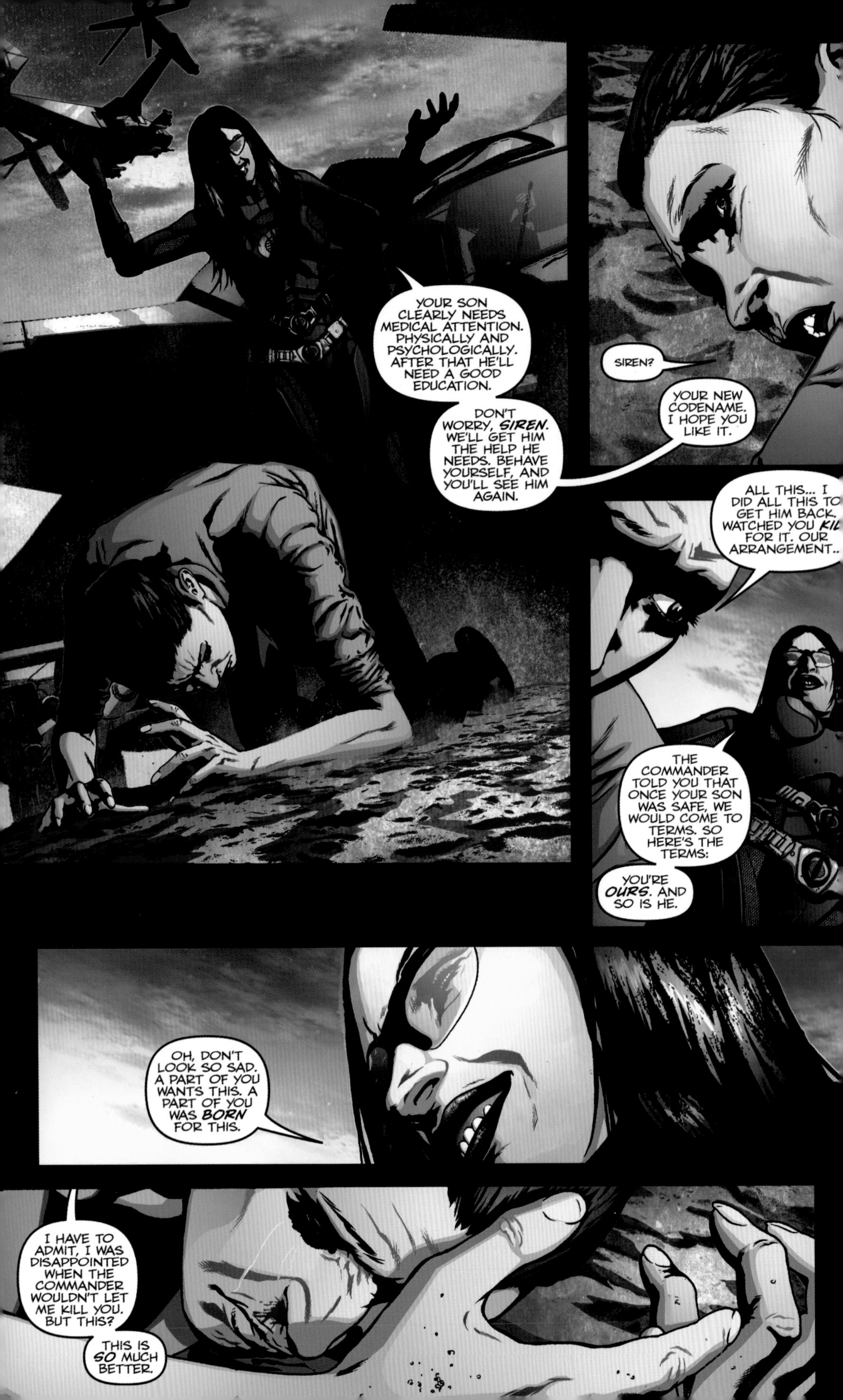
YOUR SON CLEARLY NEEDS MEDICAL ATTENTION. PHYSICALLY AND PSYCHOLOGICALLY. AFTER THAT HE'LL NEED A GOOD EDUCATION.
DON'T WORRY, SIREN. WE'LL GET HIM THE HELP HE NEEDS. BEHAVE YOURSELF, AND YOU'LL SEE HIM AGAIN.
SIREN?
YOUR NEW CODENAME. I HOPE YOU LIKE IT.
ALL THIS... I DID ALL THIS TO GET HIM BACK. WATCHED YOU KIL FOR IT. OUR ARRANGEMENT...
THE COMMANDER TOLD YOU THAT ONCE YOUR SON WAS SAFE, WE WOULD COME TO TERMS. SO HERE'S THE TERMS:
YOU'RE OURS. AND SO IS HE.
OH, DON'T LOOK SO SAD. A PART OF YOU WANTS THIS. A PART OF YOU WAS BORN FOR THIS.
I HAVE TO ADMIT, I WAS DISAPPOINTED WHEN THE COMMANDER WOULDN'T LET ME KILL YOU. BUT THIS?
THIS IS SO MUCH BETTER.

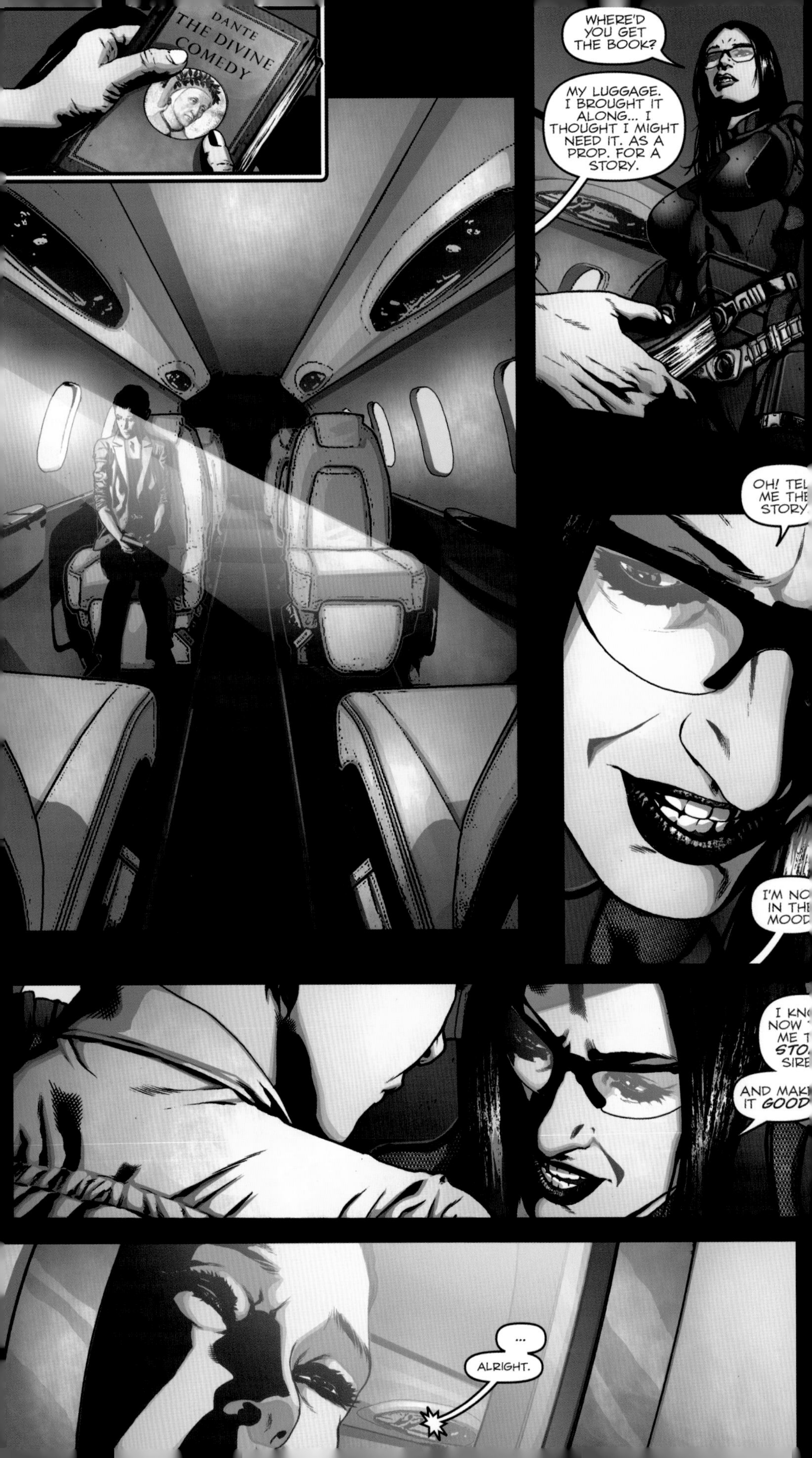
DANTE
THE DIVINE COMEDY
WHERE'D YOU GET THE BOOK?
MY LUGGAGE. I BROUGHT IT ALONG... I THOUGHT I MIGHT NEED IT. AS A PROP. FOR A STORY.
OH! TEL ME THE STORY
I'M NO IN THE MOOD
I KN NOW ME T STO SIRE
AND MAK IT GOOD
...
ALRIGHT.

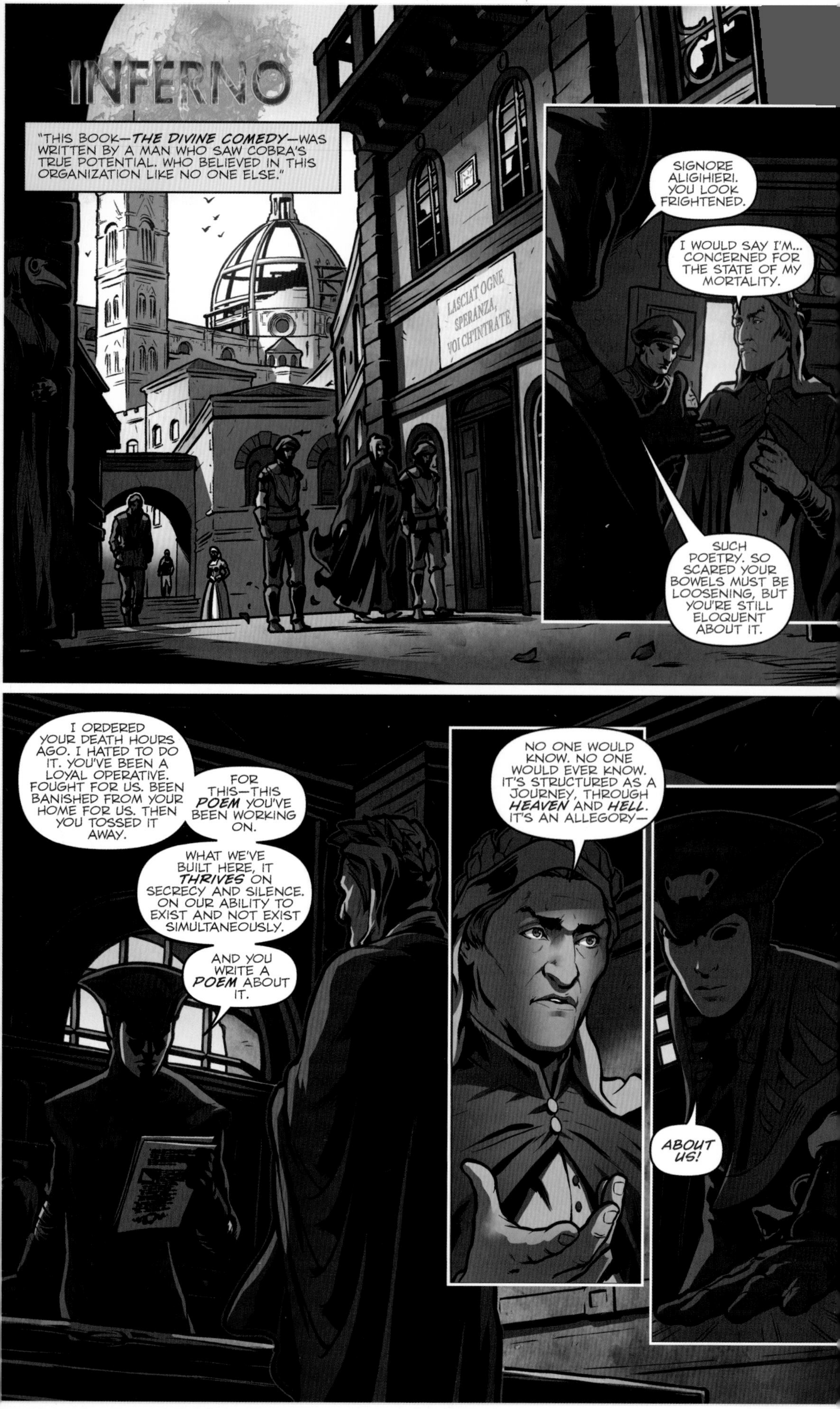
INFERNO
"THIS BOOK—THE DIVINE COMEDY—WAS WRITTEN BY A MAN WHO SAW COBRA'S TRUE POTENTIAL. WHO BELIEVED IN THIS ORGANIZATION LIKE NO ONE ELSE."
LASCIAT OGNE SPERANZA, VOI CH'INTRATE
SIGNORE ALIGIHIERI. YOU LOOK FRIGHTENED.
I WOULD SAY I'M... CONCERNED FOR THE STATE OF MY MORTALITY.
SUCH POETRY. SO SCARED YOUR BOWELS MUST BE LOOSENING, BUT YOU'RE STILL ELOQUENT ABOUT IT.
I ORDERED YOUR DEATH HOURS AGO. I HATED TO DO IT. YOU'VE BEEN A LOYAL OPERATIVE. FOUGHT FOR US. BEEN BANISHED FROM YOUR HOME FOR US. THEN YOU TOSSED IT AWAY.
FOR THIS—THIS POEM YOU'VE BEEN WORKING ON.
WHAT WE'VE BUILT HERE, IT THRIVES ON SECRECY AND SILENCE. ON OUR ABILITY TO EXIST AND NOT EXIST SIMULTANEOUSLY.
AND YOU WRITE A POEM ABOUT IT.
NO ONE WOULD KNOW. NO ONE WOULD EVER KNOW. IT'S STRUCTURED AS A JOURNEY, THROUGH HEAVEN AND HELL. IT'S AN ALLEGORY—
ABOUT US!

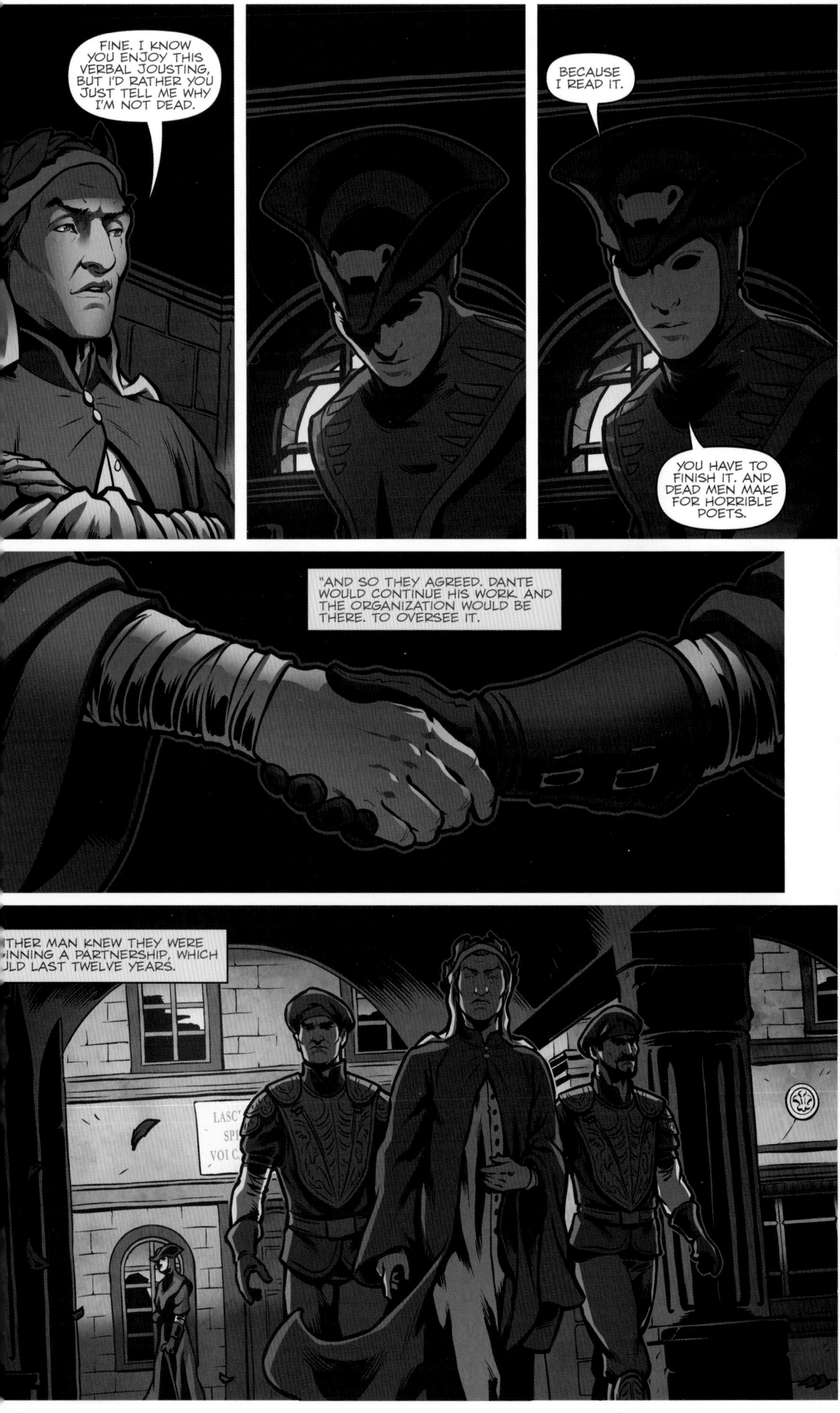
FINE. I KNOW YOU ENJOY THIS VERBAL JOUSTING, BUT I'D RATHER YOU JUST TELL ME WHY I'M NOT DEAD.
BECAUSE I READ IT.
YOU HAVE TO FINISH IT. AND DEAD MEN MAKE FOR HORRIBLE POETS.
"AND SO THEY AGREED. DANTE WOULD CONTINUE HIS WORK. AND THE ORGANIZATION WOULD BE THERE. TO OVERSEE IT.
THER MAN KNEW THEY WERE INNING A PARTNERSHIP, WHICH ULD LAST TWELVE YEARS.

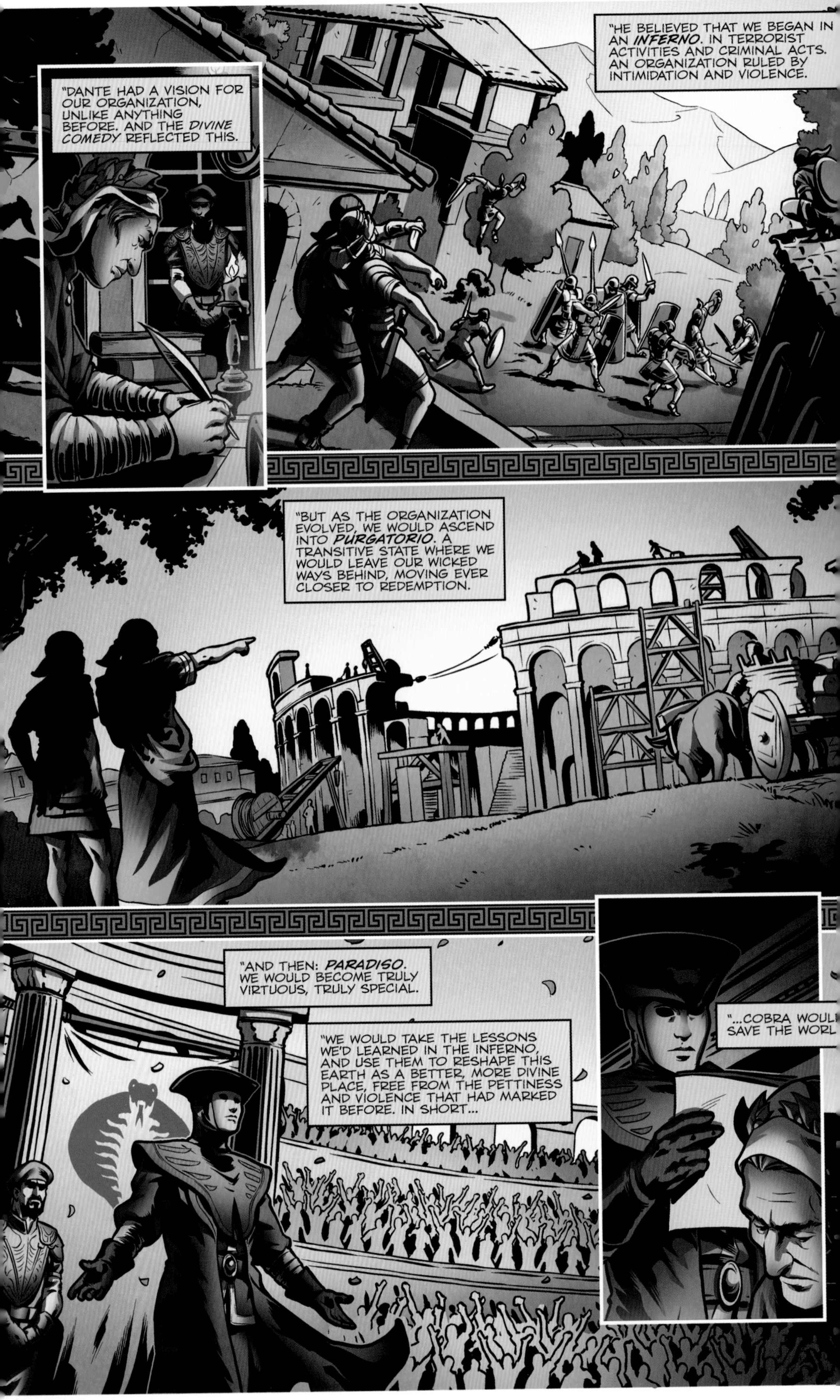
"DANTE HAD A VISION FOR OUR ORGANIZATION, UNLIKE ANYTHING BEFORE. AND THE *DIVINE COMEDY* REFLECTED THIS.
"HE BELIEVED THAT WE BEGAN IN AN ***INFERNO***. IN TERRORIST ACTIVITIES AND CRIMINAL ACTS. AN ORGANIZATION RULED BY INTIMIDATION AND VIOLENCE.
"BUT AS THE ORGANIZATION EVOLVED, WE WOULD ASCEND INTO ***PURGATORIO***. A TRANSITIVE STATE WHERE WE WOULD LEAVE OUR WICKED WAYS BEHIND, MOVING EVER CLOSER TO REDEMPTION.
"AND THEN: ***PARADISO***. WE WOULD BECOME TRULY VIRTUOUS, TRULY SPECIAL.
"WE WOULD TAKE THE LESSONS WE'D LEARNED IN THE INFERNO, AND USE THEM TO RESHAPE THIS EARTH AS A BETTER, MORE DIVINE PLACE, FREE FROM THE PETTINESS AND VIOLENCE THAT HAD MARKED IT BEFORE. IN SHORT...
"...COBRA WOUL SAVE THE WORL

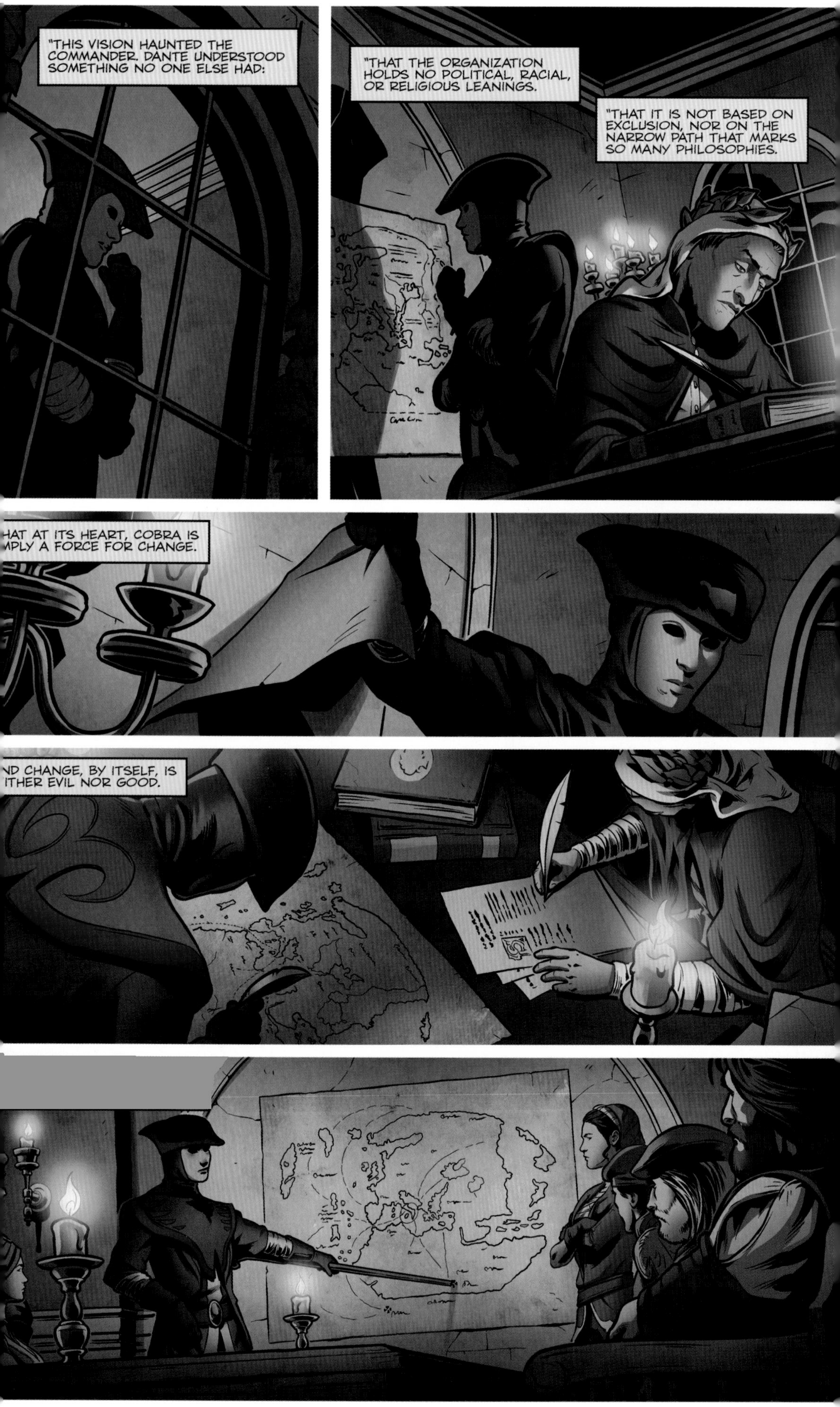
"THIS VISION HAUNTED THE COMMANDER. DANTE UNDERSTOOD SOMETHING NO ONE ELSE HAD:
"THAT THE ORGANIZATION HOLDS NO POLITICAL, RACIAL, OR RELIGIOUS LEANINGS.
"THAT IT IS NOT BASED ON EXCLUSION, NOR ON THE NARROW PATH THAT MARKS SO MANY PHILOSOPHIES.
HAT AT ITS HEART, COBRA IS MPLY A FORCE FOR CHANGE.
ND CHANGE, BY ITSELF, IS ITHER EVIL NOR GOOD.

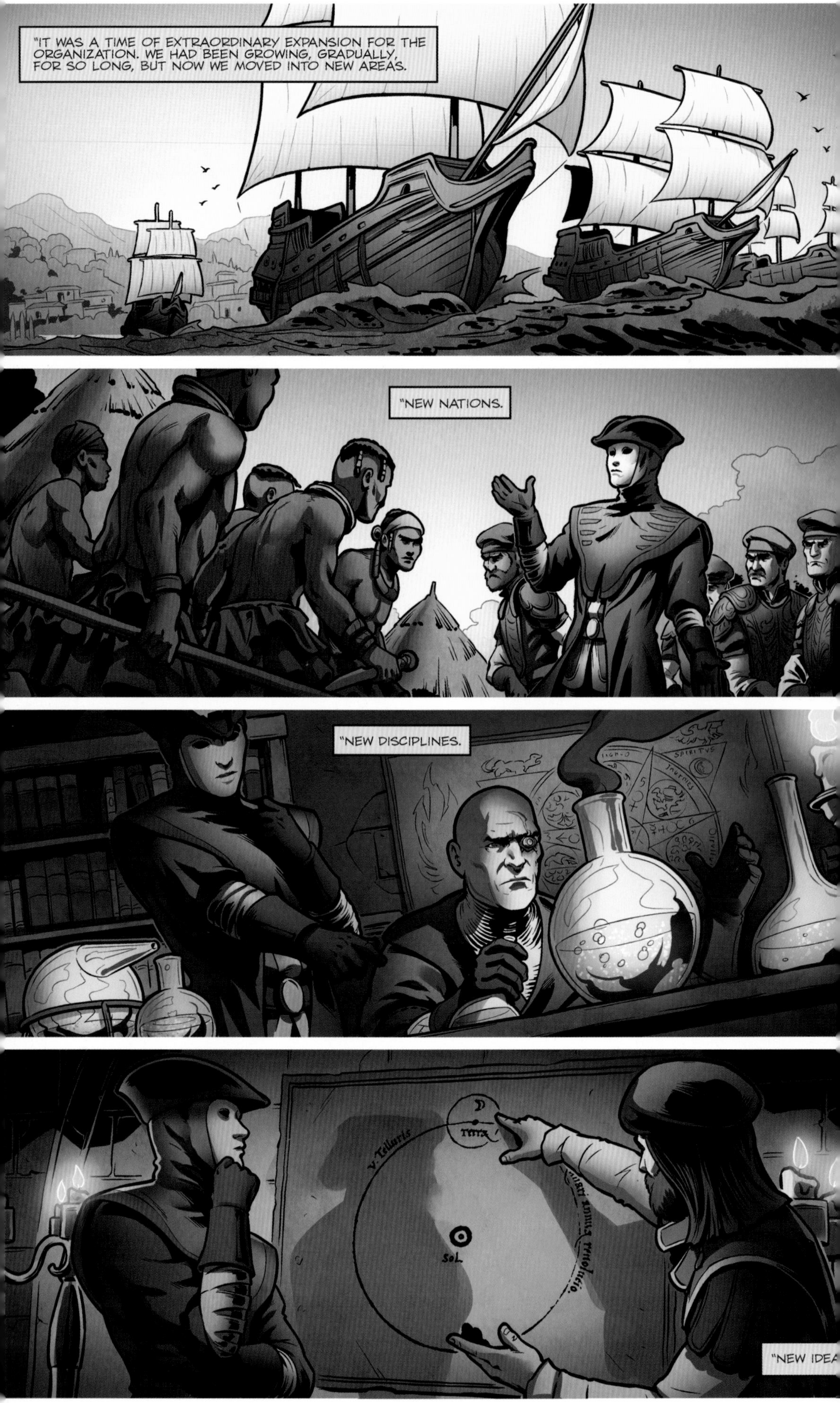
"IT WAS A TIME OF EXTRAORDINARY EXPANSION FOR THE ORGANIZATION. WE HAD BEEN GROWING, GRADUALLY, FOR SO LONG, BUT NOW WE MOVED INTO NEW AREAS.
"NEW NATIONS.
"NEW DISCIPLINES.
SPIRITVS
v. Telluris
SOL
"NEW IDEA

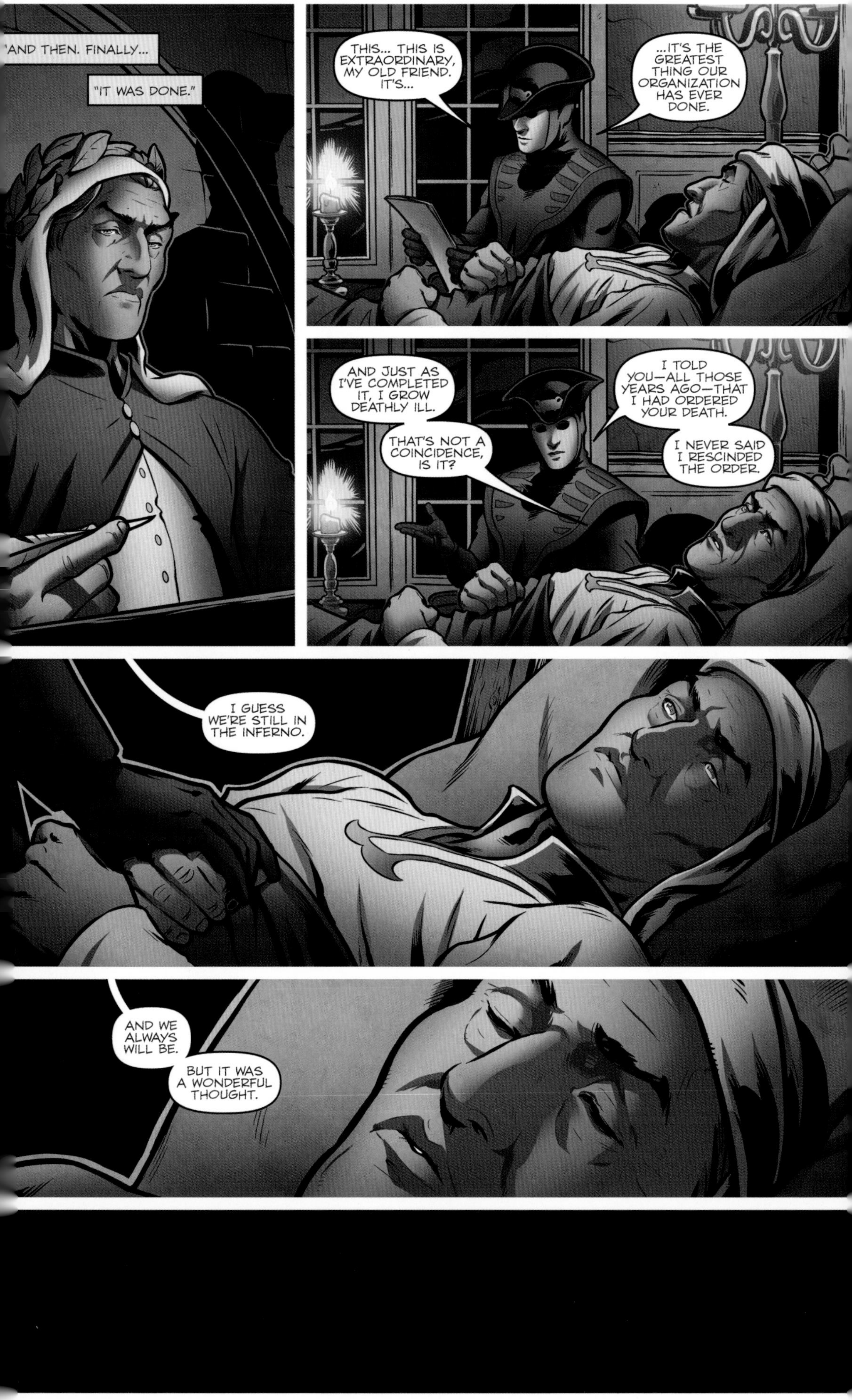
"AND THEN. FINALLY...
"IT WAS DONE."
THIS... THIS IS EXTRAORDINARY, MY OLD FRIEND. IT'S...
...IT'S THE GREATEST THING OUR ORGANIZATION HAS EVER DONE.
AND JUST AS I'VE COMPLETED IT, I GROW DEATHLY ILL.
THAT'S NOT A COINCIDENCE, IS IT?
I TOLD YOU—ALL THOSE YEARS AGO—THAT I HAD ORDERED YOUR DEATH.
I NEVER SAID I RESCINDED THE ORDER.
I GUESS WE'RE STILL IN THE INFERNO.
AND WE ALWAYS WILL BE.
BUT IT WAS A WONDERFUL THOUGHT.

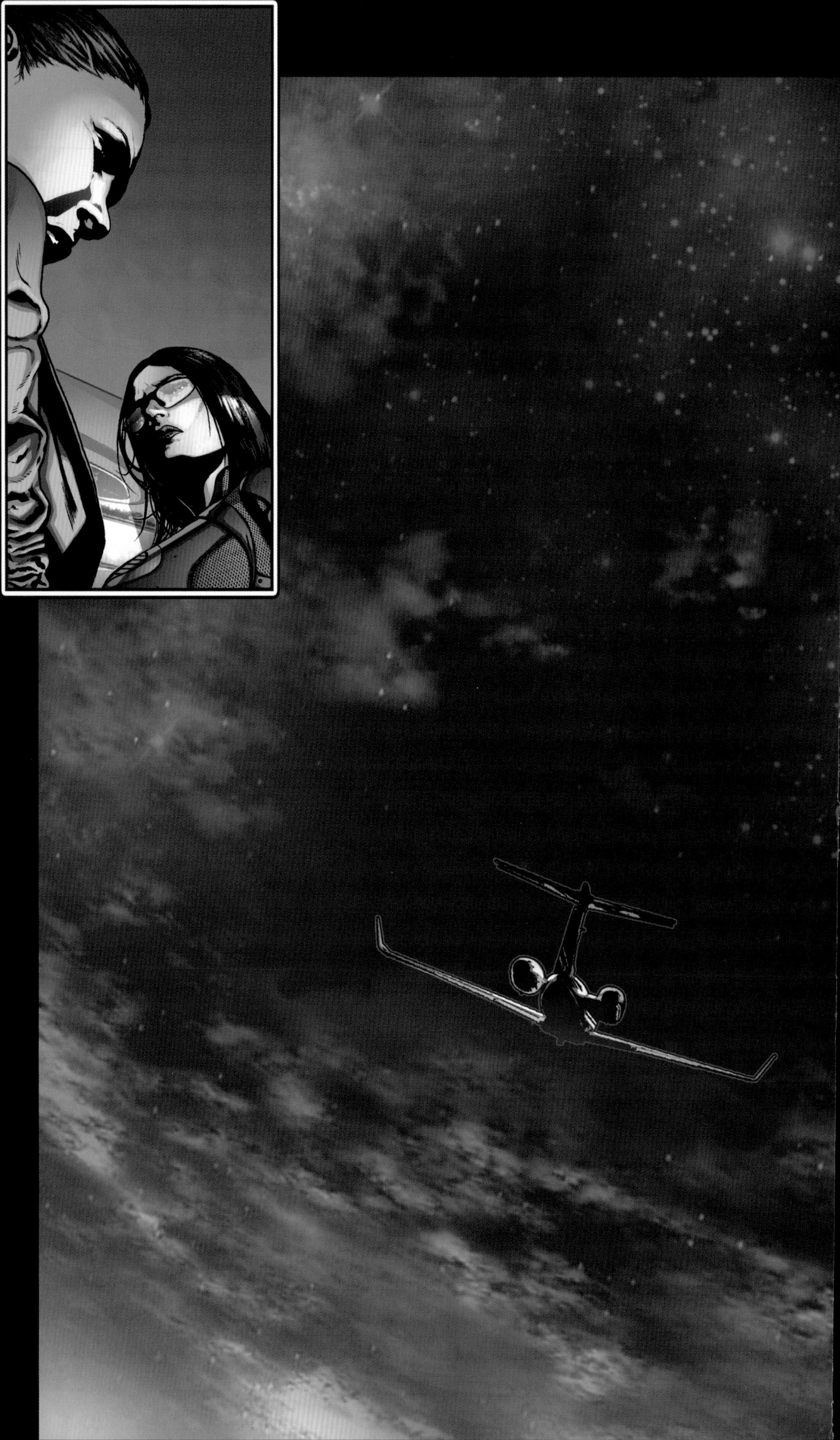

CHAPTER THREE

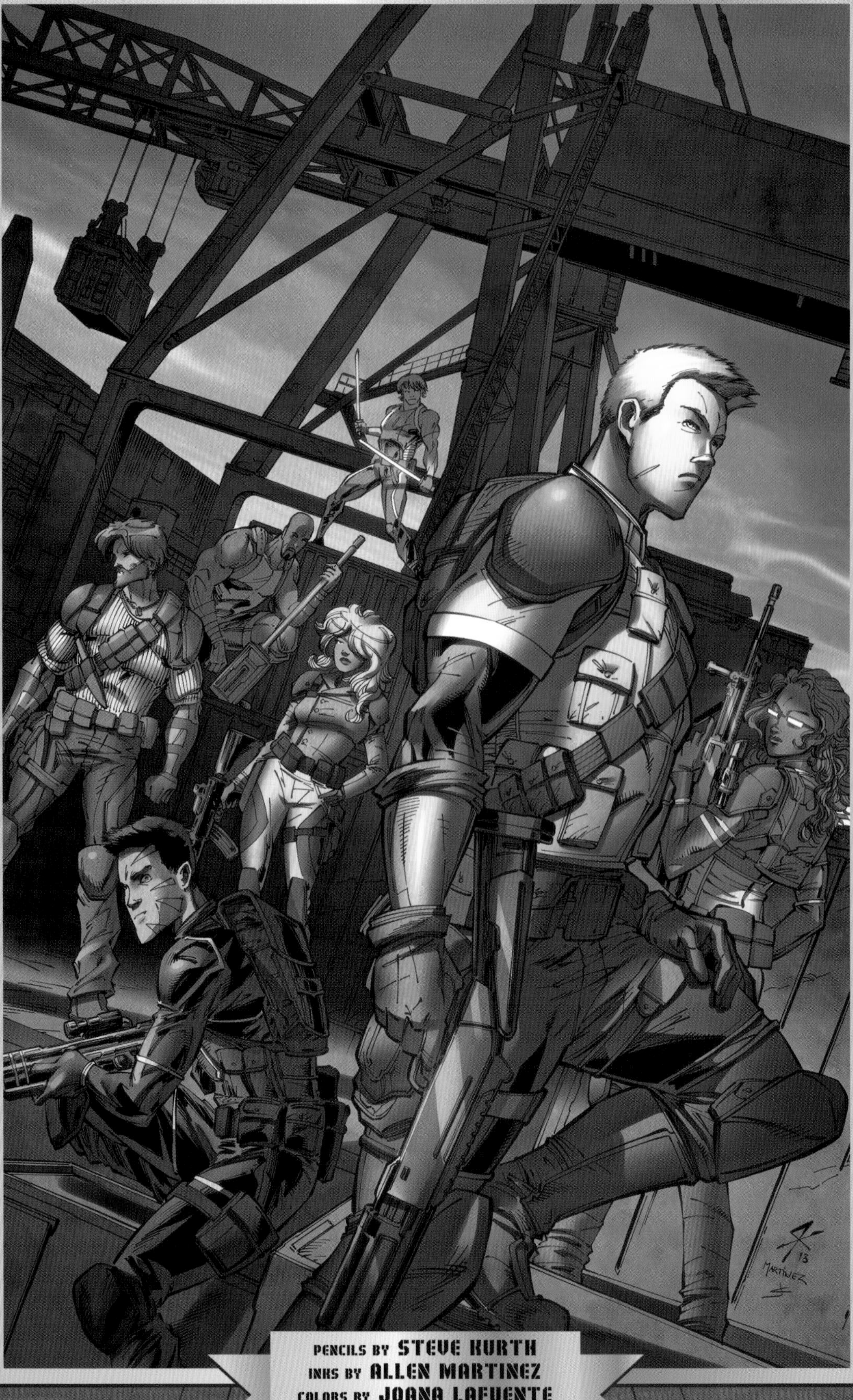
MARTINEZ '13

PENCILS BY **STEVE KURTH**
INKS BY **ALLEN MARTINEZ**
COLORS BY **JOANA LAFUENTE**

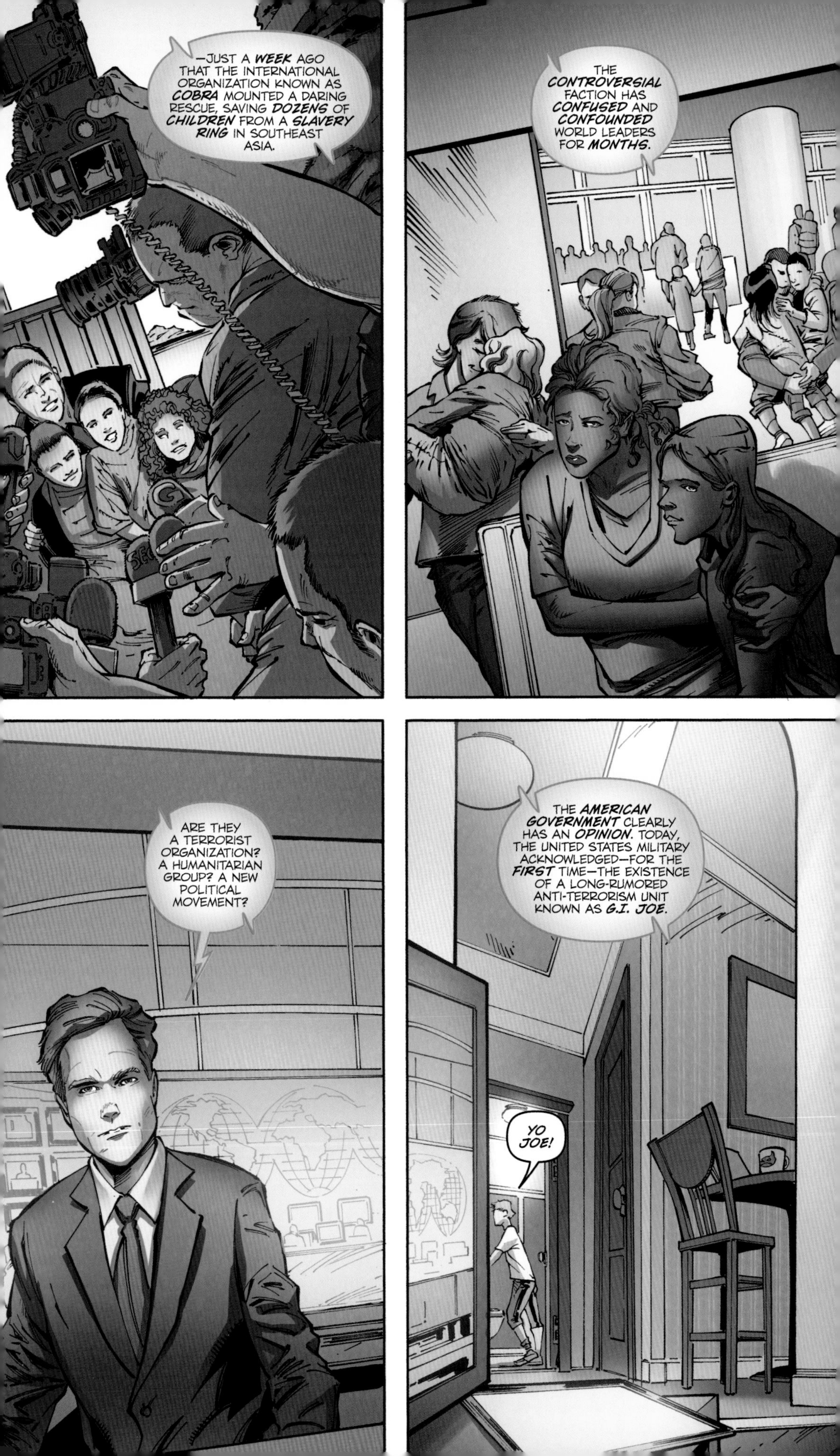
—JUST A WEEK AGO THAT THE INTERNATIONAL ORGANIZATION KNOWN AS COBRA MOUNTED A DARING RESCUE, SAVING DOZENS OF CHILDREN FROM A SLAVERY RING IN SOUTHEAST ASIA.
THE CONTROVERSIAL FACTION HAS CONFUSED AND CONFOUNDED WORLD LEADERS FOR MONTHS.
ARE THEY A TERRORIST ORGANIZATION? A HUMANITARIAN GROUP? A NEW POLITICAL MOVEMENT?
THE AMERICAN GOVERNMENT CLEARLY HAS AN OPINION. TODAY, THE UNITED STATES MILITARY ACKNOWLEDGED—FOR THE FIRST TIME—THE EXISTENCE OF A LONG-RUMORED ANTI-TERRORISM UNIT KNOWN AS G.I. JOE.
YO JOE!

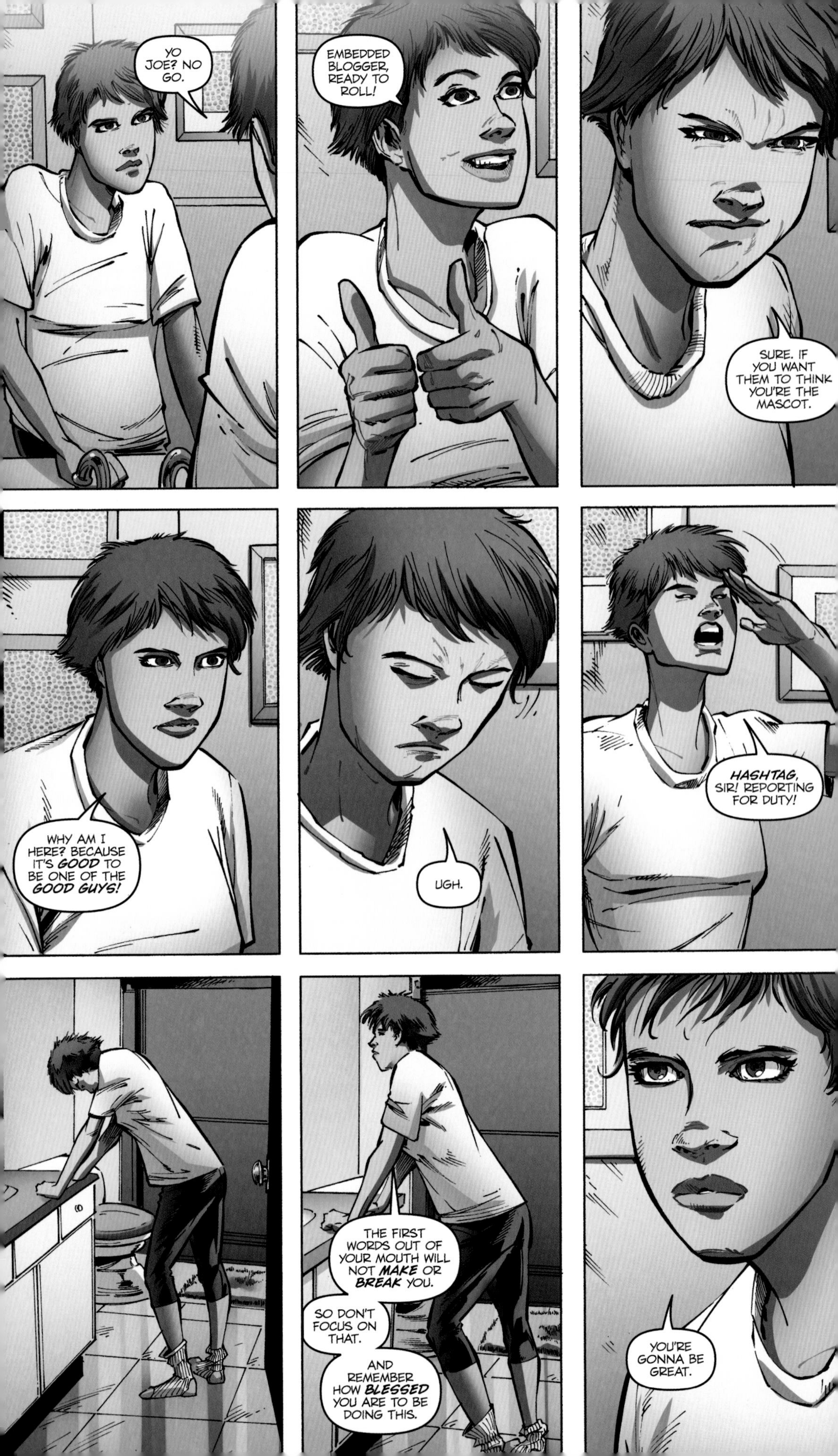
YO JOE? NO GO.
EMBEDDED BLOGGER, READY TO ROLL!
SURE. IF YOU WANT THEM TO THINK YOU'RE THE MASCOT.
WHY AM I HERE? BECAUSE IT'S **GOOD** TO BE ONE OF THE **GOOD GUYS!**
UGH.
HASHTAG, SIR! REPORTING FOR DUTY!
THE FIRST WORDS OUT OF YOUR MOUTH WILL NOT **MAKE** OR **BREAK** YOU.
SO DON'T FOCUS ON THAT.
AND REMEMBER HOW **BLESSED** YOU ARE TO BE DOING THIS.
YOU'RE GONNA BE GREAT.

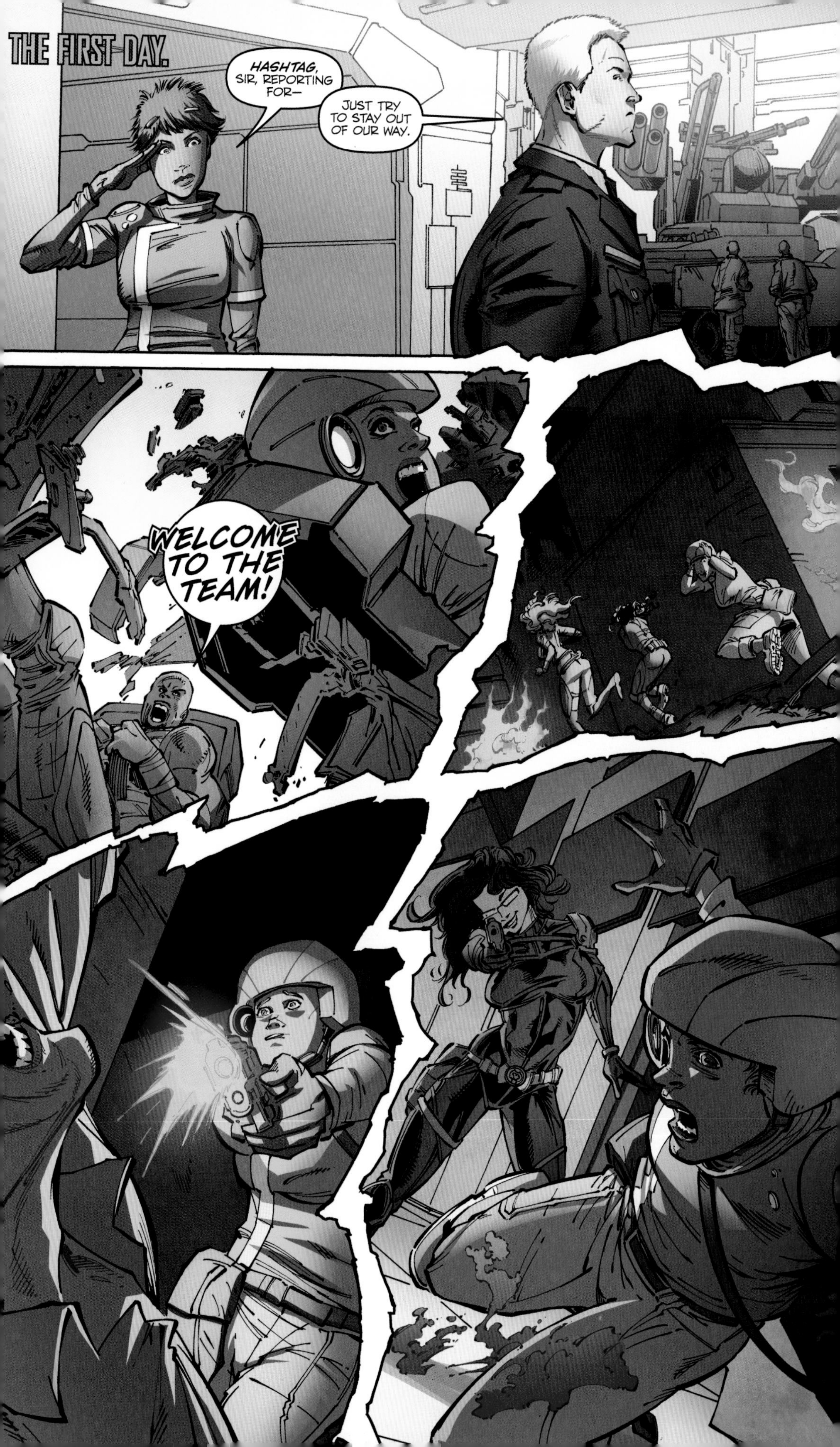
THE FIRST DAY.
HASHTAG, SIR, REPORTING FOR—
JUST TRY TO STAY OUT OF OUR WAY.
WELCOME TO THE TEAM!

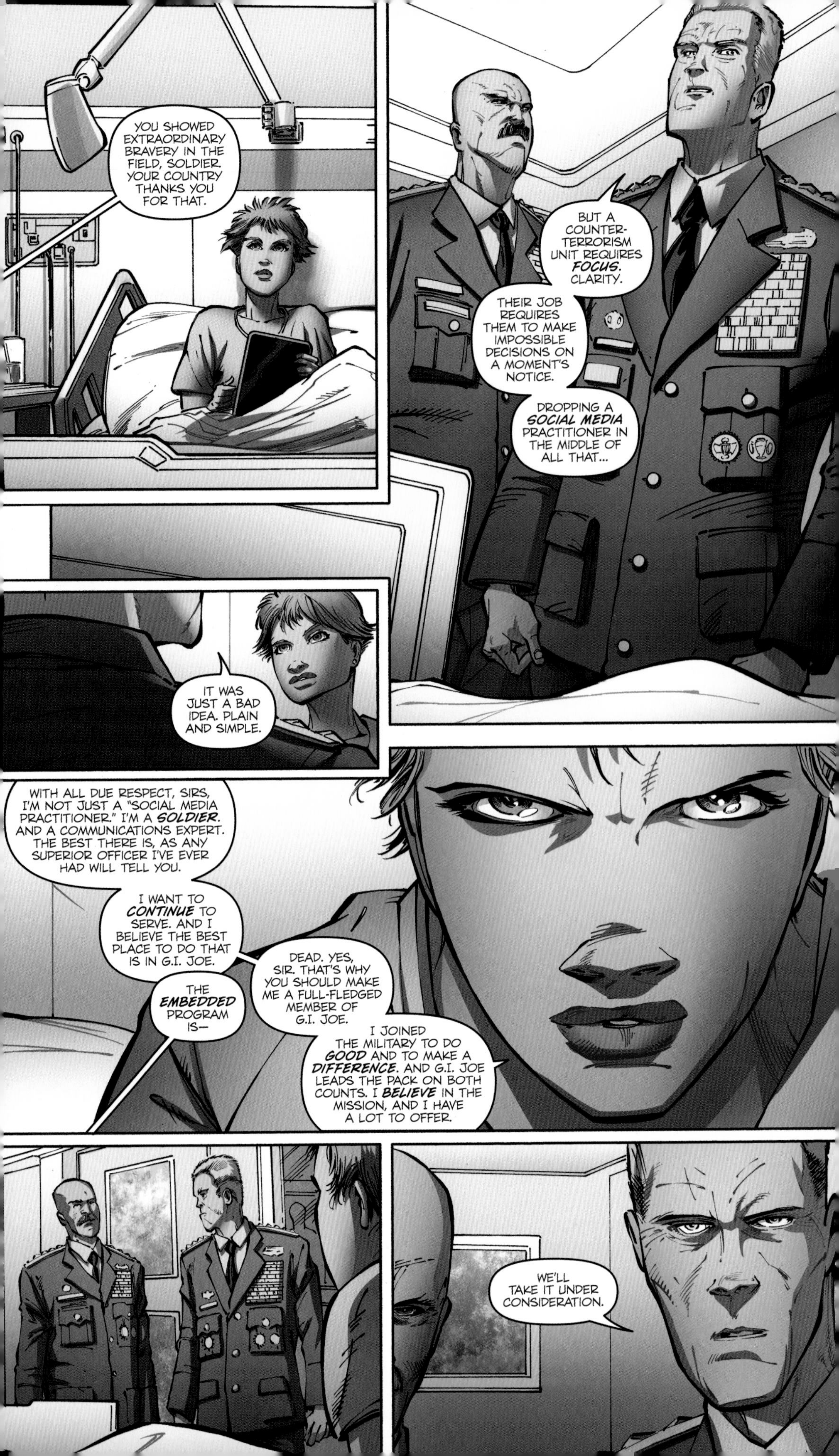
YOU SHOWED EXTRAORDINARY BRAVERY IN THE FIELD, SOLDIER. YOUR COUNTRY THANKS YOU FOR THAT.
BUT A COUNTER-TERRORISM UNIT REQUIRES FOCUS. CLARITY.
THEIR JOB REQUIRES THEM TO MAKE IMPOSSIBLE DECISIONS ON A MOMENT'S NOTICE.
DROPPING A SOCIAL MEDIA PRACTITIONER IN THE MIDDLE OF ALL THAT...
IT WAS JUST A BAD IDEA. PLAIN AND SIMPLE.
WITH ALL DUE RESPECT, SIRS, I'M NOT JUST A "SOCIAL MEDIA PRACTITIONER." I'M A SOLDIER. AND A COMMUNICATIONS EXPERT. THE BEST THERE IS, AS ANY SUPERIOR OFFICER I'VE EVER HAD WILL TELL YOU.
I WANT TO CONTINUE TO SERVE. AND I BELIEVE THE BEST PLACE TO DO THAT IS IN G.I. JOE.
THE EMBEDDED PROGRAM IS—
DEAD. YES, SIR. THAT'S WHY YOU SHOULD MAKE ME A FULL-FLEDGED MEMBER OF G.I. JOE.
I JOINED THE MILITARY TO DO GOOD AND TO MAKE A DIFFERENCE. AND G.I. JOE LEADS THE PACK ON BOTH COUNTS. I BELIEVE IN THE MISSION, AND I HAVE A LOT TO OFFER.
WE'LL TAKE IT UNDER CONSIDERATION.

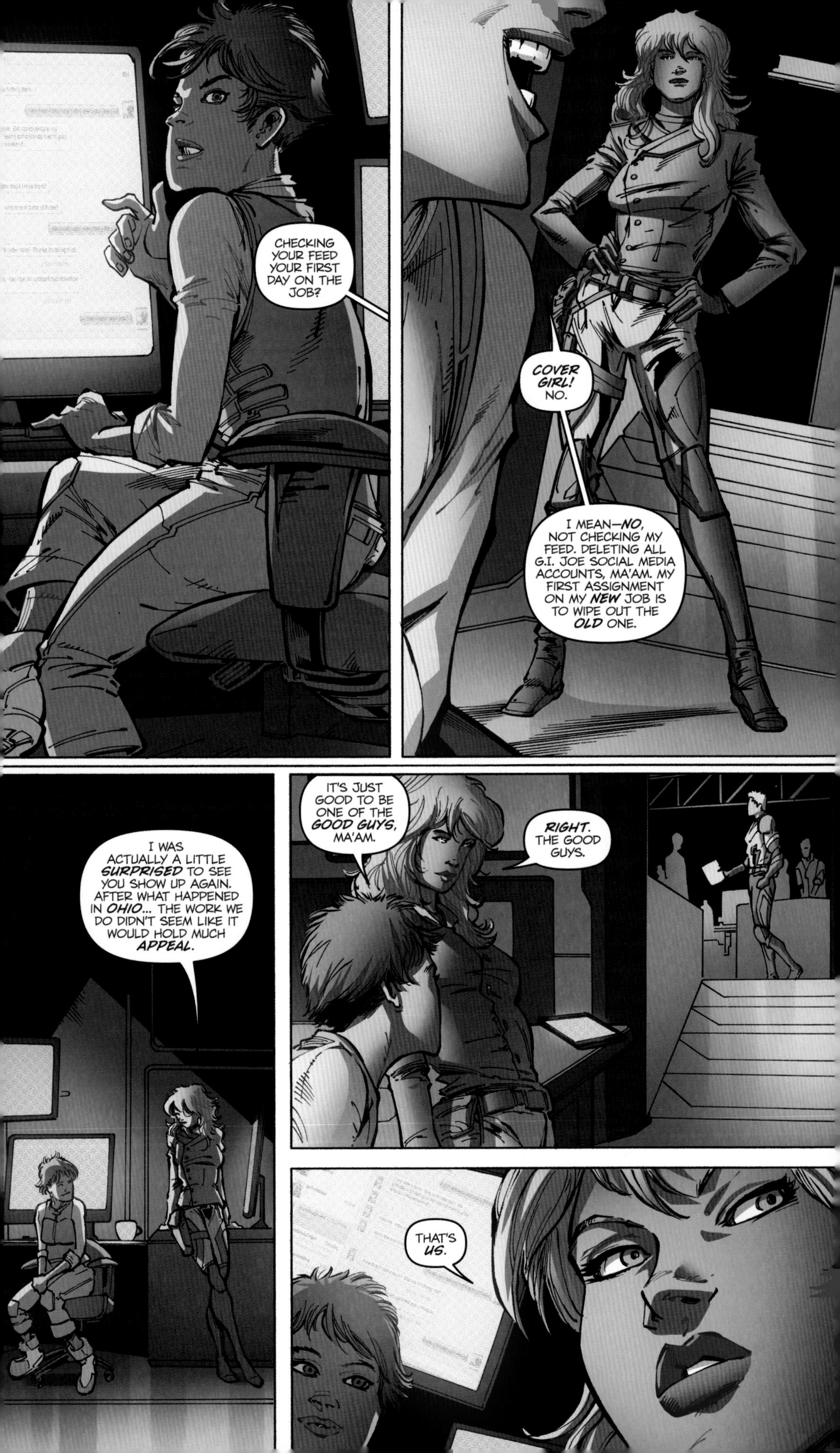
CHECKING YOUR FEED YOUR FIRST DAY ON THE JOB?
COVER GIRL! NO.
I MEAN—NO, NOT CHECKING MY FEED. DELETING ALL G.I. JOE SOCIAL MEDIA ACCOUNTS, MA'AM. MY FIRST ASSIGNMENT ON MY NEW JOB IS TO WIPE OUT THE OLD ONE.
I WAS ACTUALLY A LITTLE SURPRISED TO SEE YOU SHOW UP AGAIN. AFTER WHAT HAPPENED IN OHIO... THE WORK WE DO DIDN'T SEEM LIKE IT WOULD HOLD MUCH APPEAL.
IT'S JUST GOOD TO BE ONE OF THE GOOD GUYS, MA'AM.
RIGHT. THE GOOD GUYS.
THAT'S US.

NEW DIRECT MESSAGE FROM SINGER'S SON

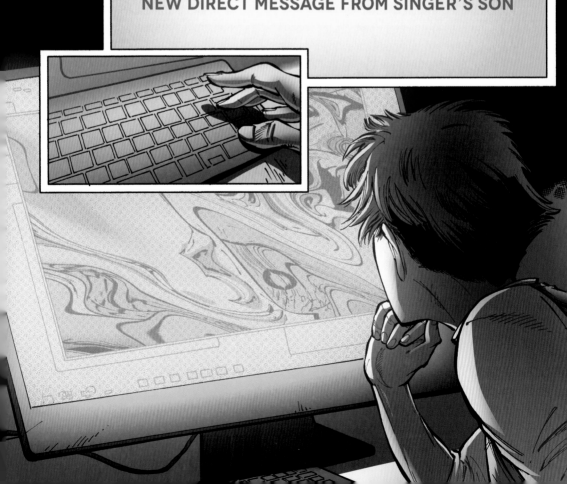

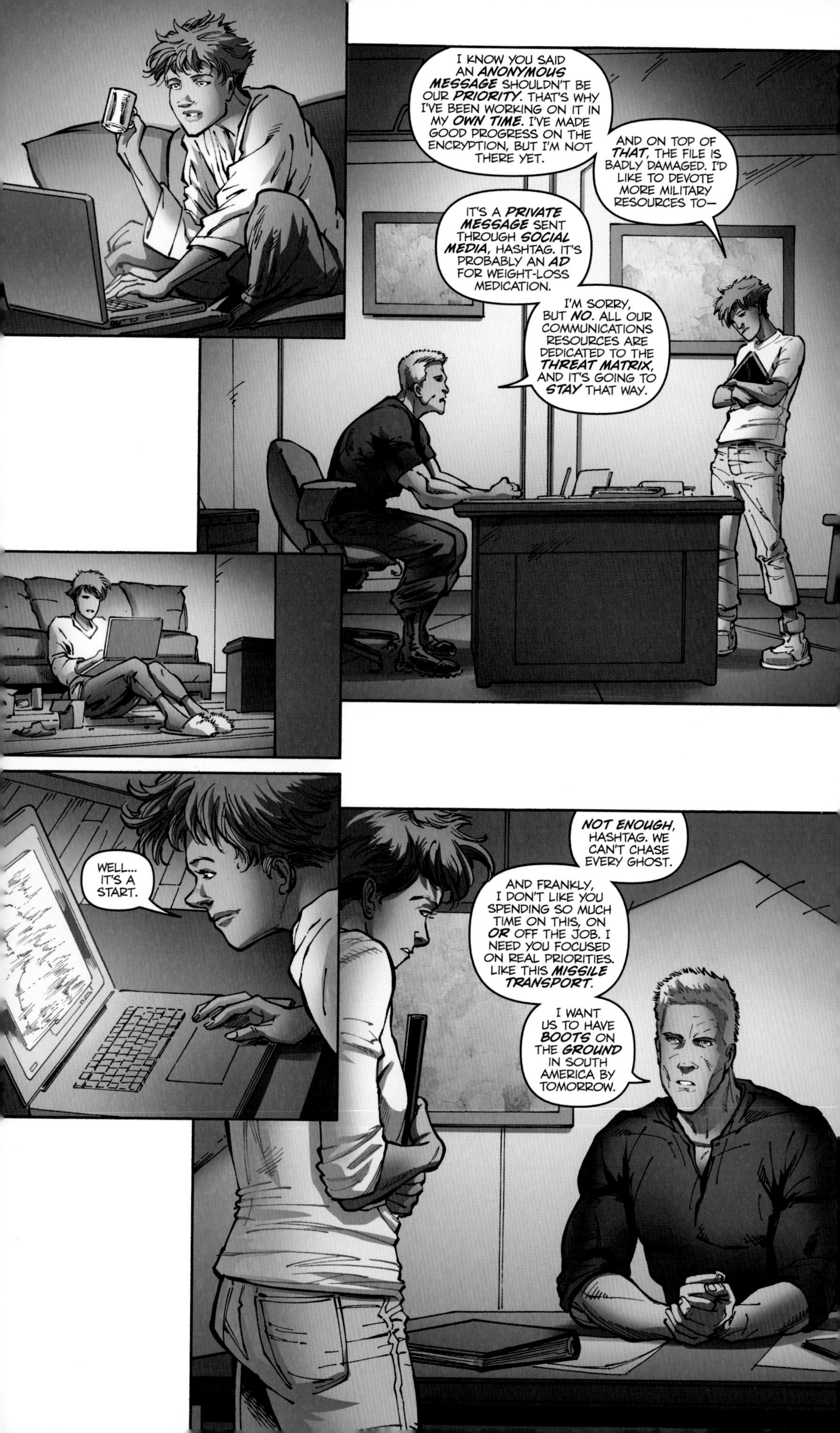

I KNOW YOU SAID AN ANONYMOUS MESSAGE SHOULDN'T BE OUR PRIORITY. THAT'S WHY I'VE BEEN WORKING ON IT IN MY OWN TIME. I'VE MADE GOOD PROGRESS ON THE ENCRYPTION, BUT I'M NOT THERE YET.
AND ON TOP OF THAT, THE FILE IS BADLY DAMAGED. I'D LIKE TO DEVOTE MORE MILITARY RESOURCES TO—
IT'S A PRIVATE MESSAGE SENT THROUGH SOCIAL MEDIA, HASHTAG. IT'S PROBABLY AN AD FOR WEIGHT-LOSS MEDICATION.
I'M SORRY, BUT NO. ALL OUR COMMUNICATIONS RESOURCES ARE DEDICATED TO THE THREAT MATRIX, AND IT'S GOING TO STAY THAT WAY.
WELL... IT'S A START.
NOT ENOUGH, HASHTAG. WE CAN'T CHASE EVERY GHOST.
AND FRANKLY, I DON'T LIKE YOU SPENDING SO MUCH TIME ON THIS, ON OR OFF THE JOB. I NEED YOU FOCUSED ON REAL PRIORITIES. LIKE THIS MISSILE TRANSPORT.
I WANT US TO HAVE BOOTS ON THE GROUND IN SOUTH AMERICA BY TOMORROW.

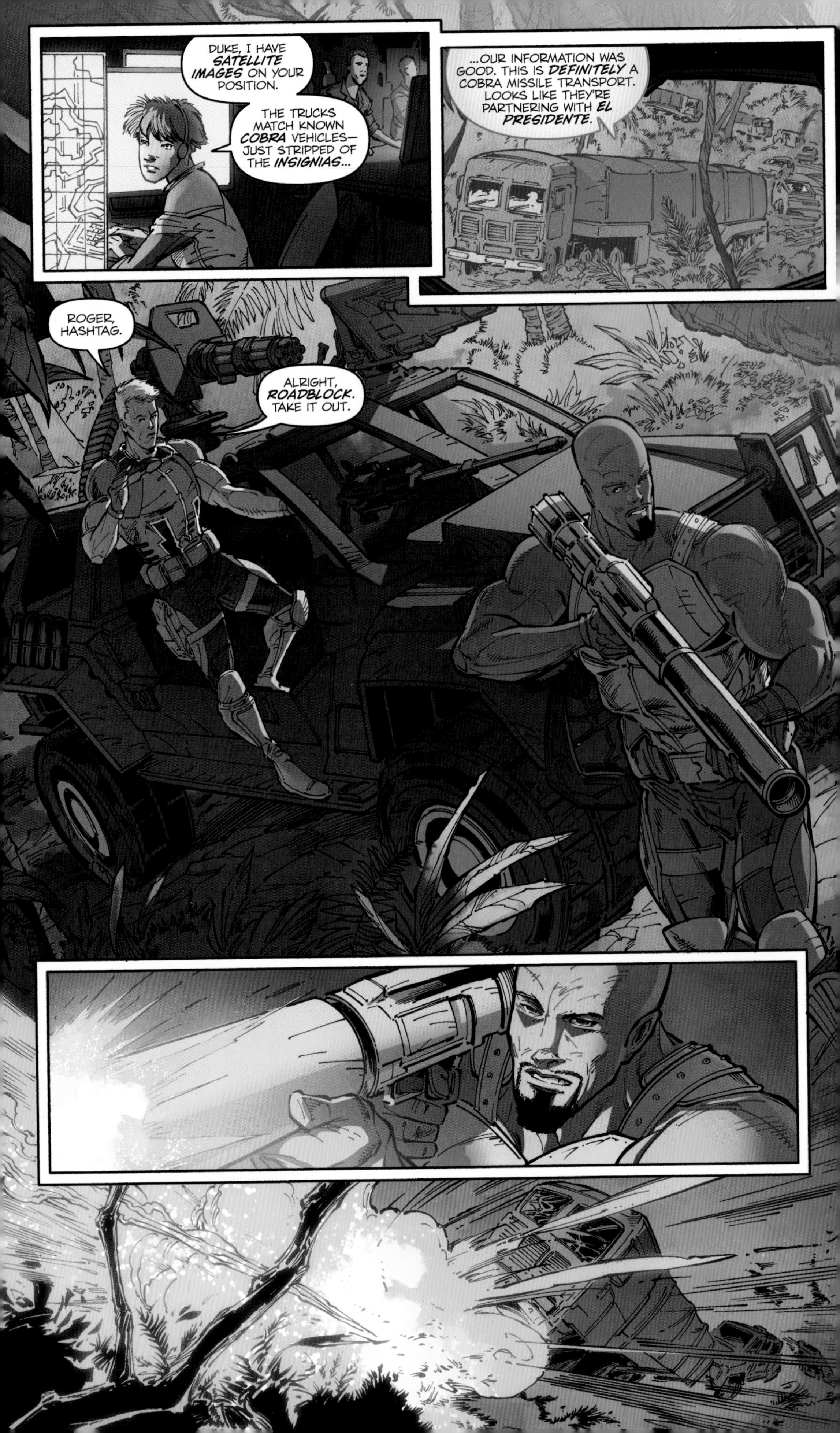
DUKE, I HAVE *SATELLITE IMAGES* ON YOUR POSITION.
THE TRUCKS MATCH KNOWN *COBRA* VEHICLES— JUST STRIPPED OF THE *INSIGNIAS*...
...OUR INFORMATION WAS GOOD. THIS IS *DEFINITELY* A COBRA MISSILE TRANSPORT. LOOKS LIKE THEY'RE PARTNERING WITH *EL PRESIDENTE*.
ROGER, HASHTAG.
ALRIGHT, *ROADBLOCK*. TAKE IT OUT.

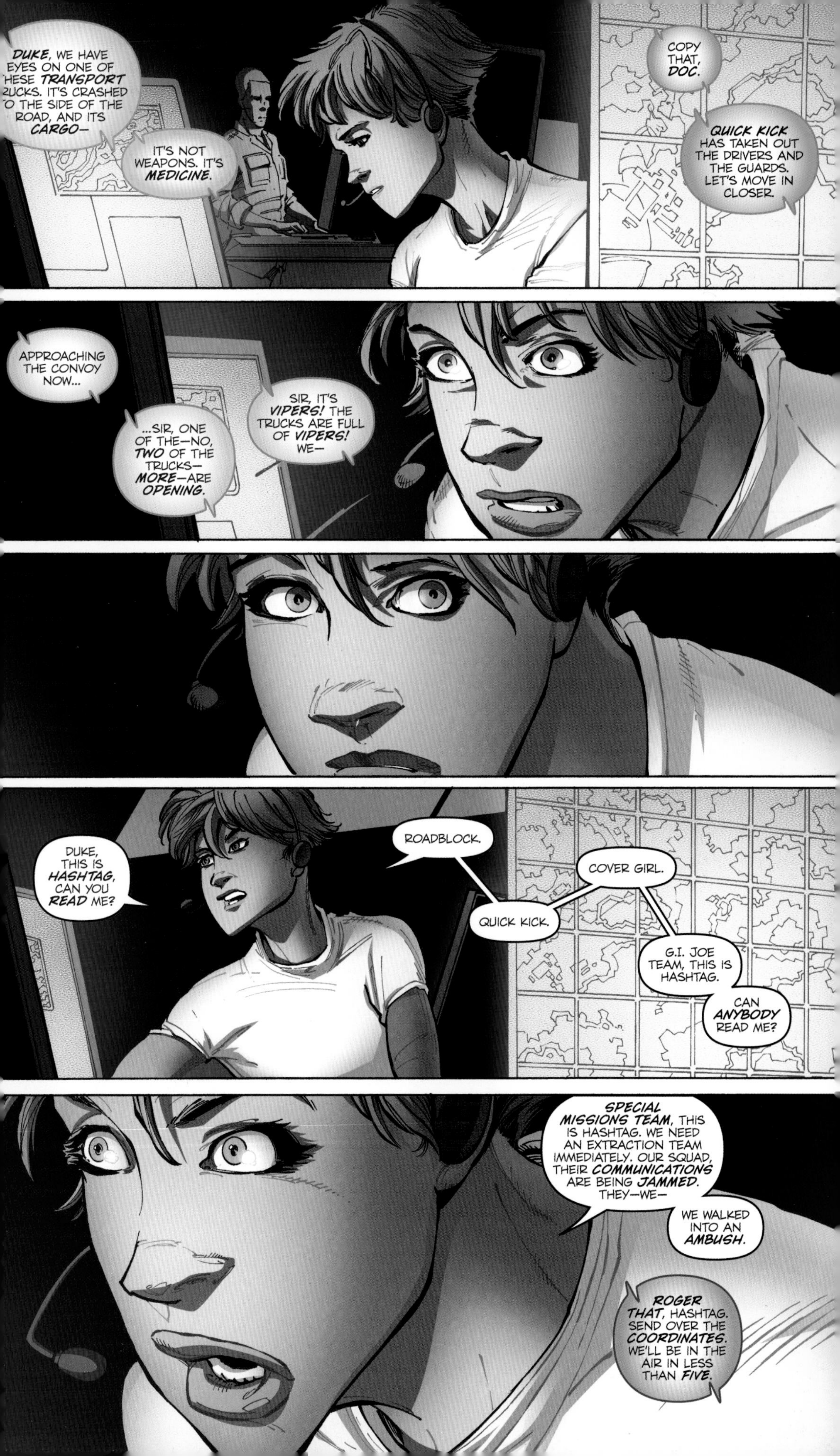
DUKE, WE HAVE EYES ON ONE OF THESE TRANSPORT TRUCKS. IT'S CRASHED TO THE SIDE OF THE ROAD, AND ITS CARGO—
IT'S NOT WEAPONS. IT'S MEDICINE.
COPY THAT, DOC.
QUICK KICK HAS TAKEN OUT THE DRIVERS AND THE GUARDS. LET'S MOVE IN CLOSER.
APPROACHING THE CONVOY NOW...
...SIR, ONE OF THE—NO, TWO OF THE TRUCKS—MORE—ARE OPENING.
SIR, IT'S VIPERS! THE TRUCKS ARE FULL OF VIPERS! WE—
DUKE, THIS IS HASHTAG, CAN YOU READ ME?
ROADBLOCK.
COVER GIRL.
QUICK KICK.
G.I. JOE TEAM, THIS IS HASHTAG.
CAN ANYBODY READ ME?
SPECIAL MISSIONS TEAM, THIS IS HASHTAG. WE NEED AN EXTRACTION TEAM IMMEDIATELY. OUR SQUAD, THEIR COMMUNICATIONS ARE BEING JAMMED. THEY—WE—
WE WALKED INTO AN AMBUSH.
ROGER THAT, HASHTAG. SEND OVER THE COORDINATES. WE'LL BE IN THE AIR IN LESS THAN FIVE.

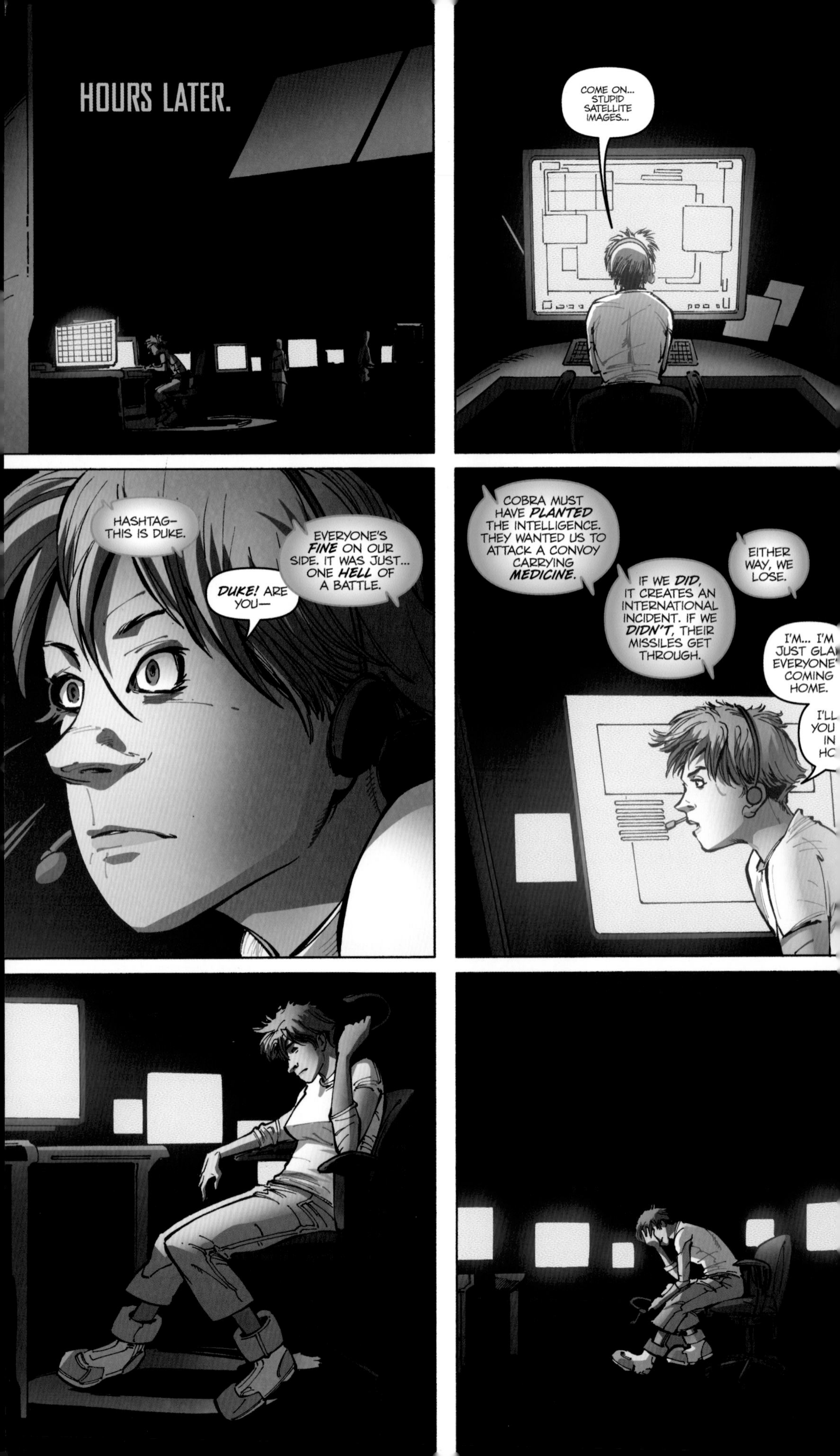
HOURS LATER.
COME ON... STUPID SATELLITE IMAGES...
HASHTAG-THIS IS DUKE.
DUKE! ARE YOU—
EVERYONE'S FINE ON OUR SIDE. IT WAS JUST... ONE HELL OF A BATTLE.
COBRA MUST HAVE PLANTED THE INTELLIGENCE. THEY WANTED US TO ATTACK A CONVOY CARRYING MEDICINE.
IF WE DID, IT CREATES AN INTERNATIONAL INCIDENT. IF WE DIDN'T, THEIR MISSILES GET THROUGH.
EITHER WAY, WE LOSE.
I'M... I'M JUST GLA
EVERYONE
COMING HOME.
I'LL
YOU
IN
HC

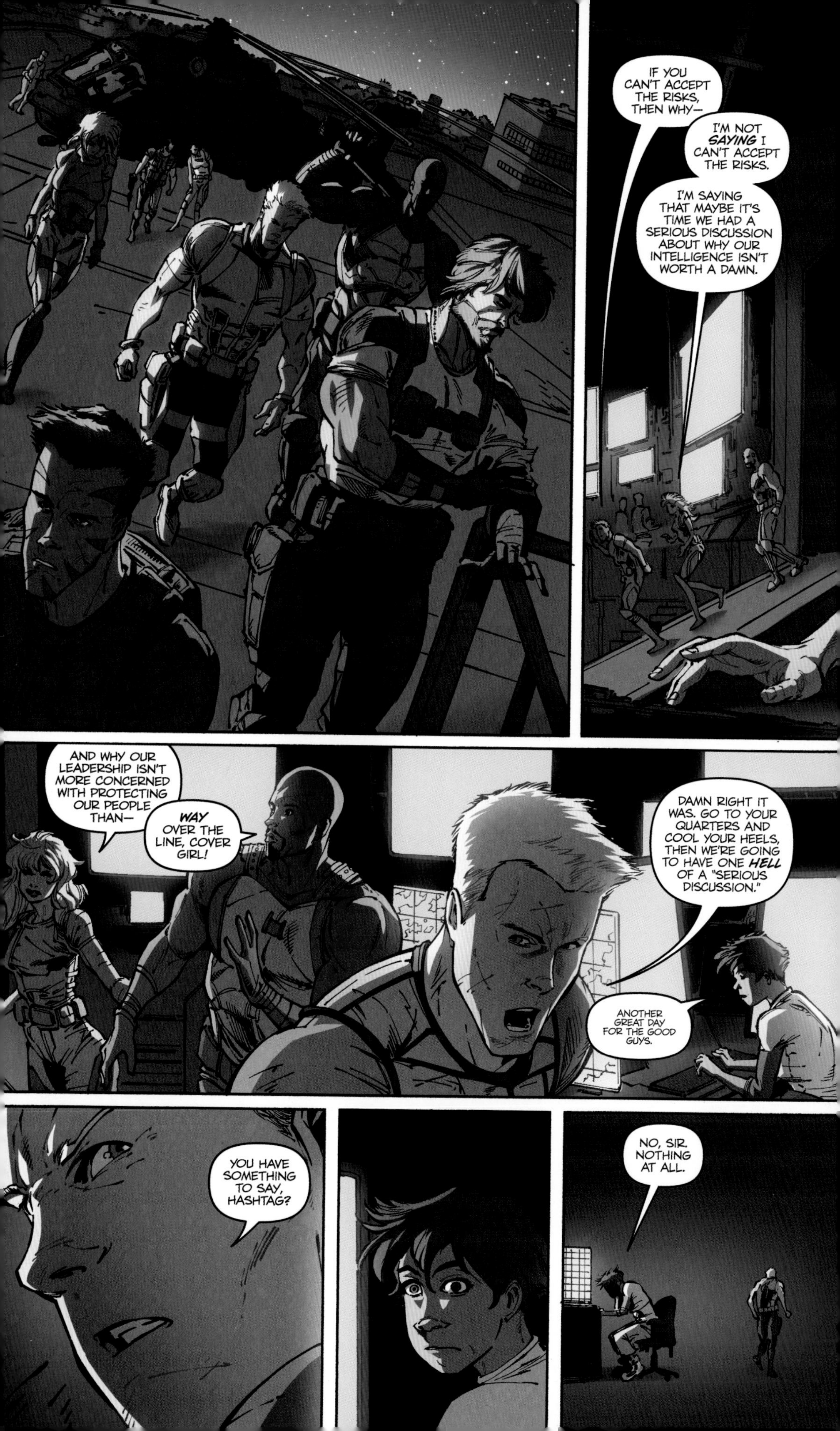
IF YOU CAN'T ACCEPT THE RISKS, THEN WHY—
I'M NOT SAYING I CAN'T ACCEPT THE RISKS.
I'M SAYING THAT MAYBE IT'S TIME WE HAD A SERIOUS DISCUSSION ABOUT WHY OUR INTELLIGENCE ISN'T WORTH A DAMN.
AND WHY OUR LEADERSHIP ISN'T MORE CONCERNED WITH PROTECTING OUR PEOPLE THAN—
WAY OVER THE LINE, COVER GIRL!
DAMN RIGHT IT WAS. GO TO YOUR QUARTERS AND COOL YOUR HEELS, THEN WE'RE GOING TO HAVE ONE HELL OF A "SERIOUS DISCUSSION."
ANOTHER GREAT DAY FOR THE GOOD GUYS.
YOU HAVE SOMETHING TO SAY, HASHTAG?
NO, SIR. NOTHING AT ALL.

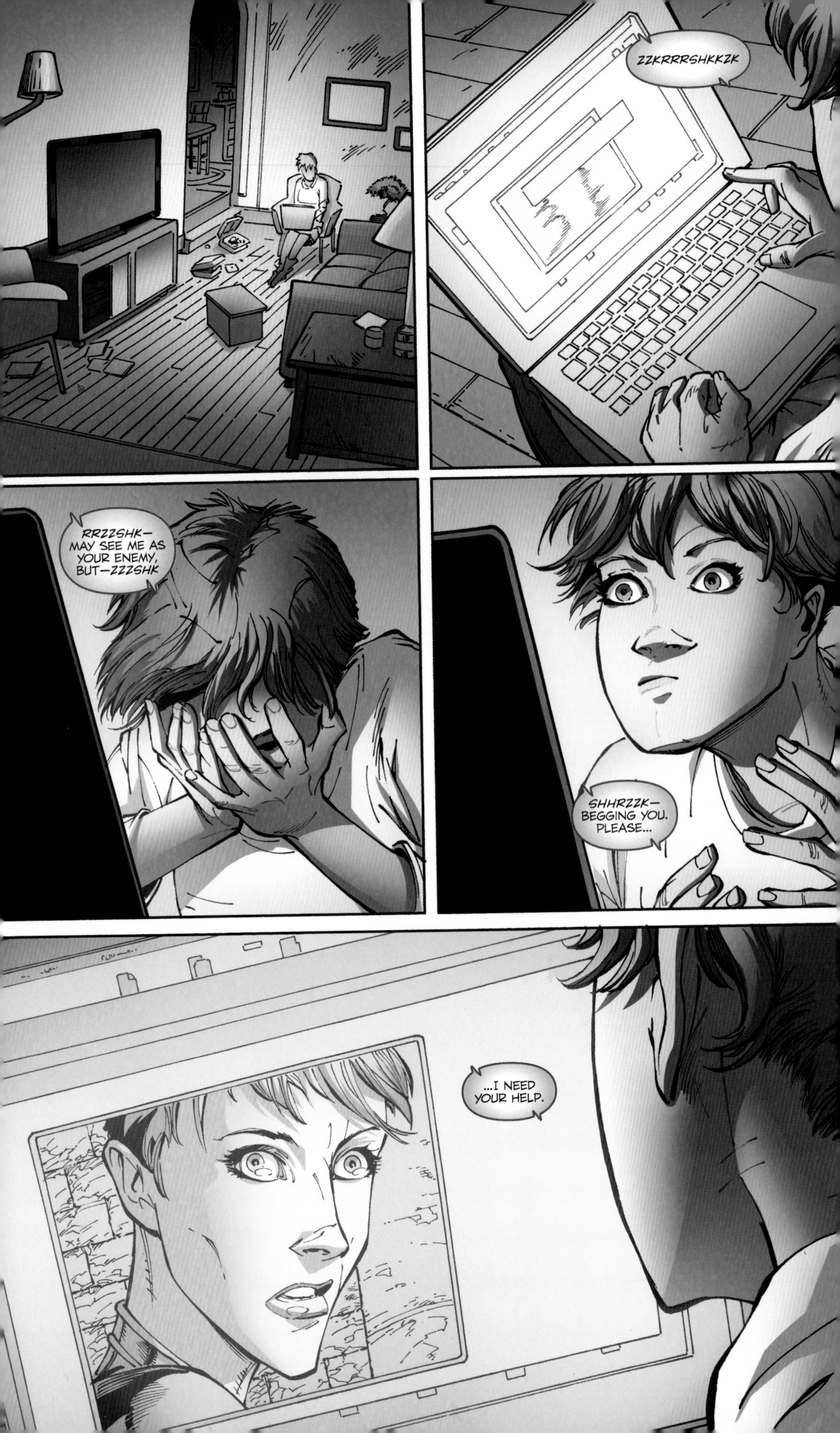
ZZKRRRSHKKZK
RRZZSHK— MAY SEE ME AS YOUR ENEMY, BUT—ZZZSHK
SHHRZZK— BEGGING YOU. PLEASE...
...I NEED YOUR HELP.

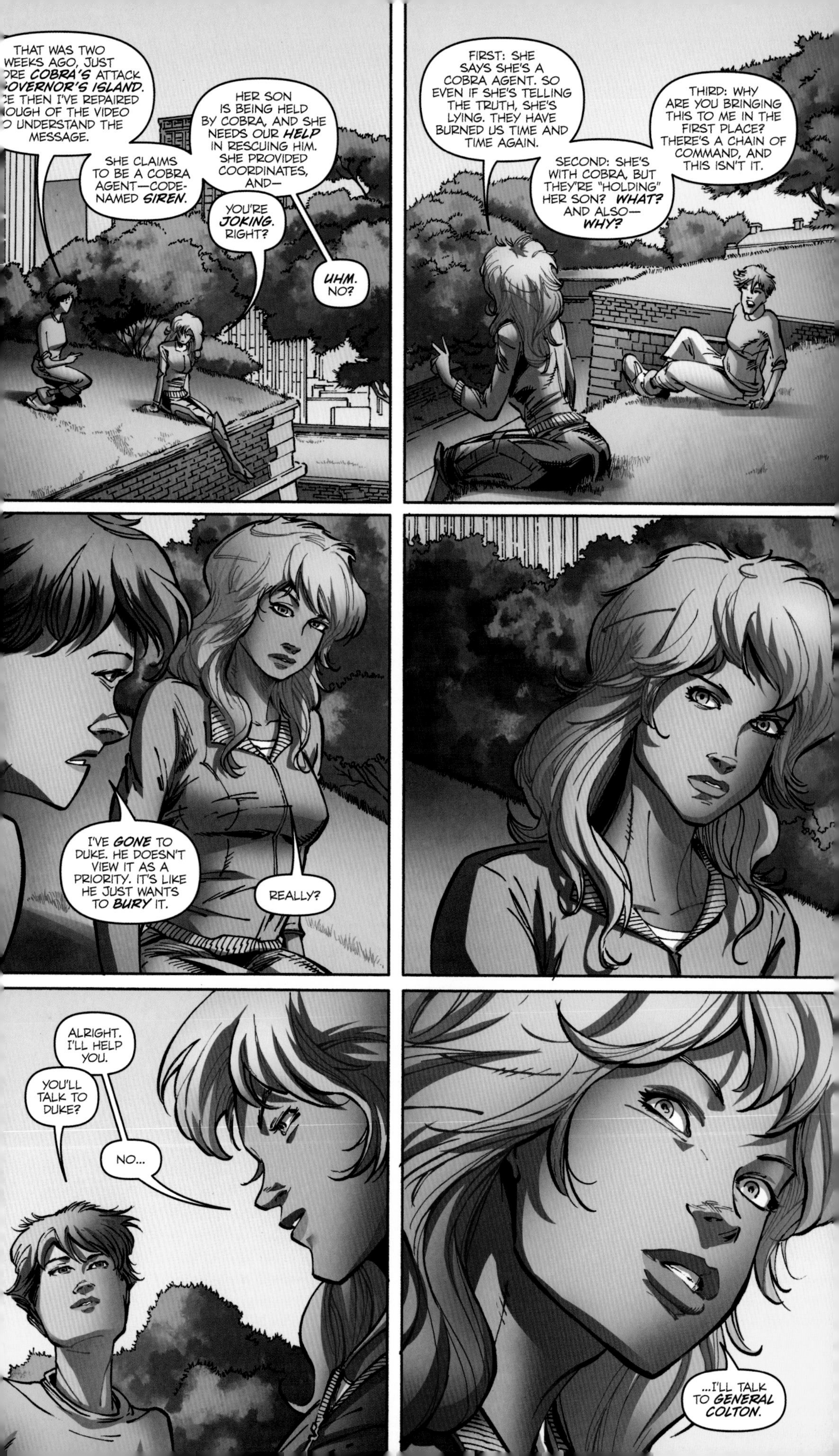

THAT WAS TWO WEEKS AGO, JUST ORE COBRA'S ATTACK GOVERNOR'S ISLAND. CE THEN I'VE REPAIRED OUGH OF THE VIDEO O UNDERSTAND THE MESSAGE.
SHE CLAIMS TO BE A COBRA AGENT—CODE-NAMED SIREN.
HER SON IS BEING HELD BY COBRA, AND SHE NEEDS OUR HELP IN RESCUING HIM. SHE PROVIDED COORDINATES, AND—
YOU'RE JOKING. RIGHT?
UHM. NO?
FIRST: SHE SAYS SHE'S A COBRA AGENT. SO EVEN IF SHE'S TELLING THE TRUTH, SHE'S LYING. THEY HAVE BURNED US TIME AND TIME AGAIN.
SECOND: SHE'S WITH COBRA, BUT THEY'RE "HOLDING" HER SON? WHAT? AND ALSO—WHY?
THIRD: WHY ARE YOU BRINGING THIS TO ME IN THE FIRST PLACE? THERE'S A CHAIN OF COMMAND, AND THIS ISN'T IT.
I'VE GONE TO DUKE. HE DOESN'T VIEW IT AS A PRIORITY. IT'S LIKE HE JUST WANTS TO BURY IT.
REALLY?
ALRIGHT. I'LL HELP YOU.
YOU'LL TALK TO DUKE?
NO...
...I'LL TALK TO GENERAL COLTON.

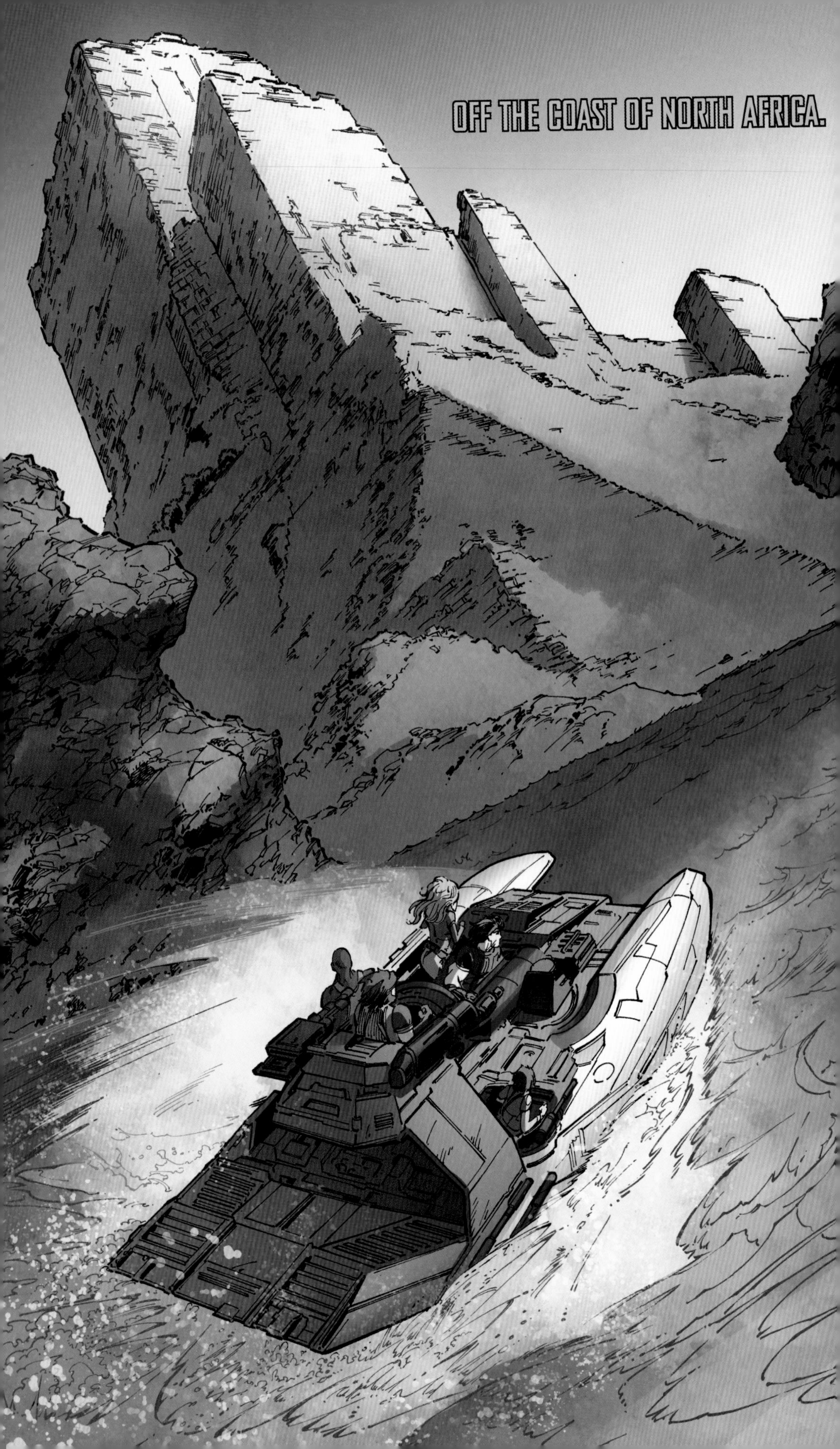
OFF THE COAST OF NORTH AFRICA.

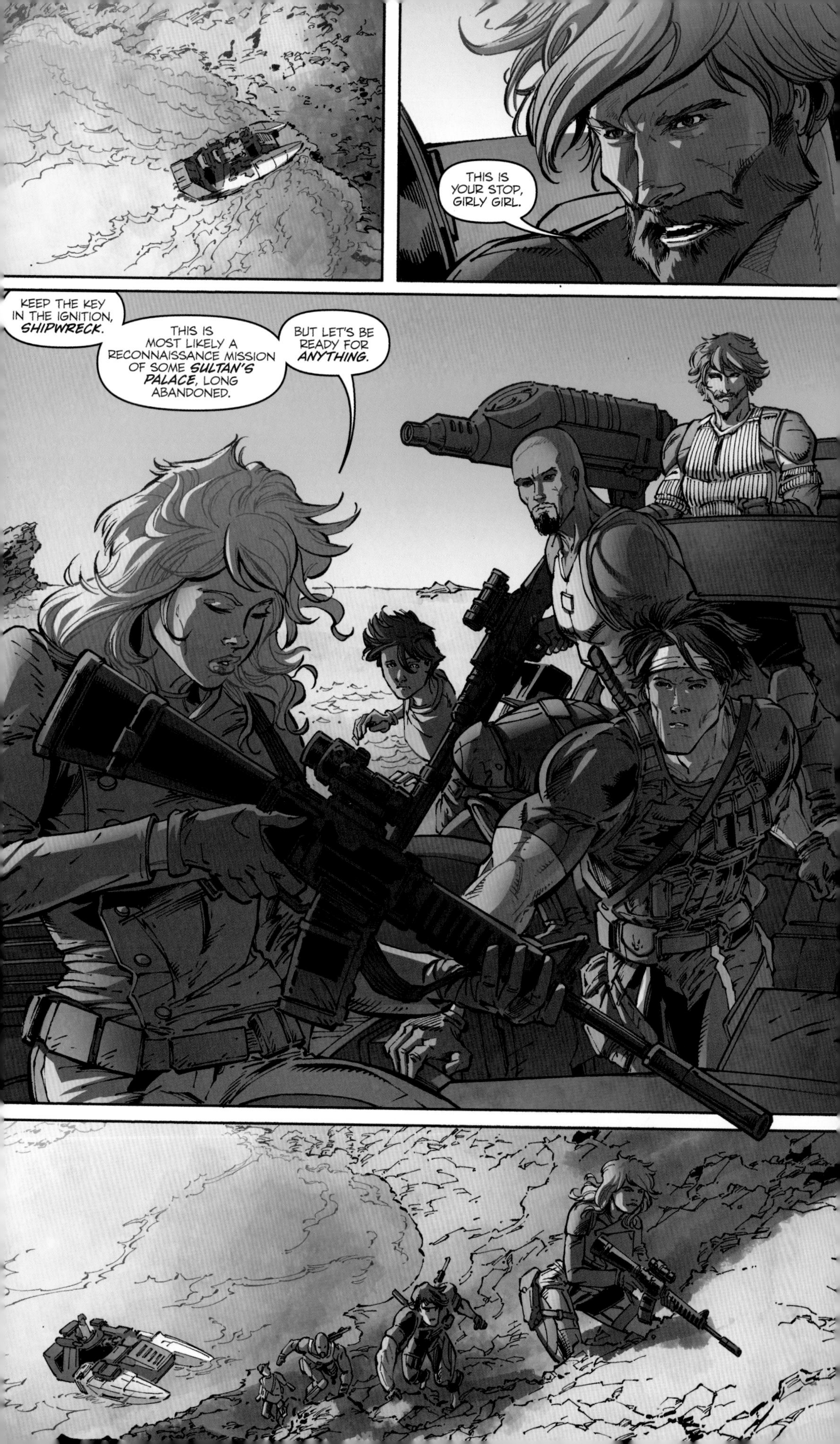
THIS IS YOUR STOP, GIRLY GIRL.
KEEP THE KEY IN THE IGNITION, SHIPWRECK.
THIS IS MOST LIKELY A RECONNAISSANCE MISSION OF SOME SULTAN'S PALACE, LONG ABANDONED.
BUT LET'S BE READY FOR ANYTHING.

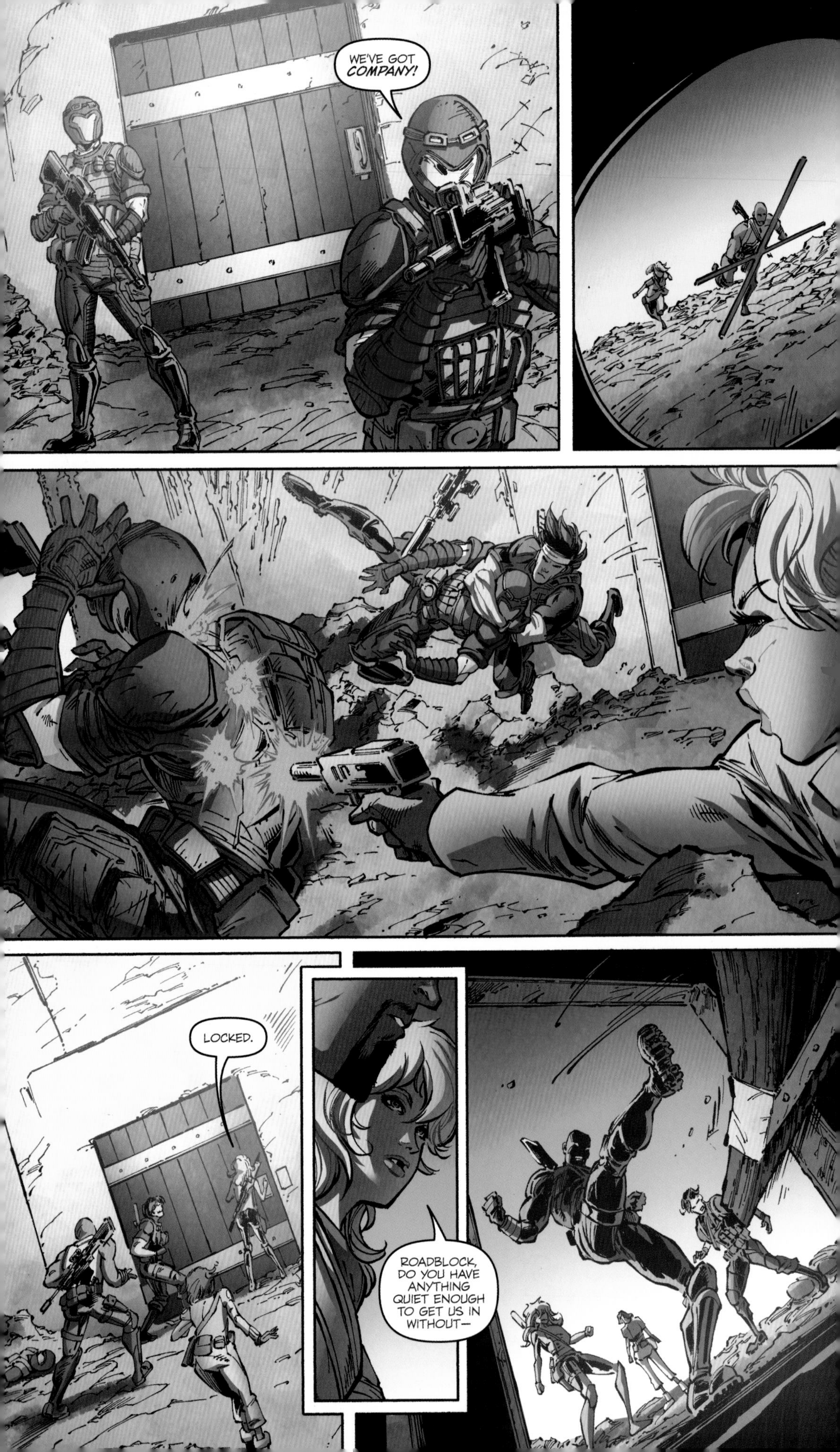
WE'VE GOT *COMPANY!*
LOCKED.
ROADBLOCK, DO YOU HAVE ANYTHING QUIET ENOUGH TO GET US IN WITHOUT—

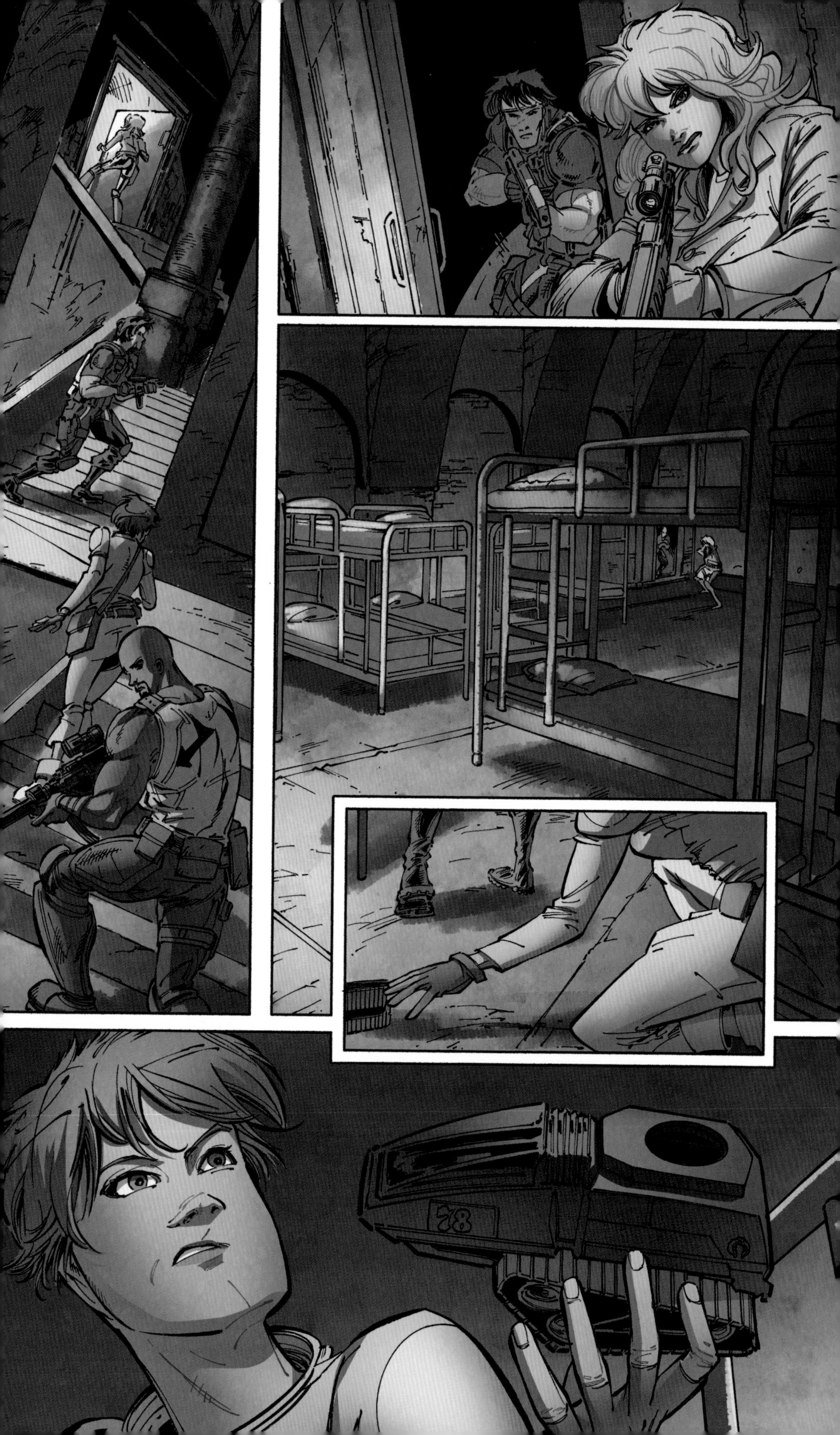

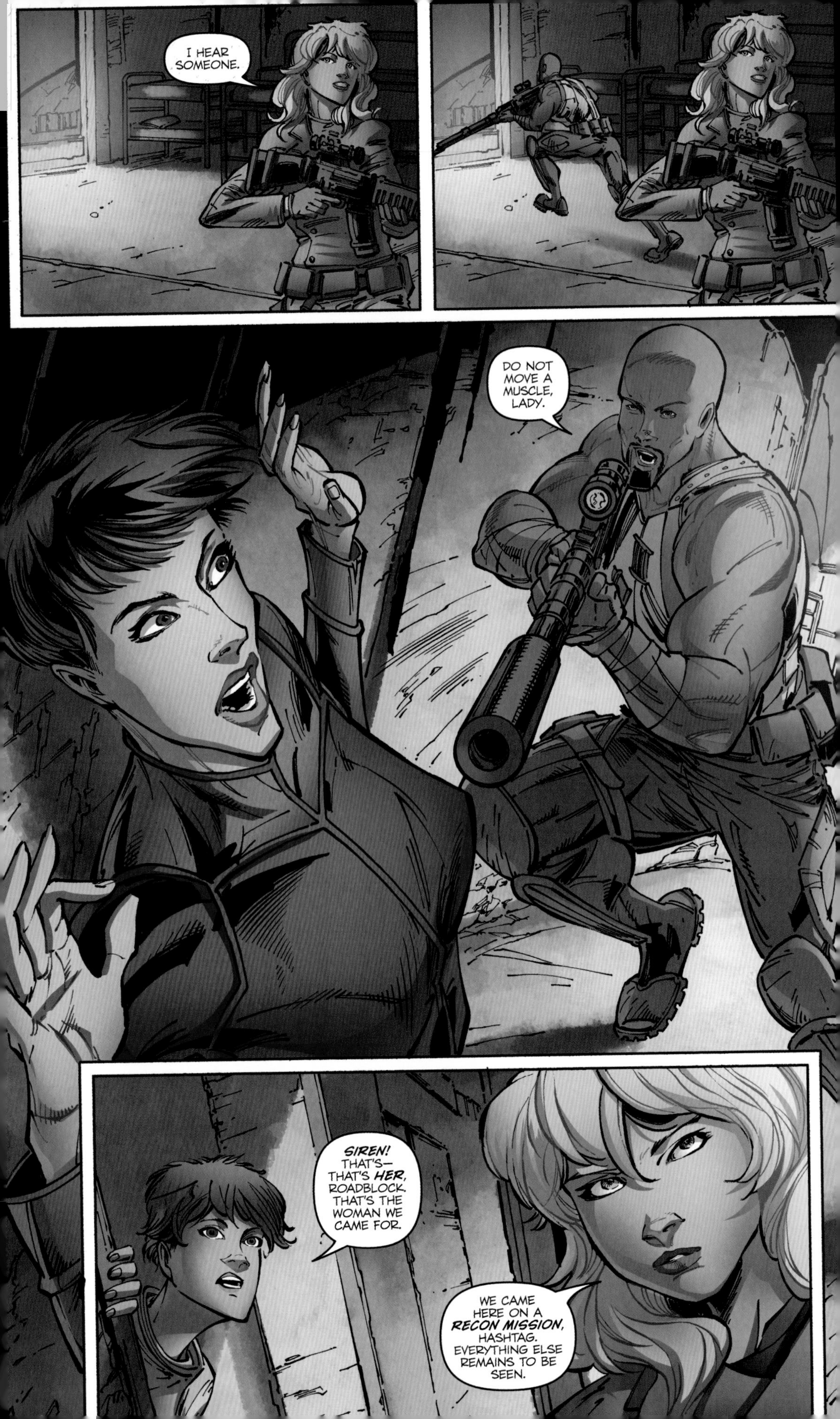
I HEAR SOMEONE.
DO NOT MOVE A MUSCLE, LADY.
SIREN! THAT'S— THAT'S HER, ROADBLOCK. THAT'S THE WOMAN WE CAME FOR.
WE CAME HERE ON A RECON MISSION, HASHTAG. EVERYTHING ELSE REMAINS TO BE SEEN.

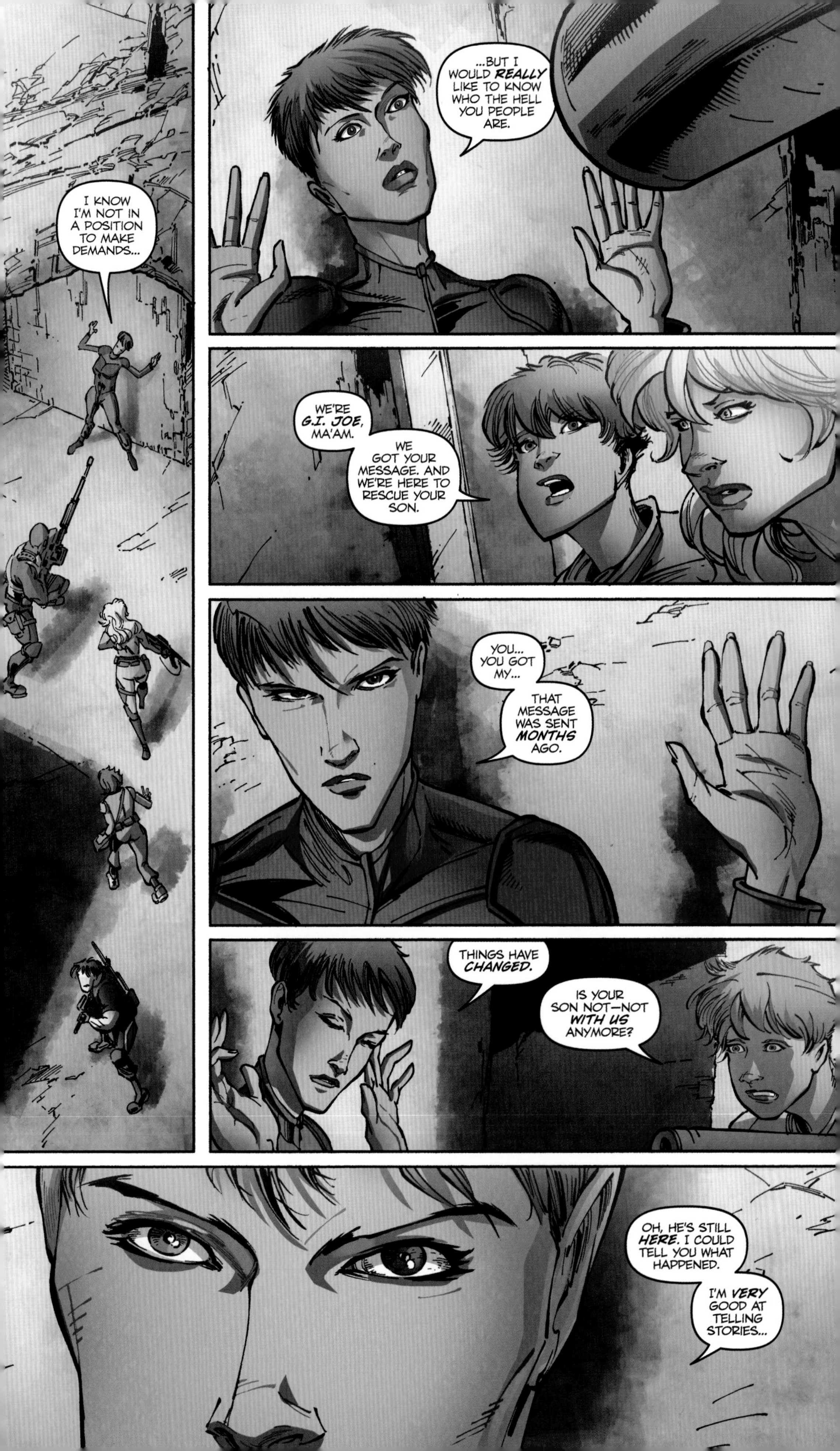
I KNOW I'M NOT IN A POSITION TO MAKE DEMANDS...
...BUT I WOULD REALLY LIKE TO KNOW WHO THE HELL YOU PEOPLE ARE.
WE'RE G.I. JOE, MA'AM.
WE GOT YOUR MESSAGE. AND WE'RE HERE TO RESCUE YOUR SON.
YOU... YOU GOT MY...
THAT MESSAGE WAS SENT MONTHS AGO.
THINGS HAVE CHANGED.
IS YOUR SON NOT—NOT WITH US ANYMORE?
OH, HE'S STILL HERE. I COULD TELL YOU WHAT HAPPENED.
I'M VERY GOOD AT TELLING STORIES...

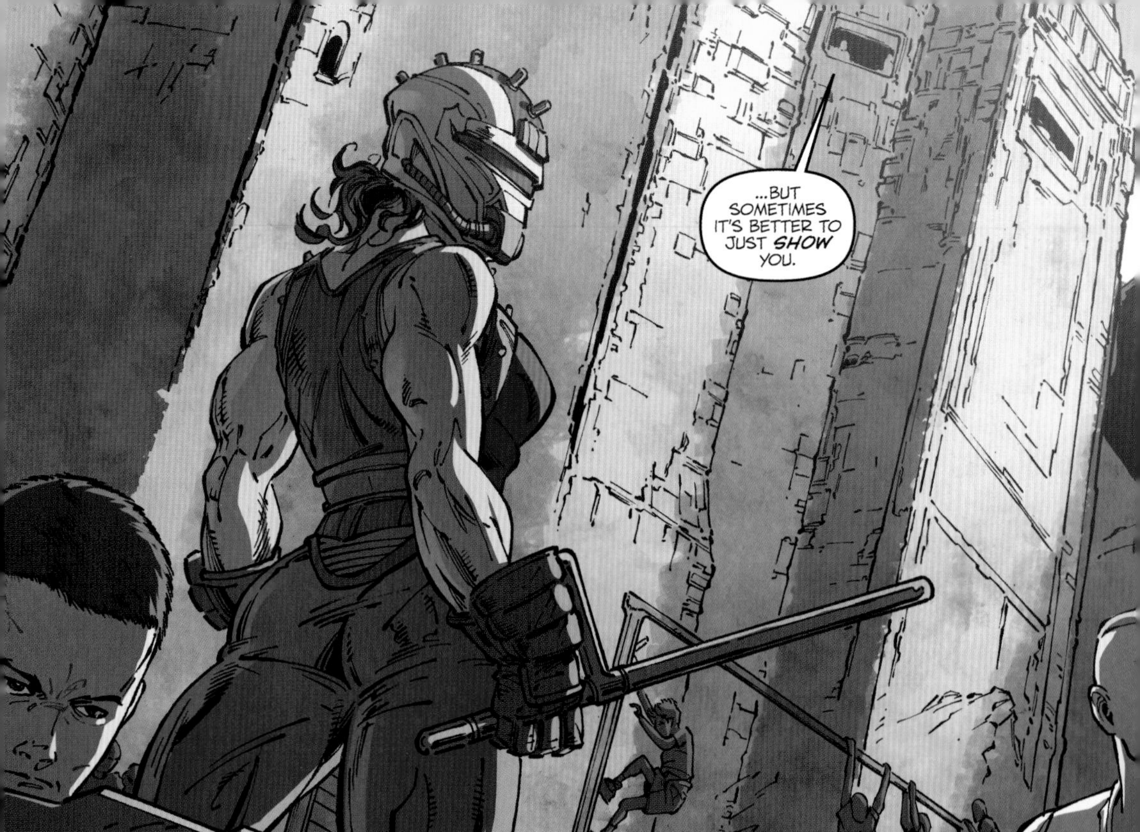
...BUT SOMETIMES IT'S BETTER TO JUST SHOW YOU.

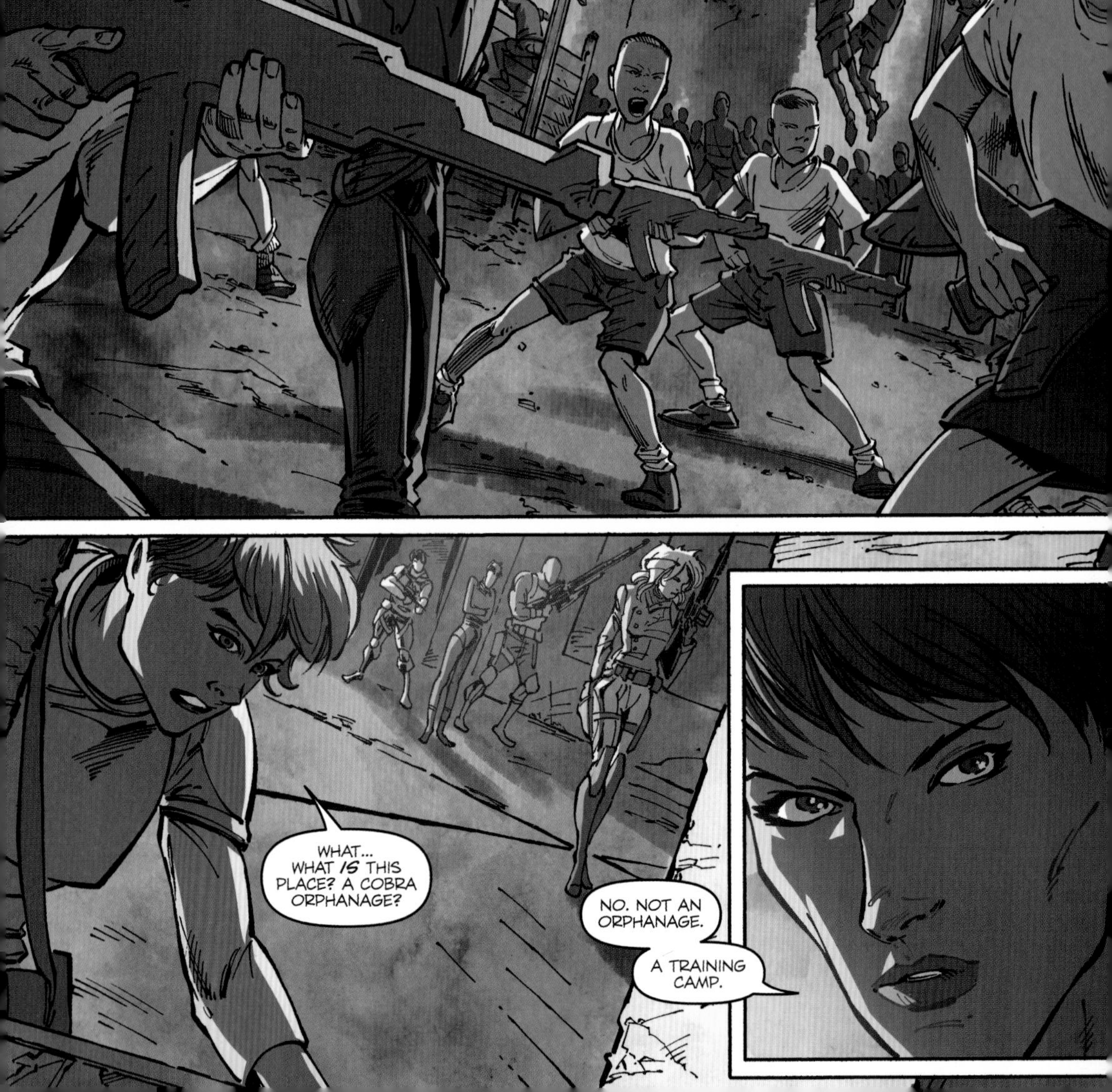
WHAT... WHAT IS THIS PLACE? A COBRA ORPHANAGE?
NO. NOT AN ORPHANAGE.
A TRAINING CAMP.

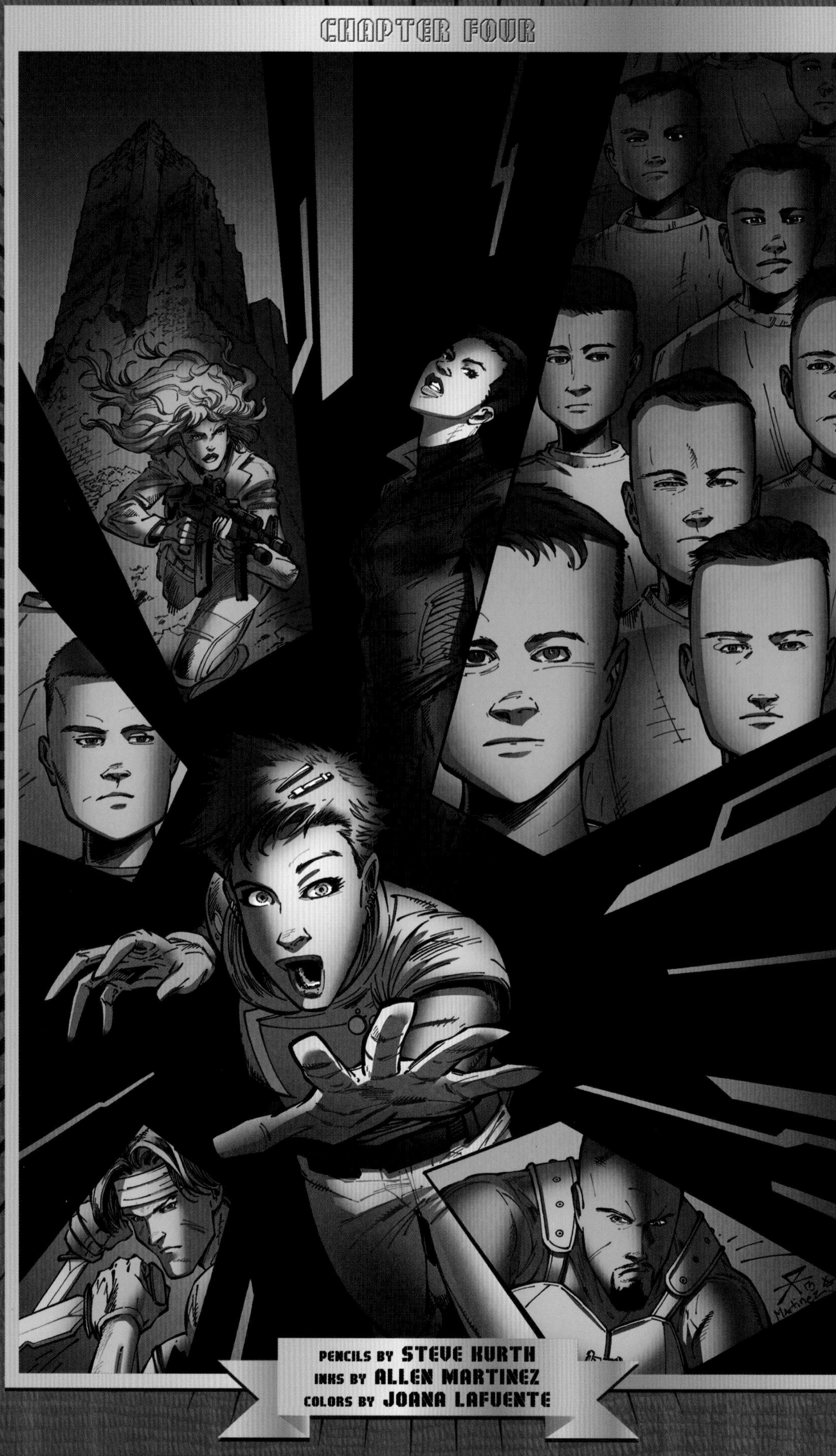
CHAPTER FOUR
PENCILS BY STEVE KURTH
INKS BY ALLEN MARTINEZ
COLORS BY JOANA LAFUENTE

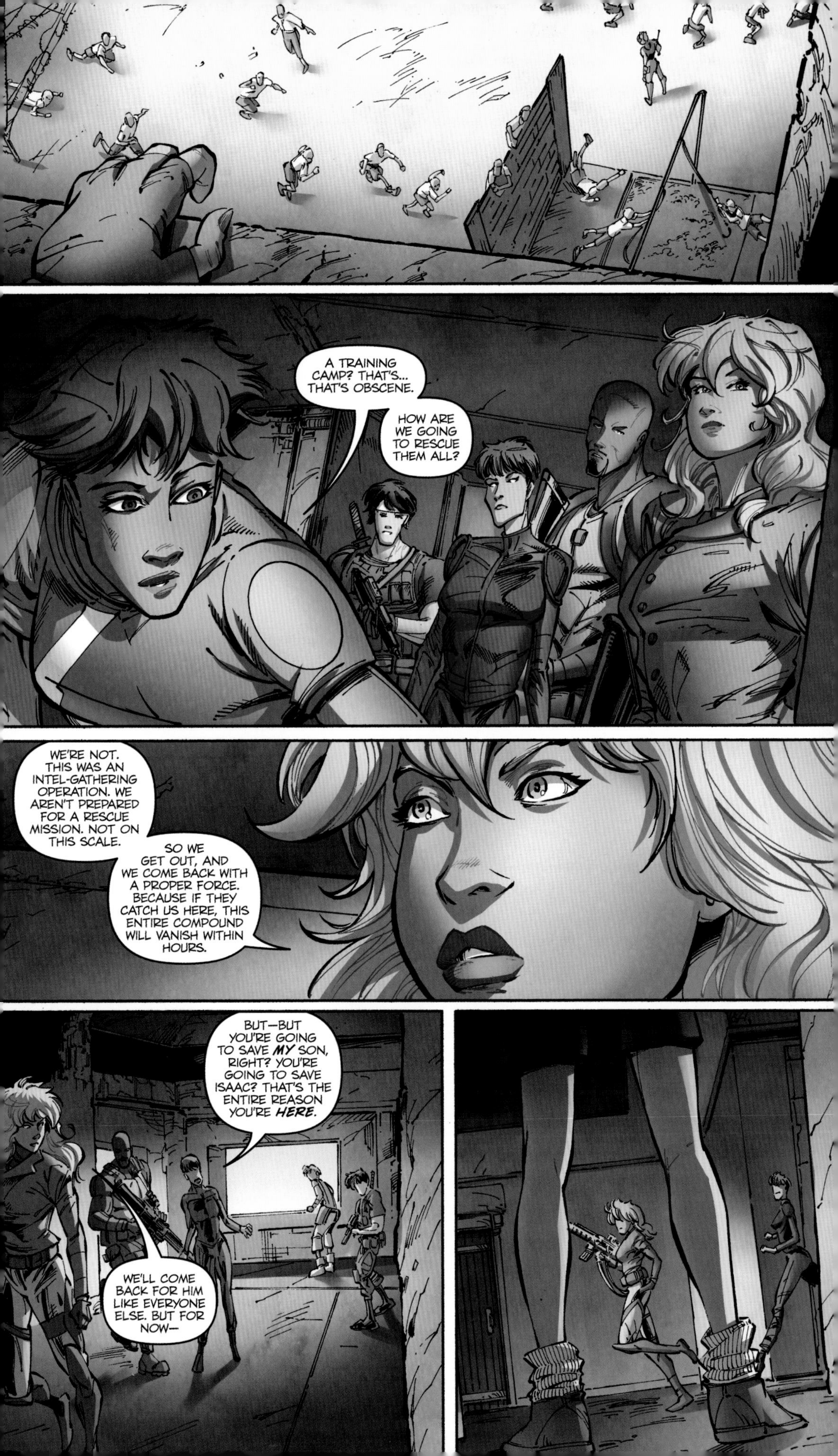
A TRAINING CAMP? THAT'S... THAT'S OBSCENE.
HOW ARE WE GOING TO RESCUE THEM ALL?
WE'RE NOT. THIS WAS AN INTEL-GATHERING OPERATION. WE AREN'T PREPARED FOR A RESCUE MISSION. NOT ON THIS SCALE.
SO WE GET OUT, AND WE COME BACK WITH A PROPER FORCE. BECAUSE IF THEY CATCH US HERE, THIS ENTIRE COMPOUND WILL VANISH WITHIN HOURS.
BUT—BUT YOU'RE GOING TO SAVE *MY* SON, RIGHT? YOU'RE GOING TO SAVE ISAAC? THAT'S THE ENTIRE REASON YOU'RE *HERE*.
WE'LL COME BACK FOR HIM LIKE EVERYONE ELSE. BUT FOR NOW—

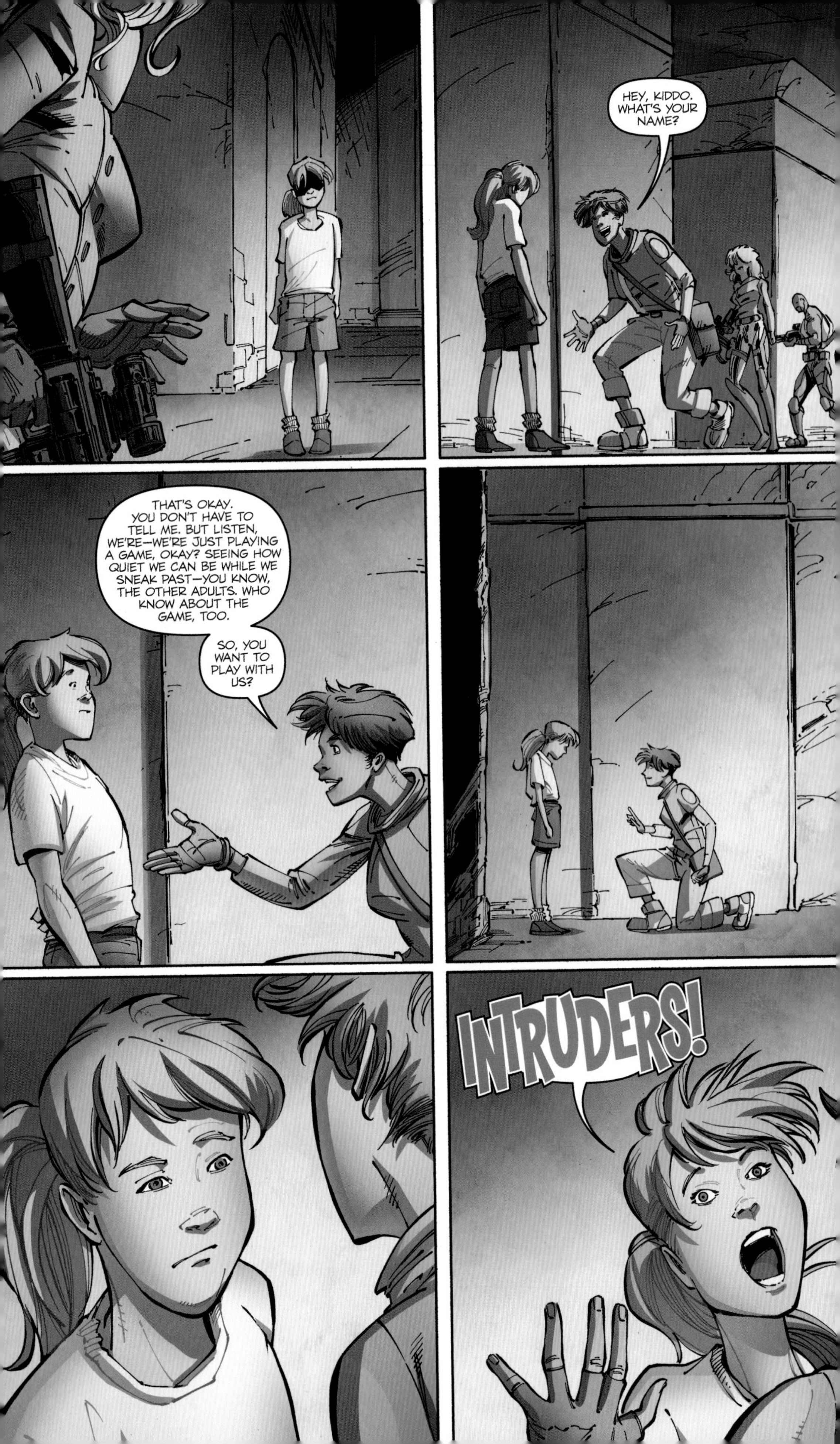
HEY, KIDDO. WHAT'S YOUR NAME?
THAT'S OKAY. YOU DON'T HAVE TO TELL ME. BUT LISTEN, WE'RE—WE'RE JUST PLAYING A GAME, OKAY? SEEING HOW QUIET WE CAN BE WHILE WE SNEAK PAST—YOU KNOW, THE OTHER ADULTS. WHO KNOW ABOUT THE GAME, TOO.
SO, YOU WANT TO PLAY WITH US?
INTRUDERS!

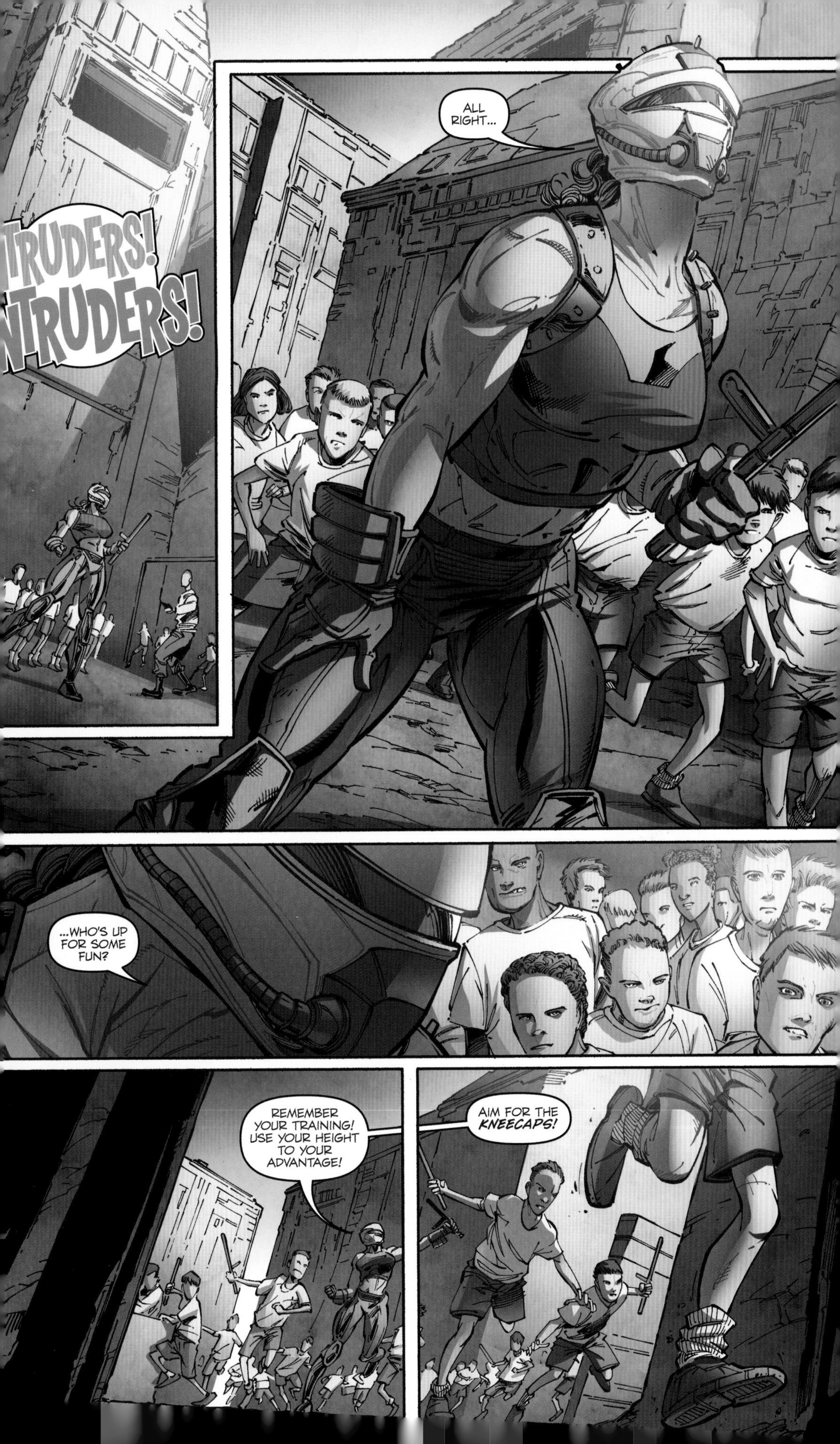

TRUDERS! NTRUDERS!
ALL RIGHT...
...WHO'S UP FOR SOME FUN?
REMEMBER YOUR TRAINING! USE YOUR HEIGHT TO YOUR ADVANTAGE!
AIM FOR THE *KNEECAPS!*

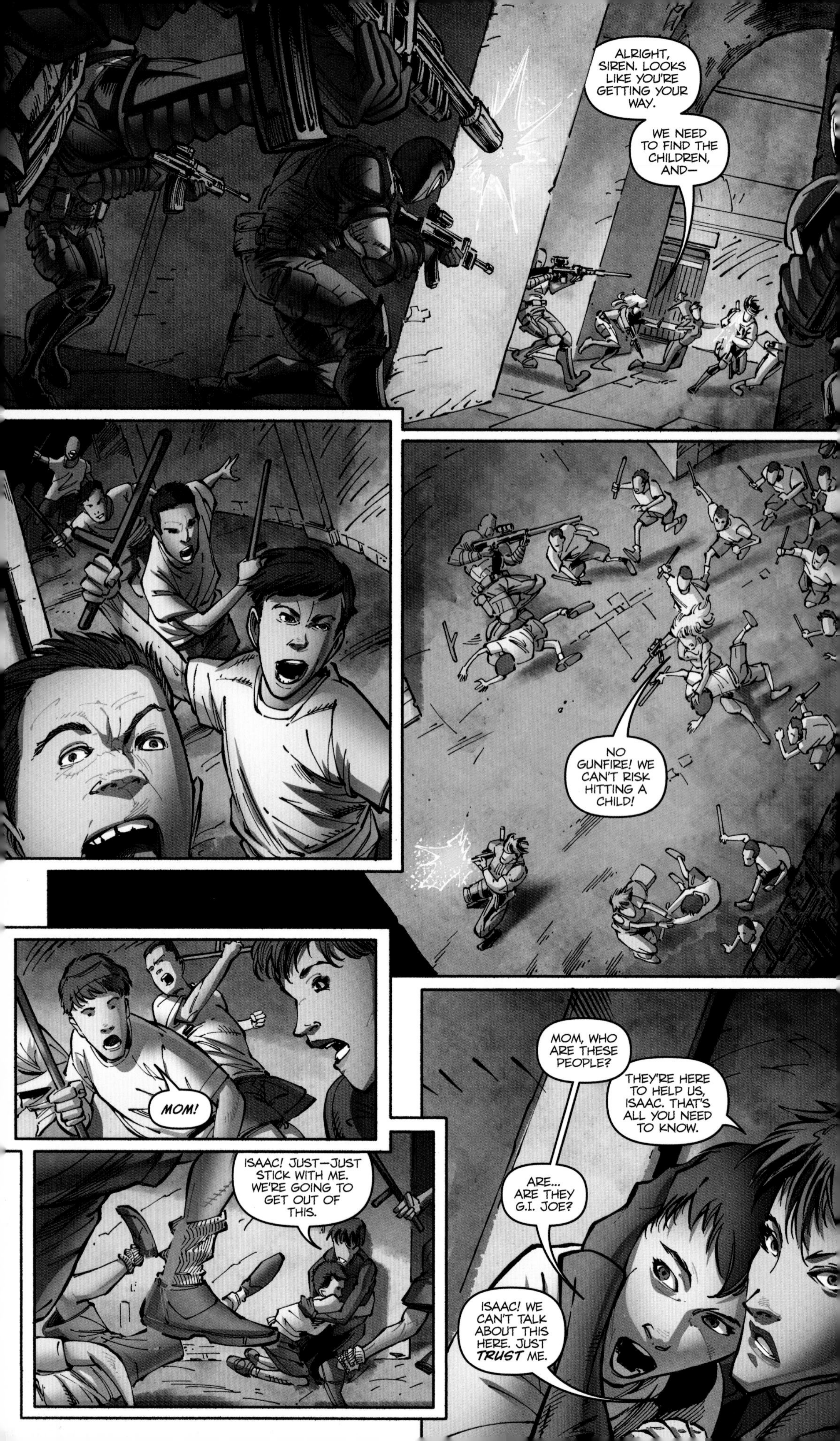
ALRIGHT, SIREN. LOOKS LIKE YOU'RE GETTING YOUR WAY.
WE NEED TO FIND THE CHILDREN, AND—
NO GUNFIRE! WE CAN'T RISK HITTING A CHILD!
MOM!
ISAAC! JUST—JUST STICK WITH ME. WE'RE GOING TO GET OUT OF THIS.
MOM, WHO ARE THESE PEOPLE?
THEY'RE HERE TO HELP US, ISAAC. THAT'S ALL YOU NEED TO KNOW.
ARE... ARE THEY G.I. JOE?
ISAAC! WE CAN'T TALK ABOUT THIS HERE. JUST TRUST ME.

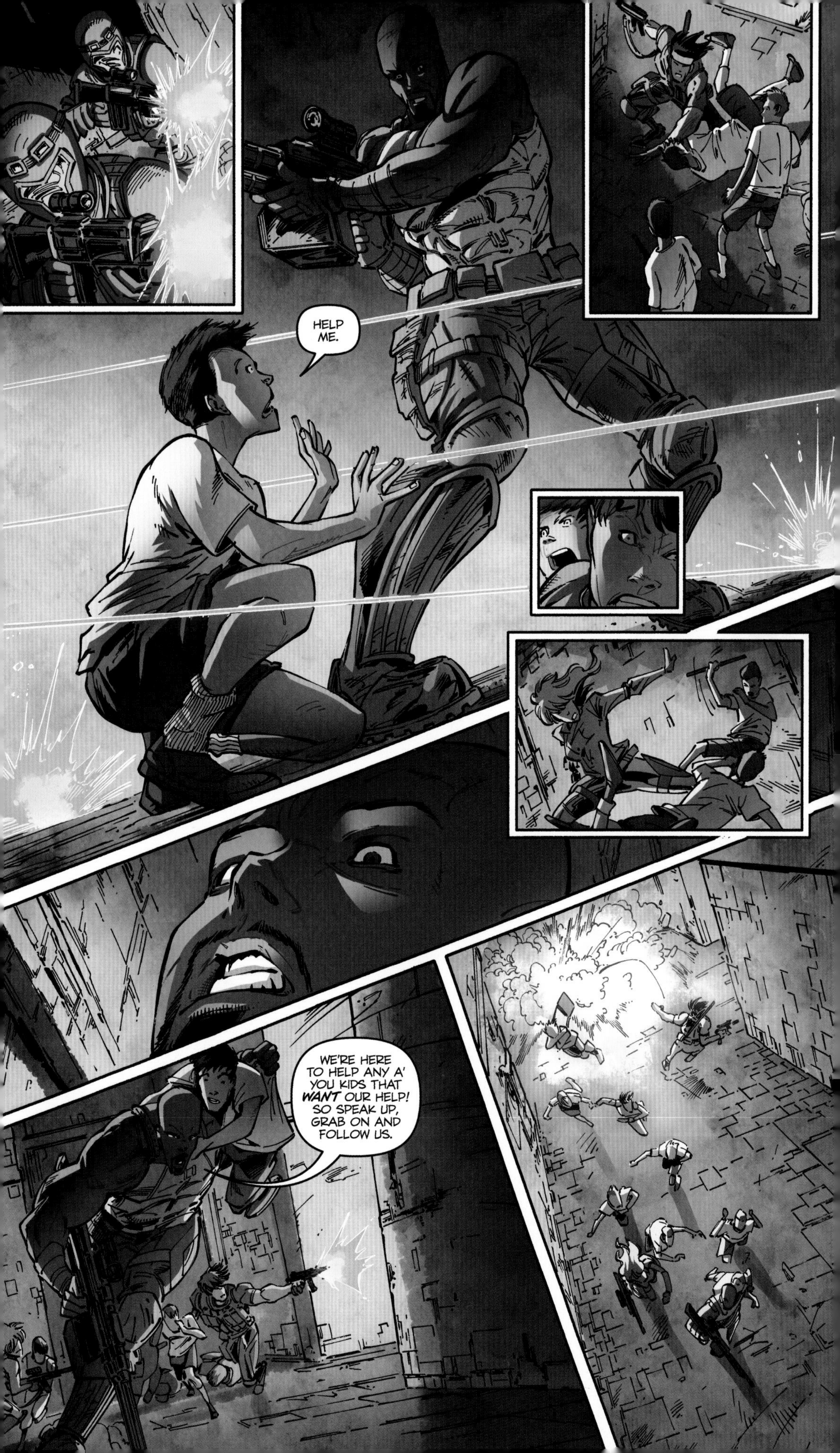
HELP ME.
WE'RE HERE TO HELP ANY A' YOU KIDS THAT *WANT* OUR HELP! SO SPEAK UP, GRAB ON AND FOLLOW US.

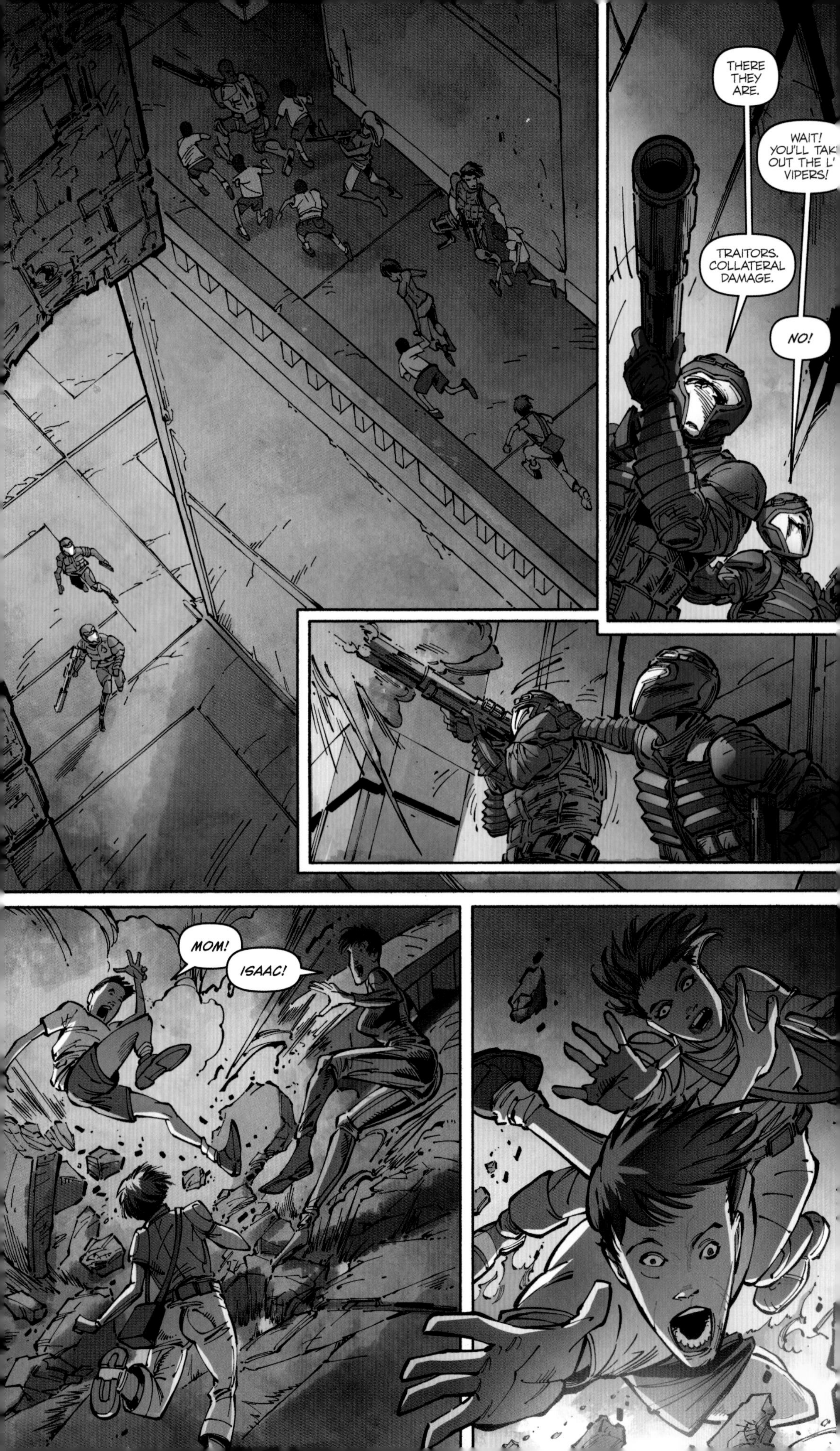
THERE THEY ARE.
WAIT! YOU'LL TAK OUT THE L' VIPERS!
TRAITORS. COLLATERAL DAMAGE.
NO!
MOM!
ISAAC!

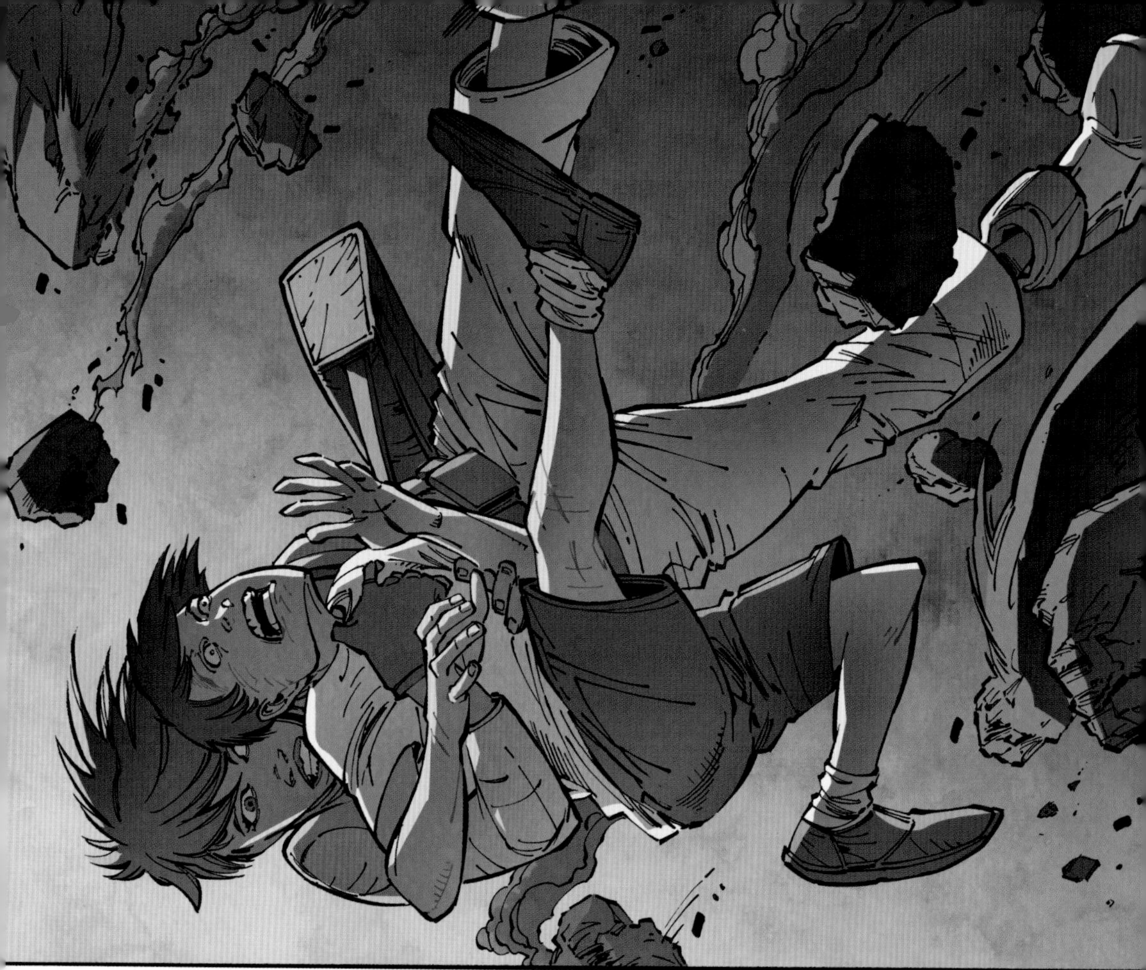

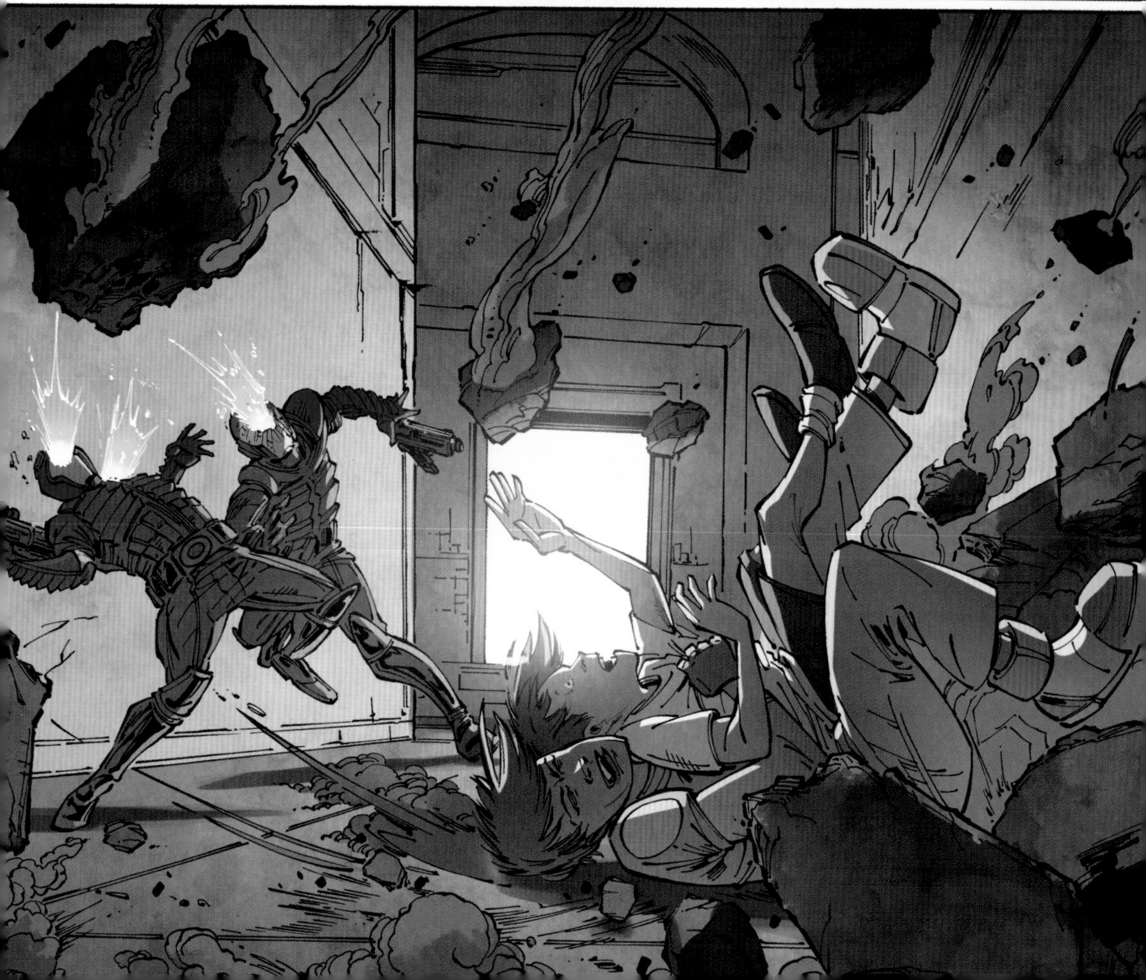

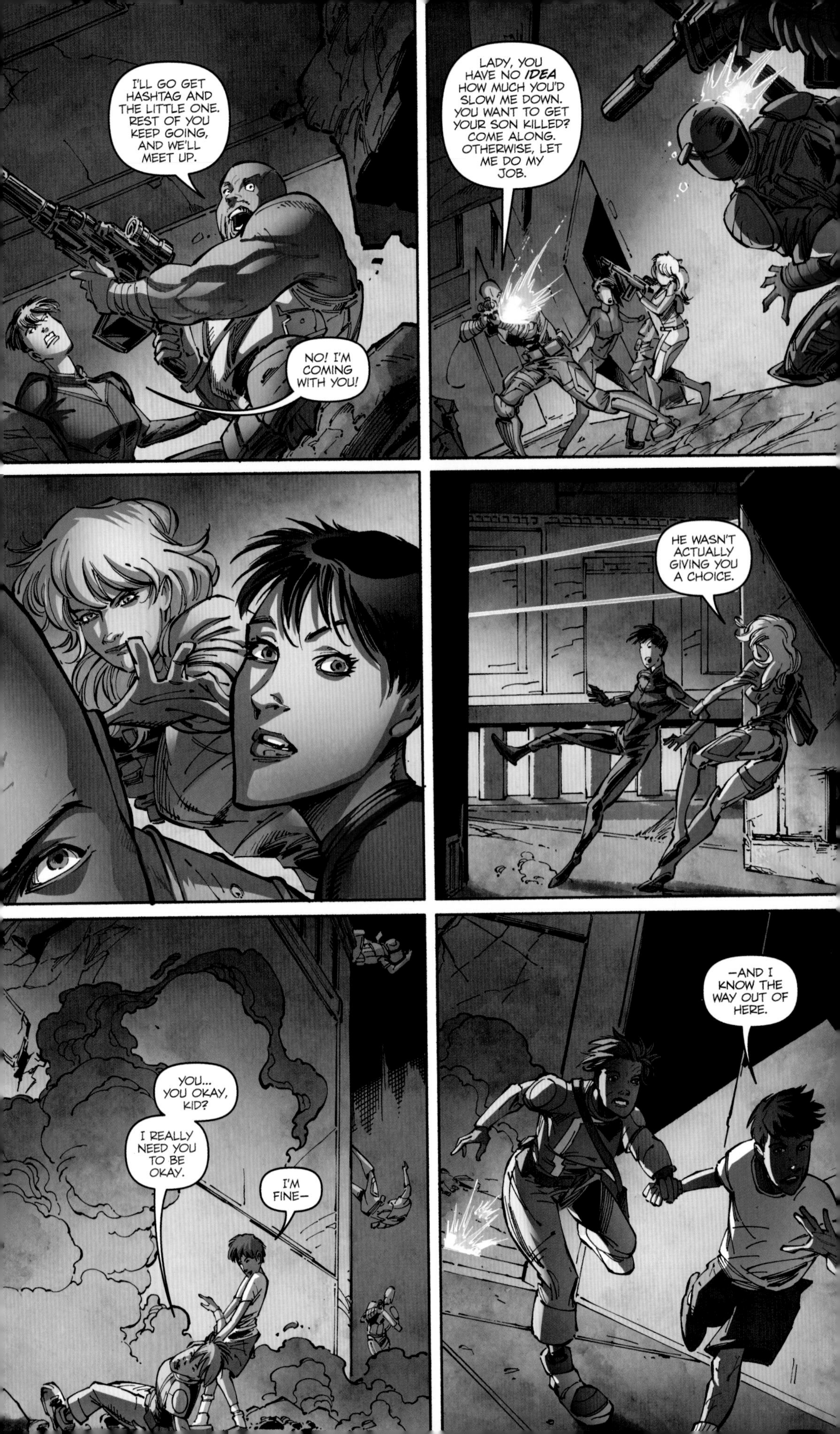
I'LL GO GET HASHTAG AND THE LITTLE ONE. REST OF YOU KEEP GOING, AND WE'LL MEET UP.
NO! I'M COMING WITH YOU!
LADY, YOU HAVE NO IDEA HOW MUCH YOU'D SLOW ME DOWN. YOU WANT TO GET YOUR SON KILLED? COME ALONG. OTHERWISE, LET ME DO MY JOB.
HE WASN'T ACTUALLY GIVING YOU A CHOICE.
YOU... YOU OKAY, KID?
I REALLY NEED YOU TO BE OKAY.
I'M FINE—
—AND I KNOW THE WAY OUT OF HERE.

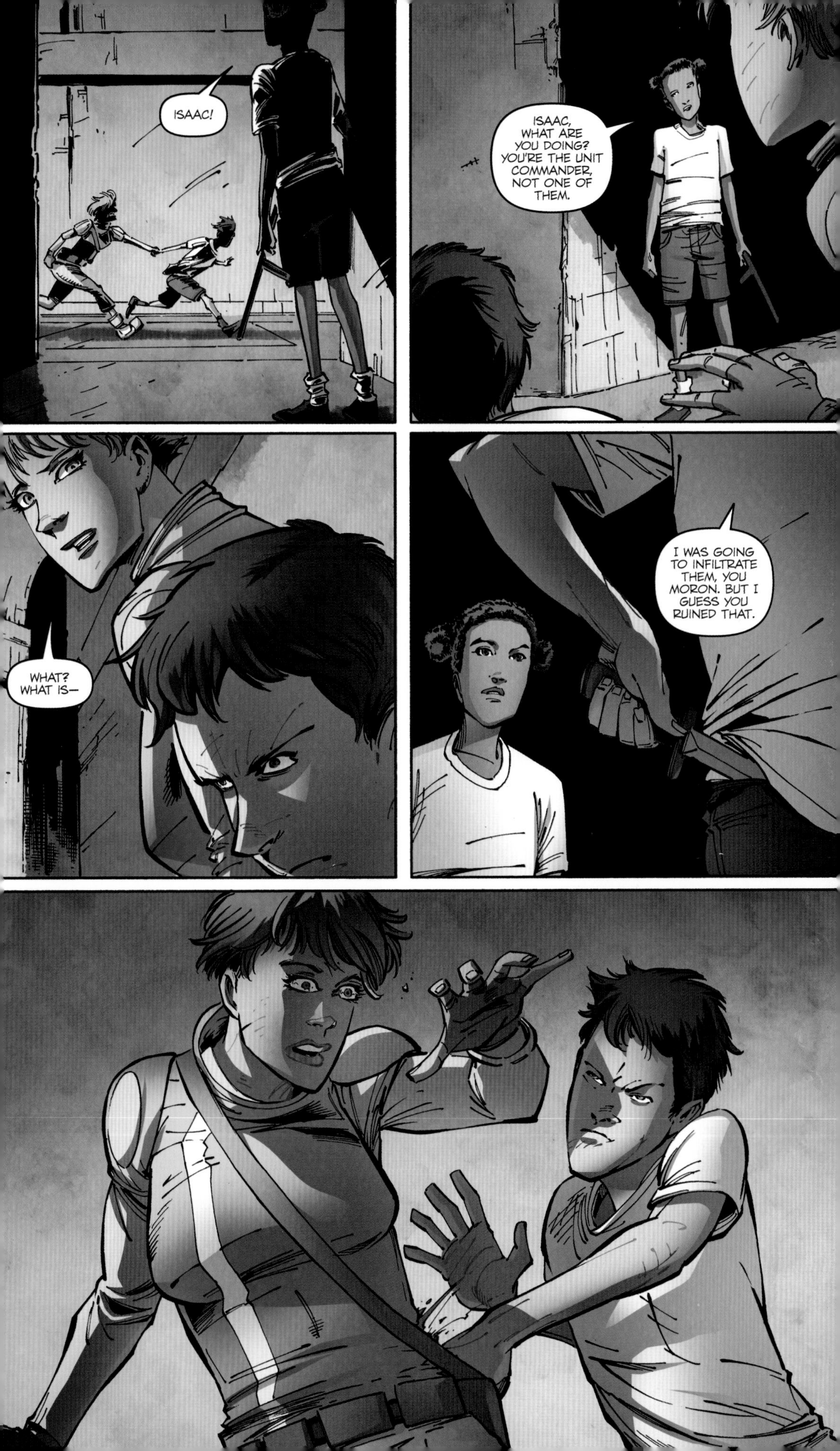
ISAAC!
ISAAC, WHAT ARE YOU DOING? YOU'RE THE UNIT COMMANDER, NOT ONE OF THEM.
WHAT? WHAT IS—
I WAS GOING TO INFILTRATE THEM, YOU MORON. BUT I GUESS YOU RUINED THAT.

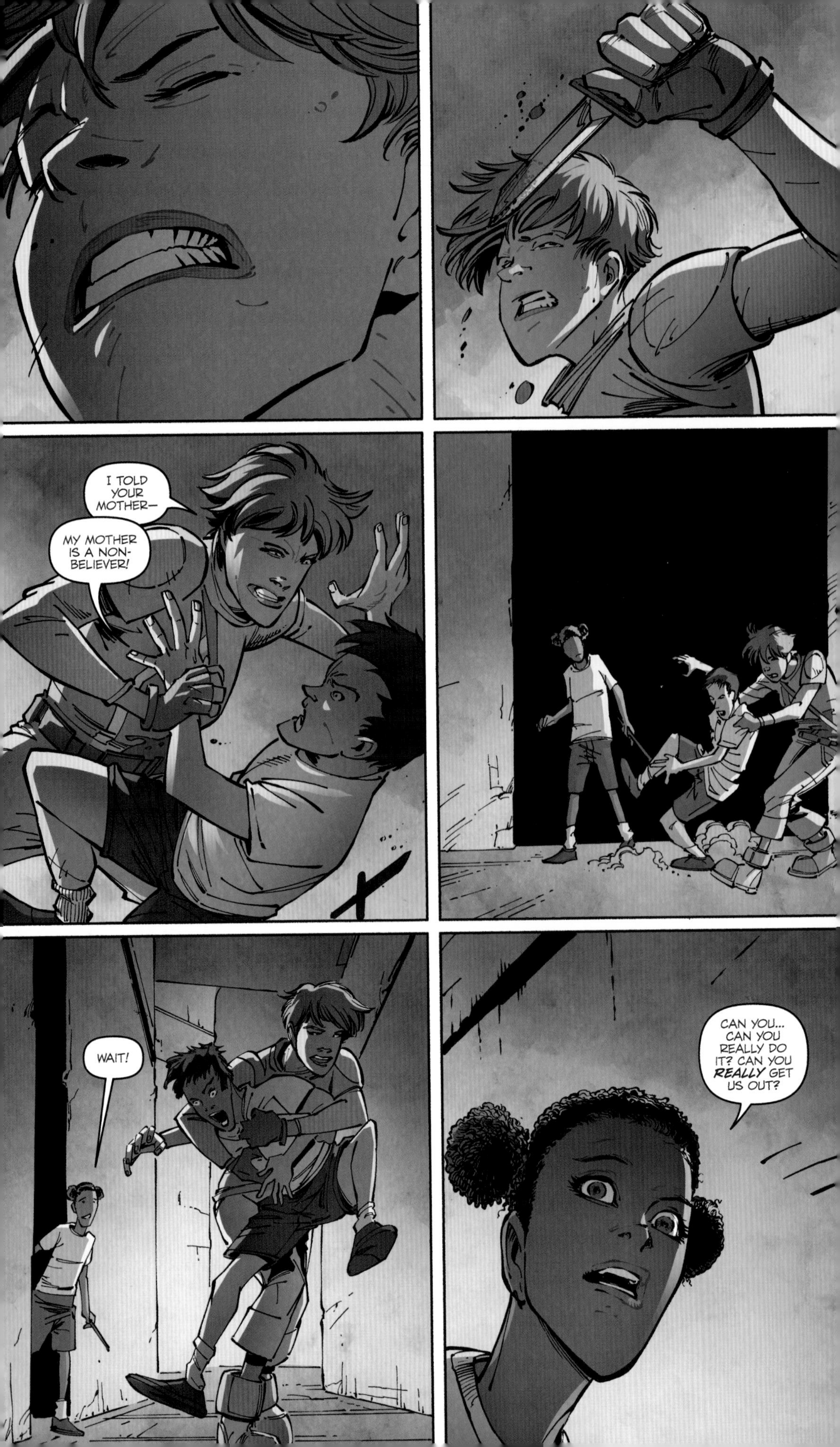
I TOLD YOUR MOTHER—
MY MOTHER IS A NON-BELIEVER!
WAIT!
CAN YOU... CAN YOU REALLY DO IT? CAN YOU *REALLY* GET US OUT?

WE CAN. OR, WE
COULD. BUT I—I
CAN'T PROTECT YOU.
IT'LL TAKE EVERY BIT
OF MY STRENGTH
JUST TO DRAG HIM
AWAY FROM—

AAAH!

I... I HAVE
BEEN WORKING
FOR MONTHS TO
SAVE YOU FROM
THESE PEOPLE.
YOU STUPID,
STUPID KID.

T I CAN'T.
AN'T SAVE
OU BOTH.

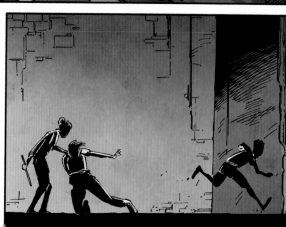

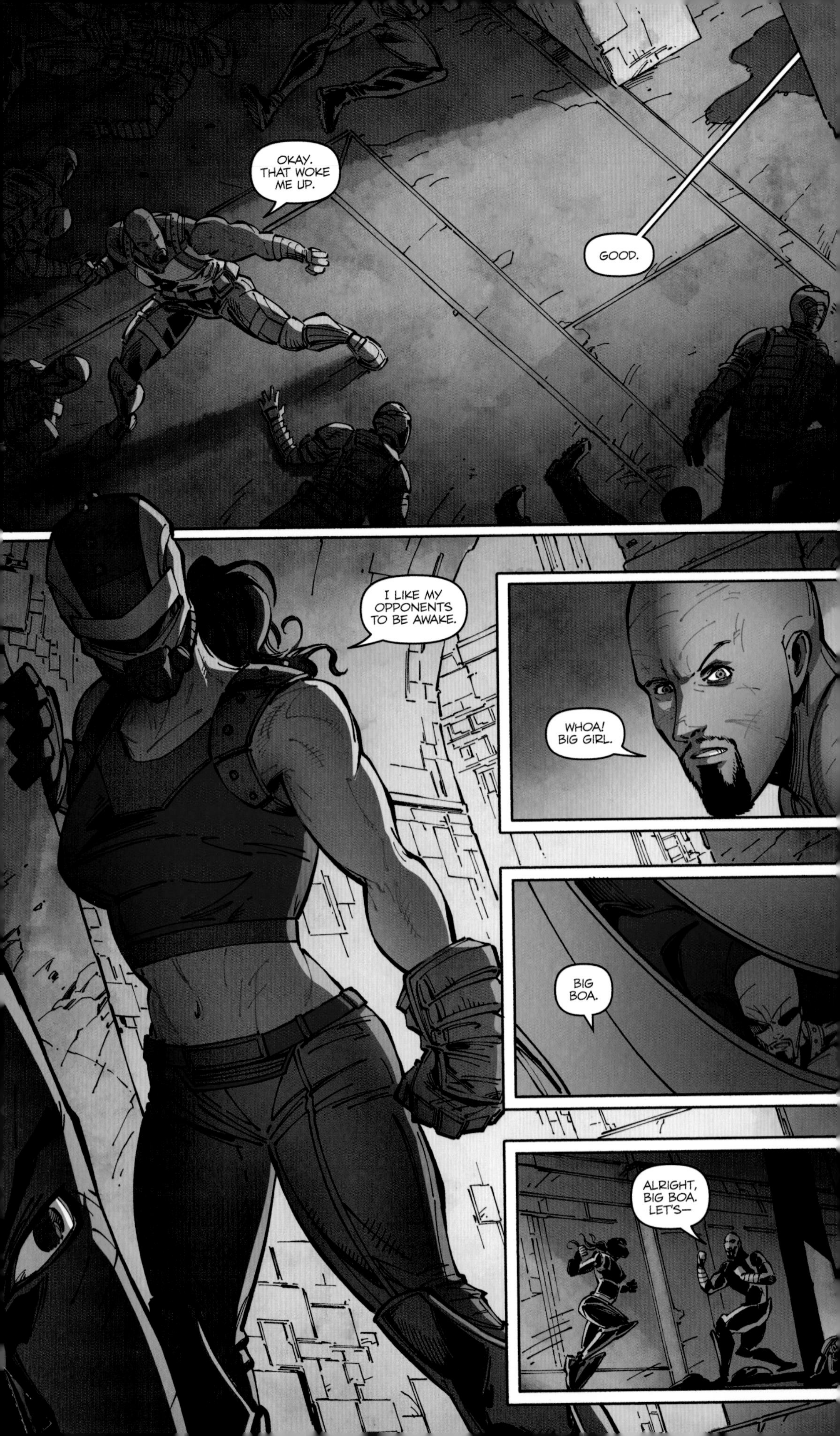
OKAY. THAT WOKE ME UP.
GOOD.
I LIKE MY OPPONENTS TO BE AWAKE.
WHOA! BIG GIRL.
BIG BOA.
ALRIGHT, BIG BOA. LET'S—

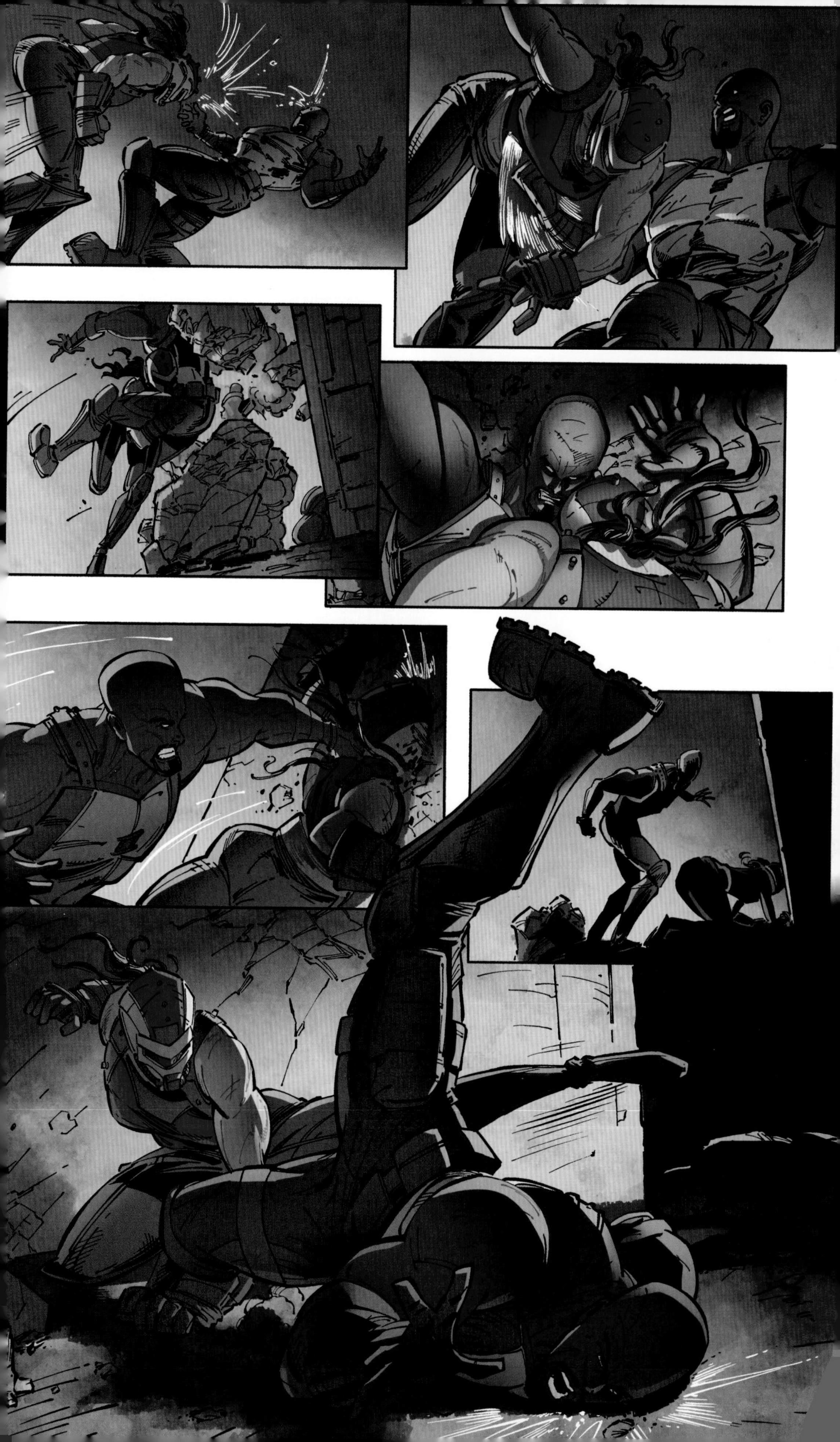

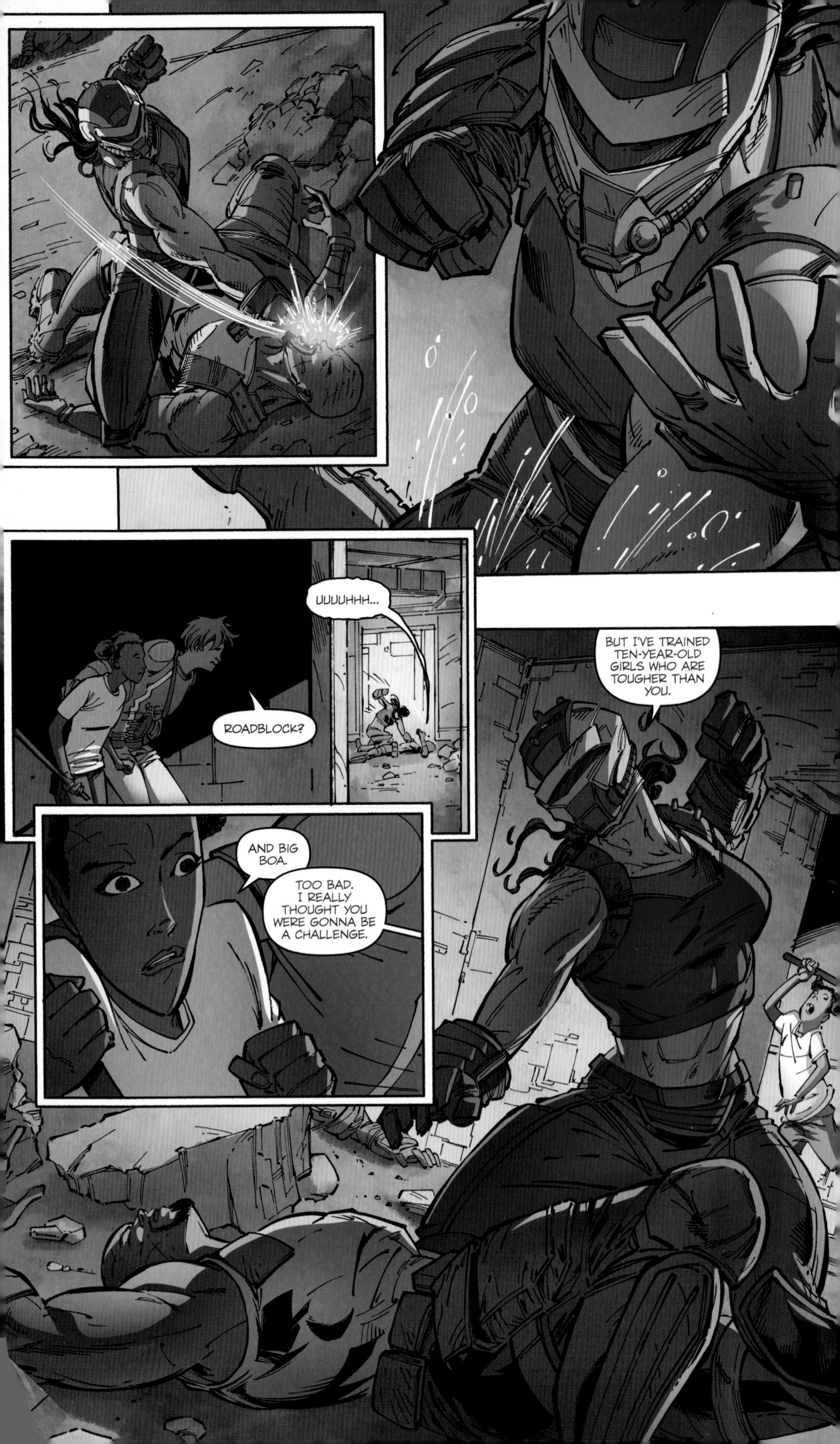
UUUUHHH...
ROADBLOCK?
AND BIG BOA.
TOO BAD. I REALLY THOUGHT YOU WERE GONNA BE A CHALLENGE.
BUT I'VE TRAINED TEN-YEAR-OLD GIRLS WHO ARE TOUGHER THAN YOU.

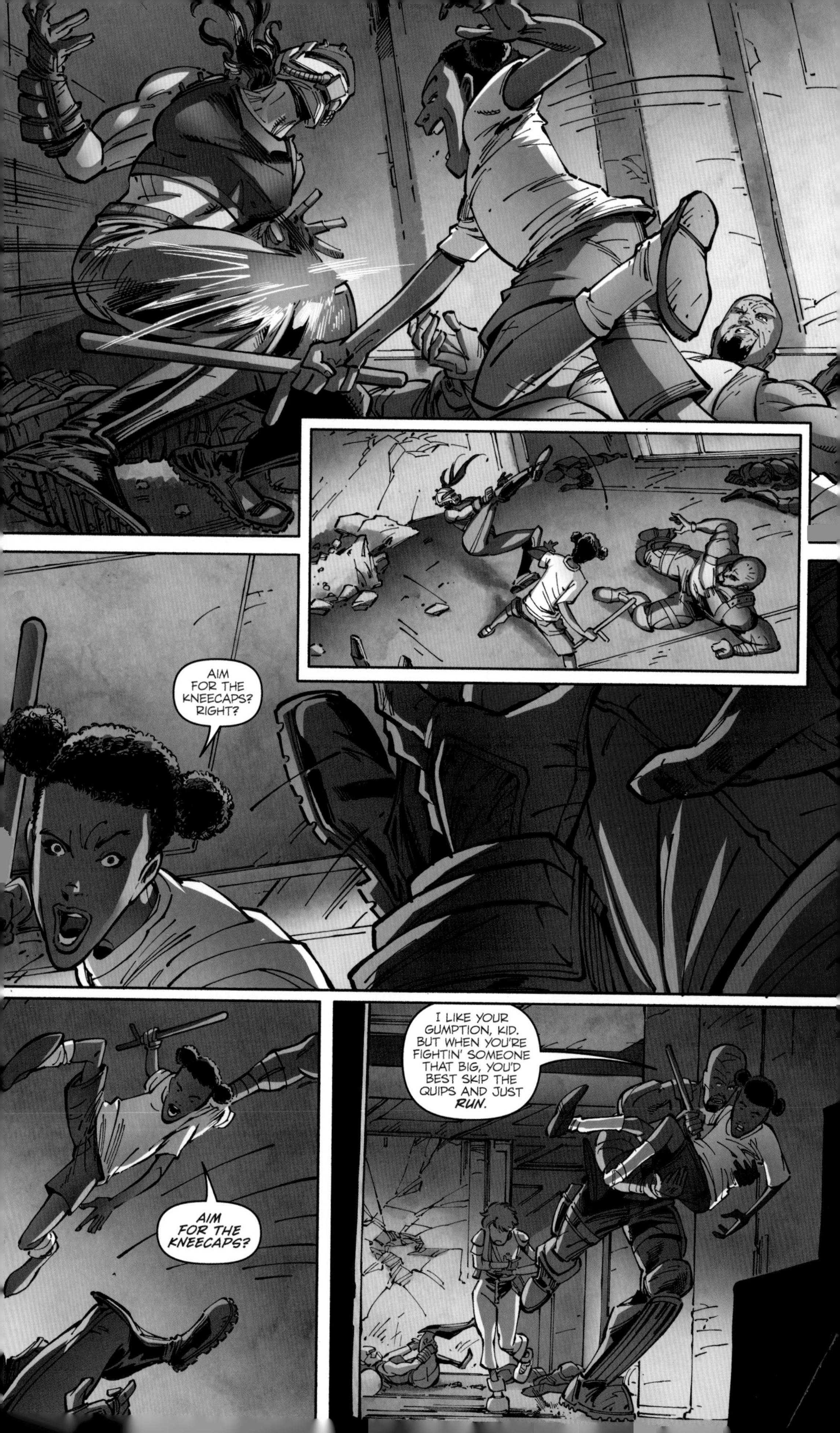
AIM FOR THE KNEECAPS? RIGHT?
AIM FOR THE KNEECAPS?
I LIKE YOUR GUMPTION, KID. BUT WHEN YOU'RE FIGHTIN' SOMEONE THAT BIG, YOU'D BEST SKIP THE QUIPS AND JUST *RUN*.

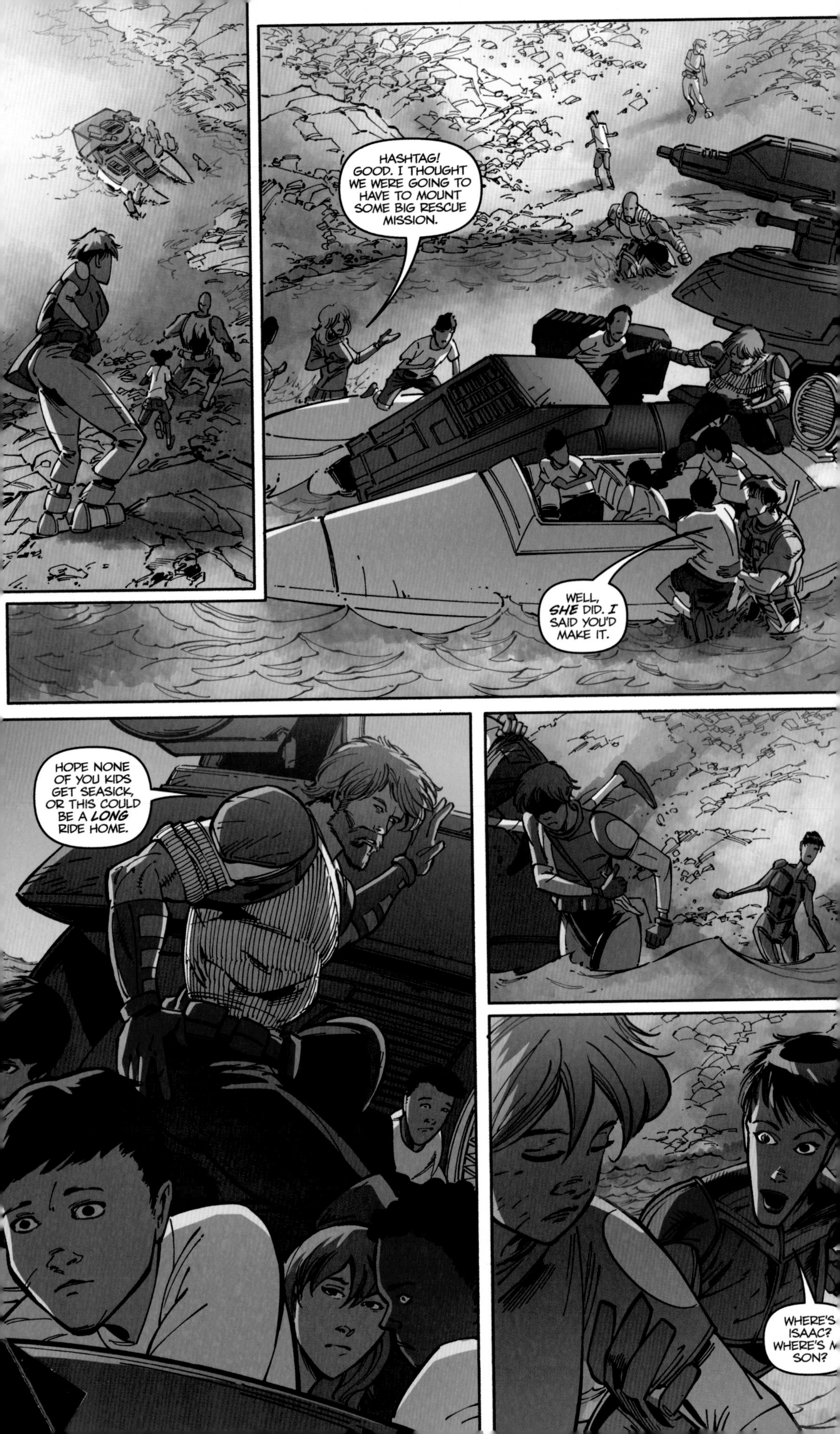
HASHTAG! GOOD. I THOUGHT WE WERE GOING TO HAVE TO MOUNT SOME BIG RESCUE MISSION.
WELL, SHE DID. I SAID YOU'D MAKE IT.
HOPE NONE OF YOU KIDS GET SEASICK, OR THIS COULD BE A LONG RIDE HOME.
WHERE'S ISAAC? WHERE'S M SON?

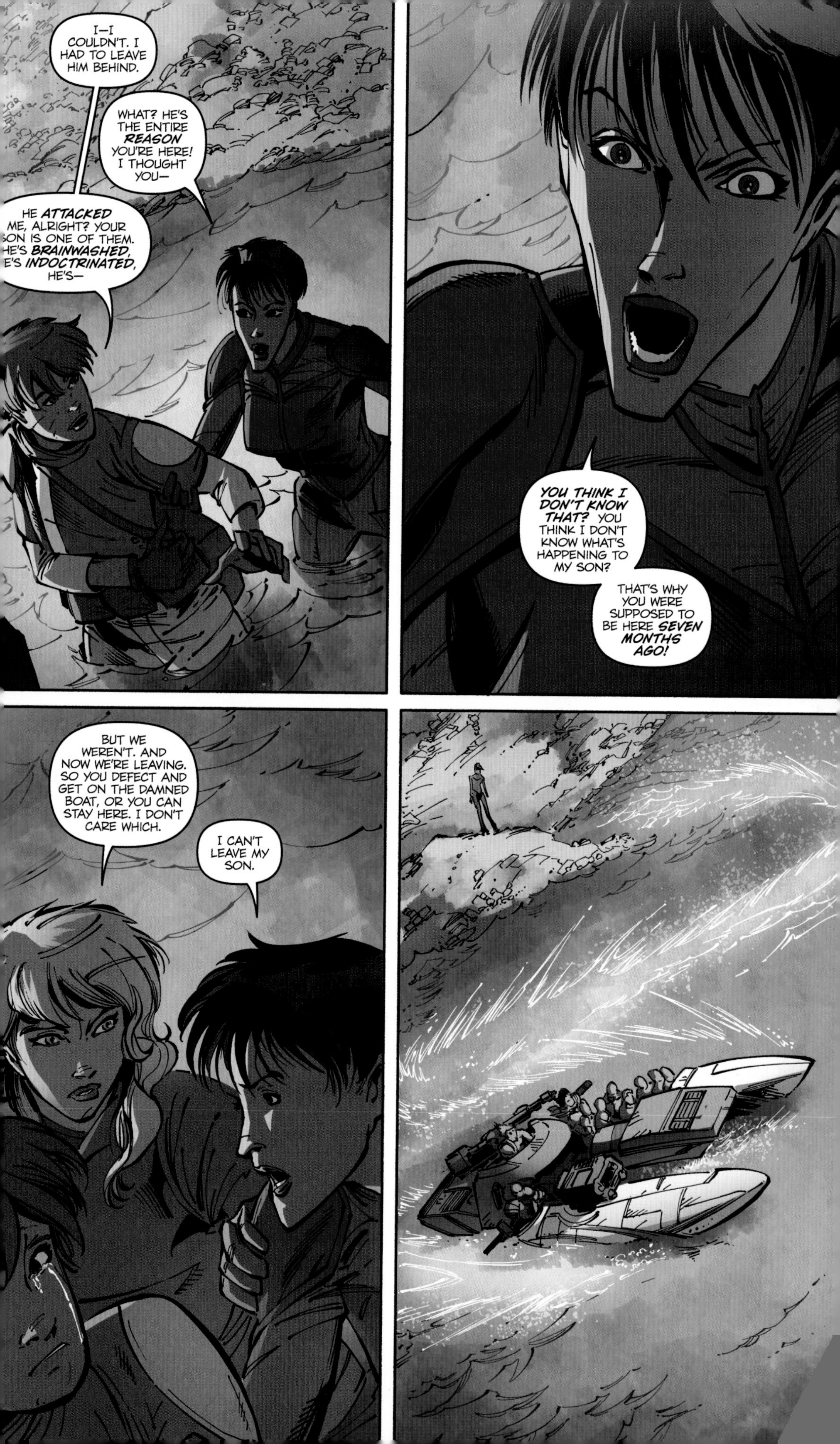
I—I COULDN'T. I HAD TO LEAVE HIM BEHIND.
WHAT? HE'S THE ENTIRE REASON YOU'RE HERE! I THOUGHT YOU—
HE ATTACKED ME, ALRIGHT? YOUR SON IS ONE OF THEM. HE'S BRAINWASHED, HE'S INDOCTRINATED, HE'S—
YOU THINK I DON'T KNOW THAT? YOU THINK I DON'T KNOW WHAT'S HAPPENING TO MY SON?
THAT'S WHY YOU WERE SUPPOSED TO BE HERE SEVEN MONTHS AGO!
BUT WE WEREN'T. AND NOW WE'RE LEAVING. SO YOU DEFECT AND GET ON THE DAMNED BOAT, OR YOU CAN STAY HERE. I DON'T CARE WHICH.
I CAN'T LEAVE MY SON.

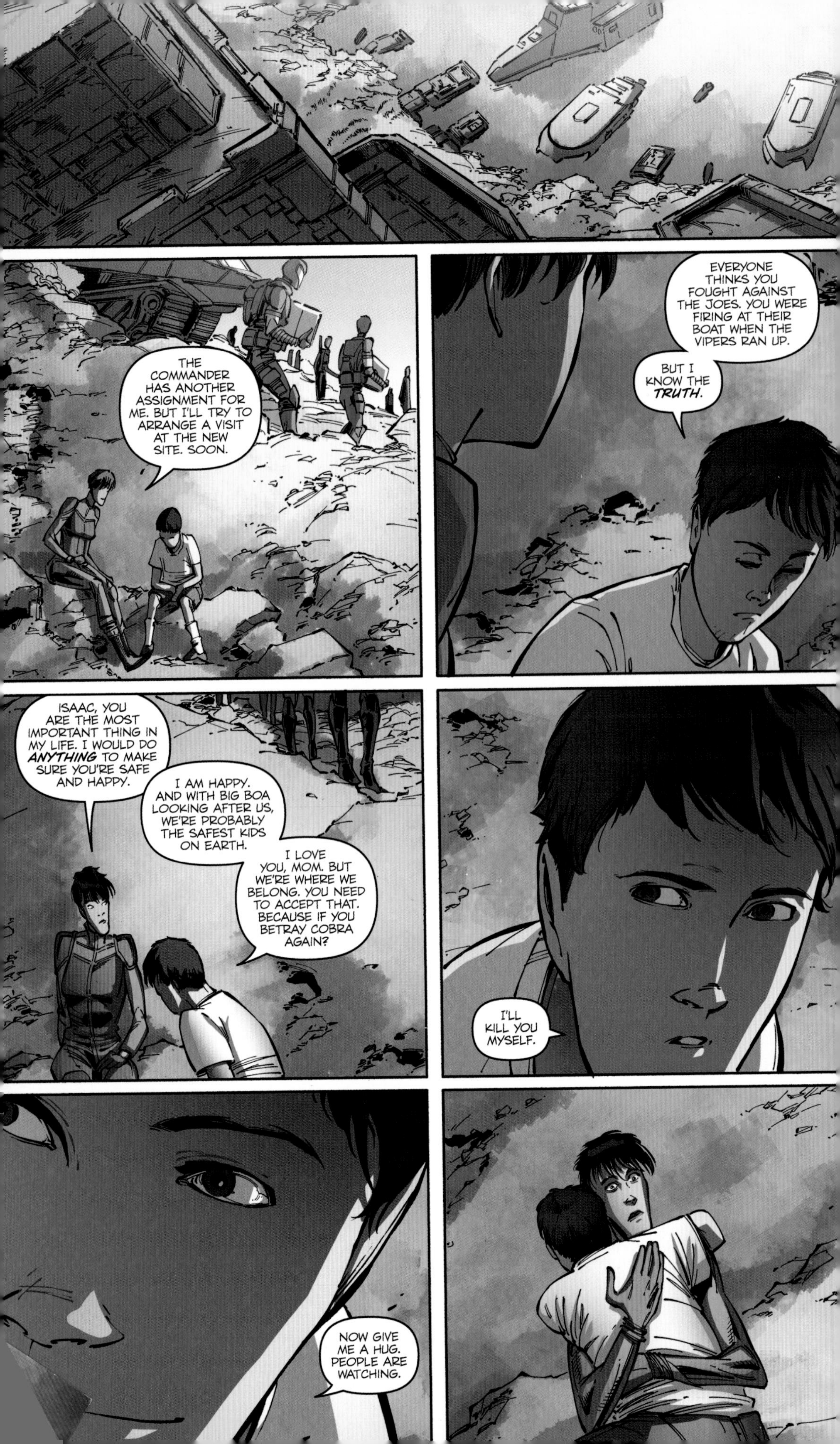
THE COMMANDER HAS ANOTHER ASSIGNMENT FOR ME. BUT I'LL TRY TO ARRANGE A VISIT AT THE NEW SITE. SOON.
EVERYONE THINKS YOU FOUGHT AGAINST THE JOES. YOU WERE FIRING AT THEIR BOAT WHEN THE VIPERS RAN UP.
BUT I KNOW THE *TRUTH*.
ISAAC, YOU ARE THE MOST IMPORTANT THING IN MY LIFE. I WOULD DO ***ANYTHING*** TO MAKE SURE YOU'RE SAFE AND HAPPY.
I AM HAPPY. AND WITH BIG BOA LOOKING AFTER US, WE'RE PROBABLY THE SAFEST KIDS ON EARTH.
I LOVE YOU, MOM. BUT WE'RE WHERE WE BELONG. YOU NEED TO ACCEPT THAT. BECAUSE IF YOU BETRAY COBRA AGAIN?
I'LL KILL YOU MYSELF.
NOW GIVE ME A HUG. PEOPLE ARE WATCHING.

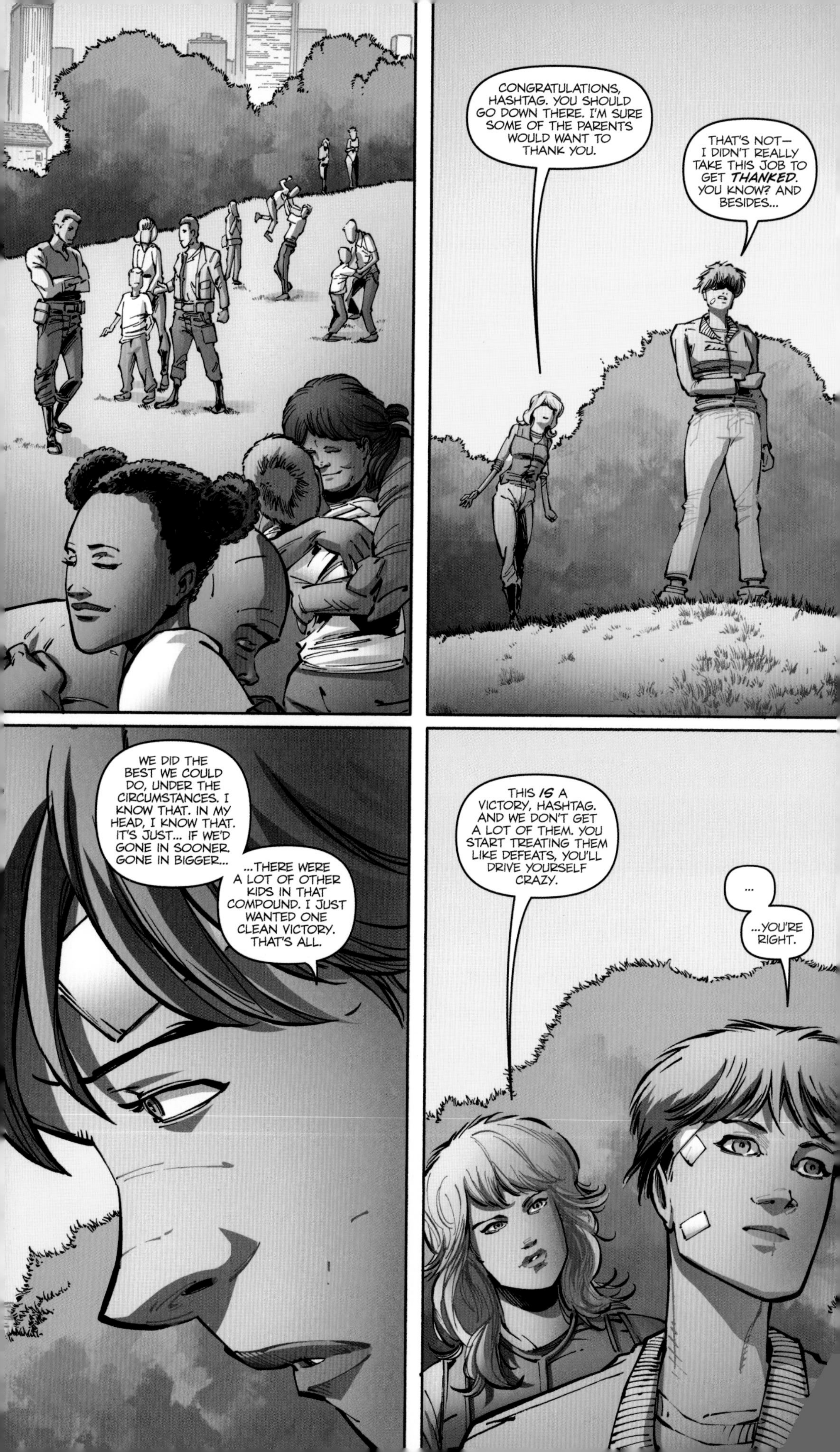
CONGRATULATIONS, HASHTAG. YOU SHOULD GO DOWN THERE. I'M SURE SOME OF THE PARENTS WOULD WANT TO THANK YOU.
THAT'S NOT— I DIDN'T REALLY TAKE THIS JOB TO GET *THANKED*. YOU KNOW? AND BESIDES...
WE DID THE BEST WE COULD DO, UNDER THE CIRCUMSTANCES. I KNOW THAT. IN MY HEAD, I KNOW THAT. IT'S JUST... IF WE'D GONE IN SOONER. GONE IN BIGGER...
...THERE WERE A LOT OF OTHER KIDS IN THAT COMPOUND. I JUST WANTED ONE CLEAN VICTORY. THAT'S ALL.
THIS *IS* A VICTORY, HASHTAG. AND WE DON'T GET A LOT OF THEM. YOU START TREATING THEM LIKE DEFEATS, YOU'LL DRIVE YOURSELF CRAZY.
...
...YOU'RE RIGHT.

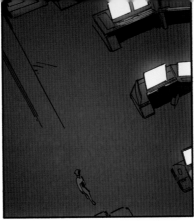

THIS MESSAGE IS FOR THE UNITED STATES MILITARY UNIT KNOWN AS G.I. JOE.

MY NAME IS MARY CRAFT. CODE-NAMED SIREN. I'M A COBRA AGENT. AND I'M A MOTHER. SO, PLEASE. *PLEASE* PAY ATTENTION TO THIS MESSAGE. BECAUSE I'M DESPERATE

AND I NEED YOUR HELP.

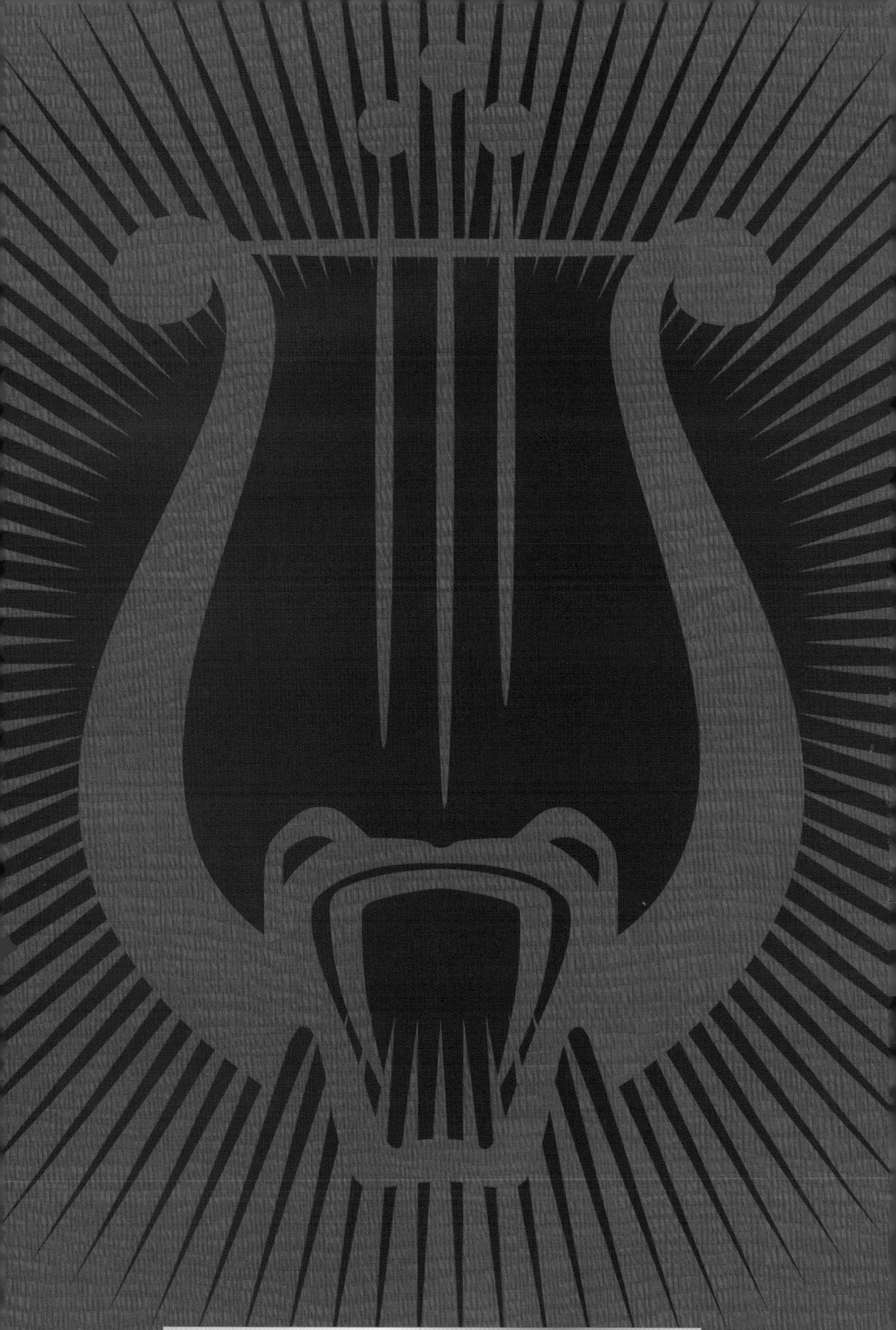

COVER GALLERY

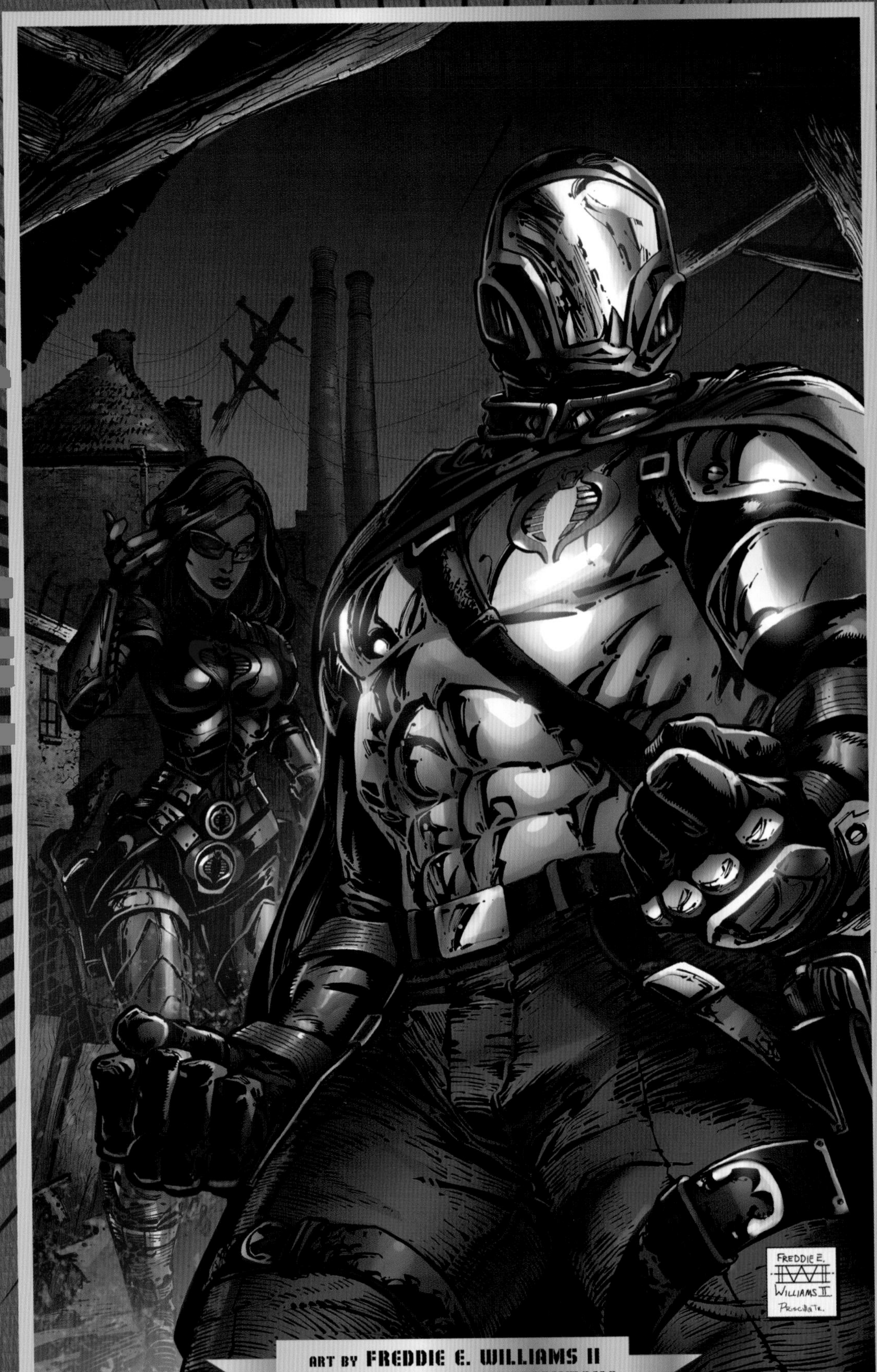
FREDDIE E. WILLIAMS II

ART BY FREDDIE E. WILLIAMS II
COLORS BY PRISCILLA TRAMONTANO

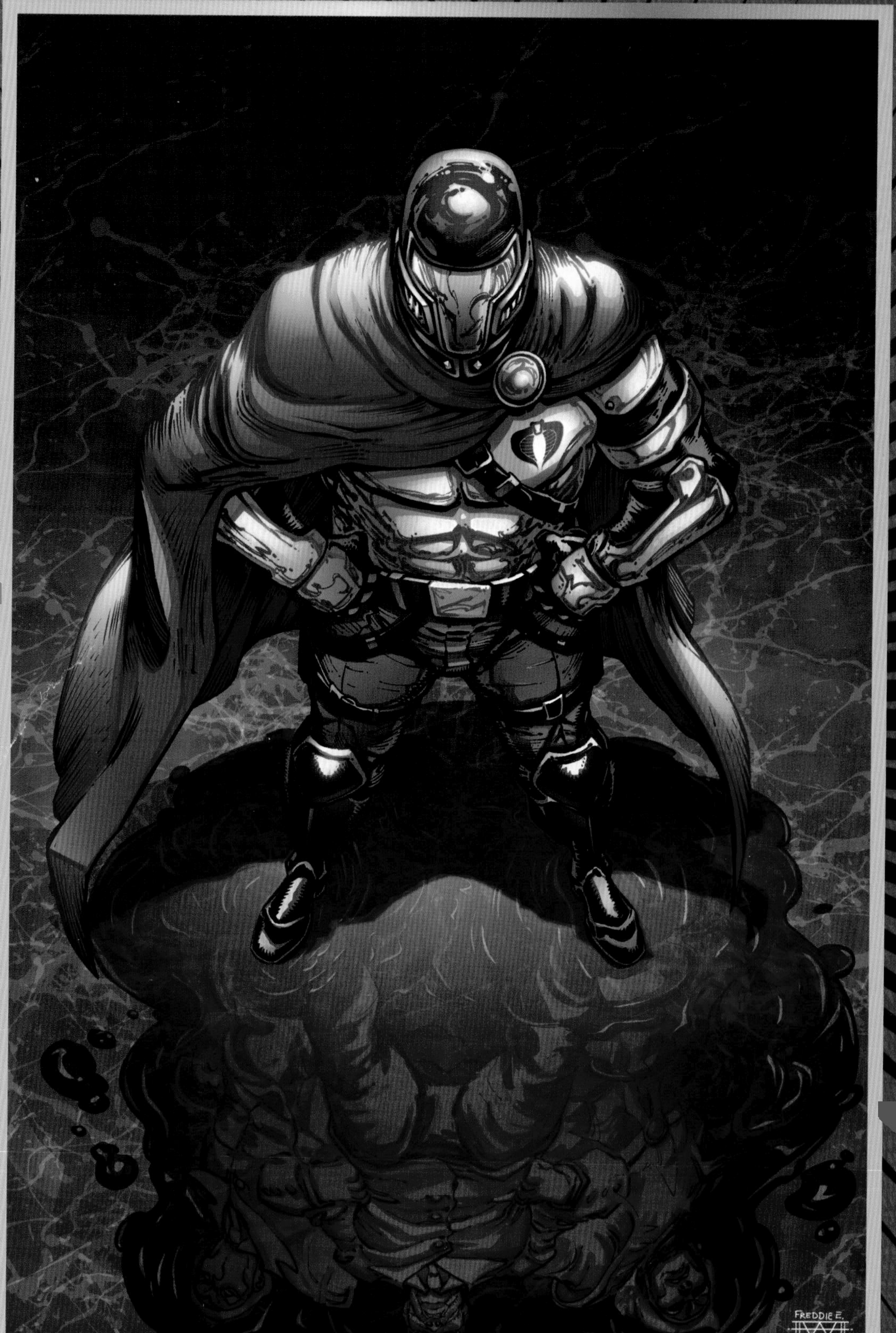
FREDDIE E. WILLIAMS II
DD

ART BY FREDDIE E. WILLIAMS II
COLORS BY DAVID GARCIA CRUZ

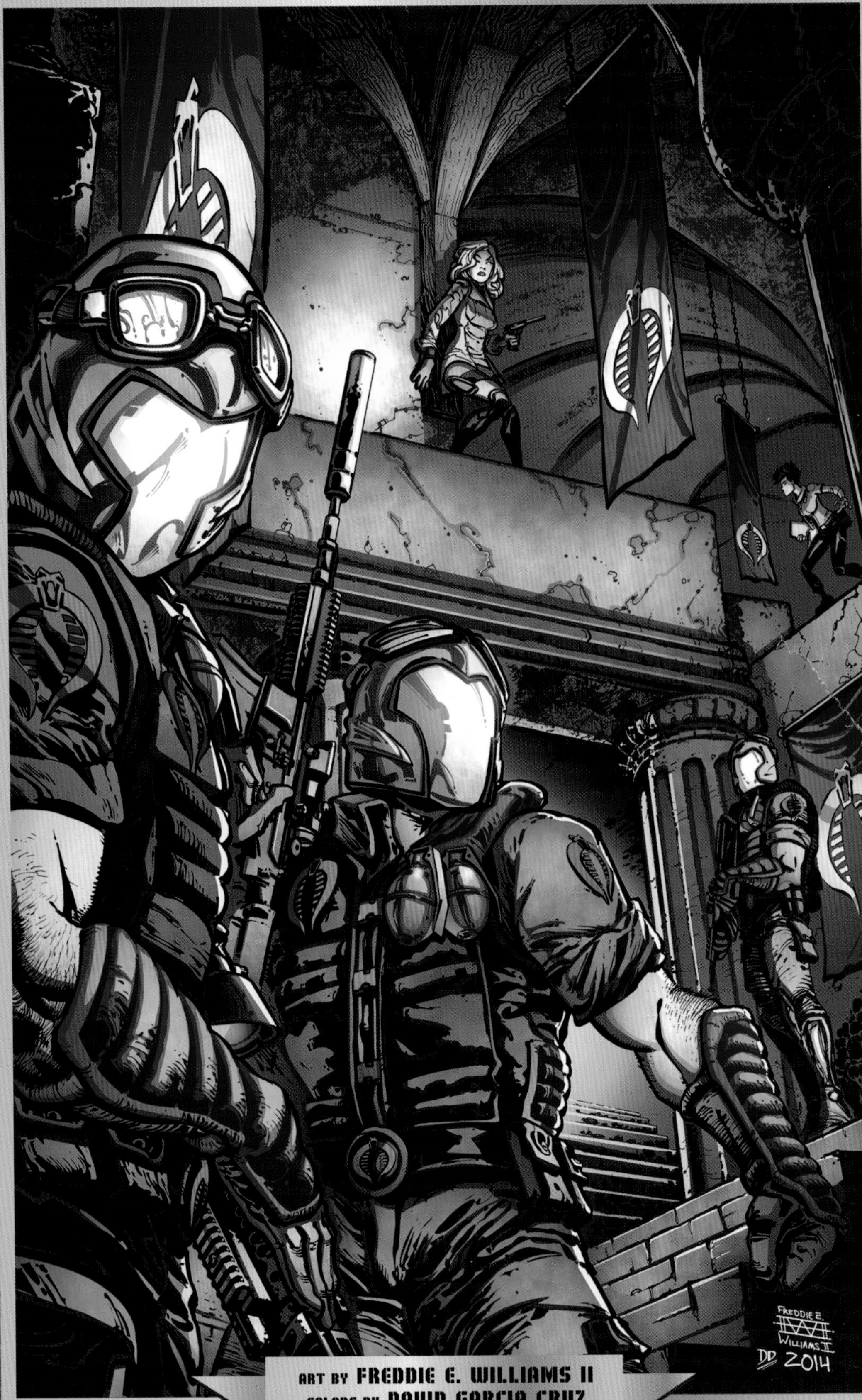
FREDDIE E. WILLIAMS II
DD 2014

ART BY FREDDIE E. WILLIAMS II
COLORS BY DAVID GARCIA CRUZ

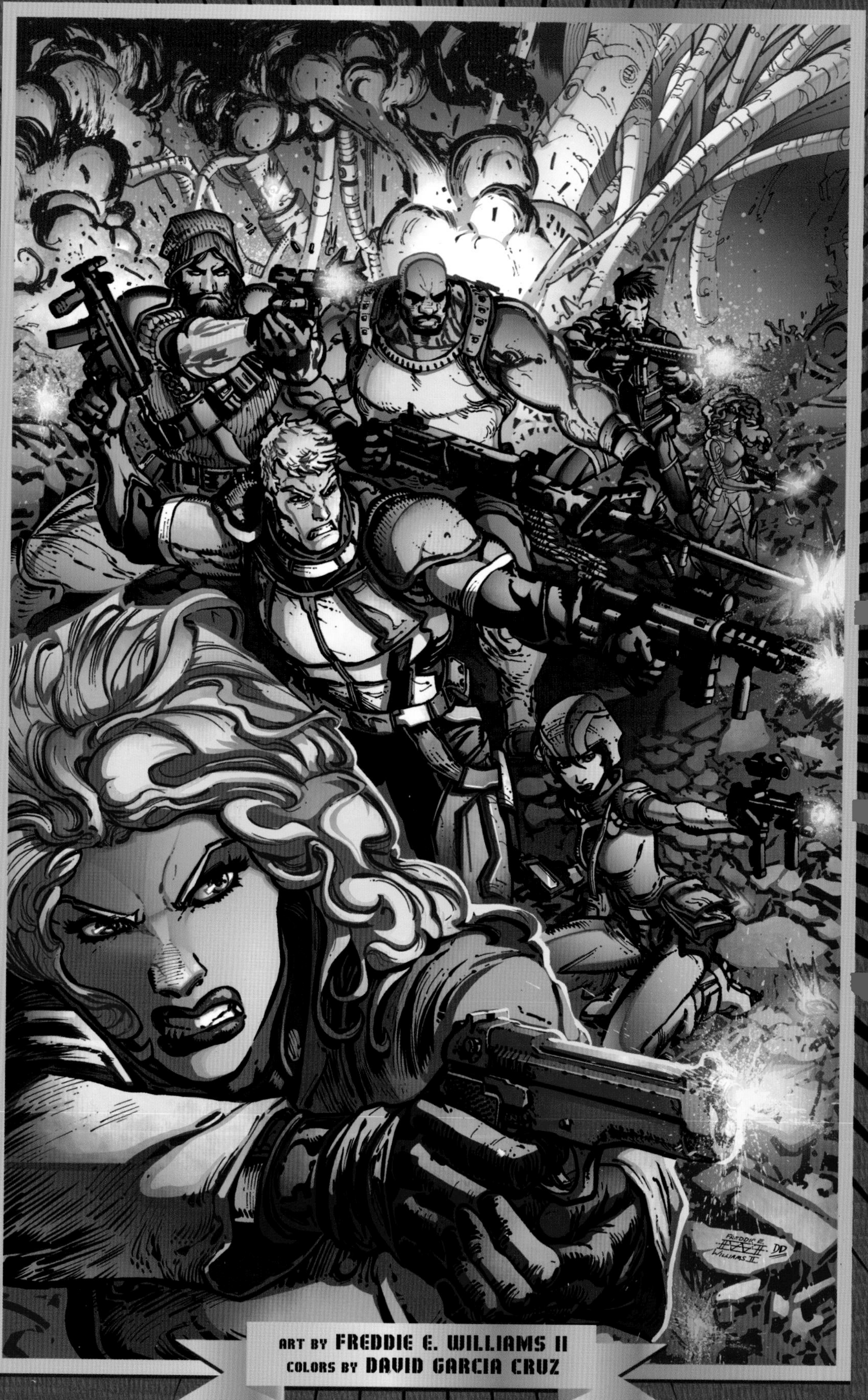

ART BY FREDDIE E. WILLIAMS II
COLORS BY DAVID GARCIA CRUZ

THE MISSION CONTINUES!

G.I. JOE
VOLUME 2: THREAT MATRIX

G.I. JOE, VOL. 2: THREAT MATRIX
ISBN: 978-1-61377-866-1

G.I. JOE
THE COBRA FILES
VOLUME 2

G.I. JOE: THE COBRA FILES, VOL. 2
ISBN: 978-1-61377-918-7

COBRA
THE LAST LAUGH

COBRA: THE LAST LAUGH
ISBN: 978-1-61377-523-3

G.I. JOE
SPECIAL MISSIONS

G.I. JOE: SPECIAL MISSIONS, VOL. 3
ISBN: 978-1-61377-976-7

G.I. JOE
The Complete Collection
☆004☆

G.I. JOE: THE COMPLETE COLLECTION, VOL. 4
ISBN: 978-1-61377-848-7

G.I. JOE
THE IDW COLLECTION

G.I. JOE: THE IDW COLLECTION, VOL. 4
ISBN: 978-1-61377-931-6

IDW

Licensed By: Hasbro

WWW.IDWPUBLISHING.COM